MAKING THE
WORLD
WORK BETTER

MAKING THE WORLD WORK BETTER

THE IDEAS THAT SHAPED A CENTURY AND A COMPANY

IBM Press – Pearson plc

Upper Saddle River, NJ / Boston / Indianapolis / San Francisco
New York / Toronto / Montreal / London / Munich / Paris / Madrid
Cape Town / Sydney / Tokyo / Singapore / Mexico City

ibmpressbooks.com

© Copyright 2011
by International Business Machines Corporation.

Cover and interior design:
VSA Partners, Inc.

Editor:
Mike Wing

Copy editor:
Pennie Rossini

Fact checker:
Janet Byrne

Indexer:
Robert Swanson

Library of Congress Cataloging-in-Publication Data is on file.

ISBN-10: 0-13-275510-6
ISBN-13: 978-0-13-275510-8

Text printed in the United States on recycled paper at R.R. Donnelley in Crawfordsville, Indiana.

First printing June 2011

Of Change and Progress
Samuel J. Palmisano

CHAIRMAN, PRESIDENT AND CHIEF EXECUTIVE OFFICER
IBM CORPORATION

One simple way to assess the impact of any organization is to answer the question: how is the world different because it existed?

The date of this volume's publication, June 16, 2011, is a meaningful one for IBM. On it, we celebrate our centennial as a corporation. For IBMers today—women and men who have lived through an eventful part of that history—that means reconnecting to a storied past, and understanding its implications for a still-unfolding story.

But we believe the lessons of our history apply more broadly. Whether you seek to understand the trajectory of technology or to build and sustain a successful enterprise or to make the world work better, there is much to learn from IBM's experience. And because these lessons have significance that goes far beyond our company— and because we wish to understand them better ourselves—we decided to do something different from a typical commemorative publication.

Rather than simply chronicle the company's long list of achievements, we reached out to three journalists who have covered our industry for years. In fact, all of them have interviewed me at one time or another. They have a wealth of knowledge about technology, business and history, and each one offers a distinct perspective on what it all means. Plus, they're all crack reporters. We asked them to take a deep dive into three aspects of how the world has changed and to explore IBM's role in that change.

I have been fascinated by the results of their research—in particular, the underlying beliefs they discovered. Our company, of course, became famous for Thomas Watson Sr.'s Basic Beliefs, the principles that were intended to guide IBMers' behavior. And in recent years, we have come together as a workforce to reexamine and redefine our core values. Interestingly, what the research for this book uncovered was another set of ideas that were never written down, but that nonetheless have pervaded IBM from its birth up to the present day.

One of those has to do with the nature of computation and information science. Kevin Maney's exploration of the history of this technology and the industry it spawned reminds us that it is a lot richer and more nuanced than most people today realize. If your knowledge comes from the media, you might think that the story of IT is divided into two phases—hardware and software. Or that it all falls into pre-Internet and post-Internet eras. Kevin's longer lens does much to clarify the far more multidimensional history of computation, IBM's role in shaping it and how its foundational components are advancing and recombining today.

But he does even more. As Kevin argues, the core elements of computing mirror key dimensions of the human brain. The story of their evolution shows how our thinking changes the tools we create, and how the tools we create then change the way we think. And this deeper understanding makes it clear that scientific truth isn't either/or, and discovery isn't simply before-and-after. At the start of the twenty-first century, we find ourselves at an inflection point in both scientific thought and technological capability—a moment whose implications leaders and citizens must study if they wish to ride the waves of our planet's information-shaped future.

Similarly, Steve Hamm's look at IBM's growth into a new kind of business institution doesn't just chronicle the triumphs, mistakes and repeated reinvention of one company. Steve offers intriguing new perspectives on some well-worn truisms. For one: the emergence of an information-based economy. We are all familiar with the shift from atoms to bits as the source of economic value. But it has further implications. Because information knows no borders, it also leads inevitably toward a global economy—and toward the increasing convergence of business and society. We learn how becoming global is about a lot more than geography, a lot more than simply having a presence all around the world. Finally, this narrative underscores how an enduring organizational culture isn't just a fact of nature but a deliberate act of its people—one that involves a lot more than dress codes and team-building exercises.

Neither Thomas Watson nor his son had available to him the sophisticated language we use today to describe this complex system—much less the scientific and business disciplines that have arisen over the past half century to study it. What they did have was the intention to build a particular kind of enterprise—a set of gut impulses, if you will, about what a business should be. As a result of those impulses, IBM's experience through the twentieth century did much to shape the modern corporation. And as Steve's essay persuasively argues, what IBM is still becoming offers interesting perspectives on the new ways any organization—in business, government, education or beyond—can answer basic questions like: How does it create value? How does it attract, develop and retain people? How does it organize and manage itself? What role does it play in society at large? What makes it unique?

Finally, Jeff O'Brien's research reveals compelling examples of what is required to accomplish the hard work of progress in an increasingly complex and interconnected world. When you look at the work IBM and others have done decade after decade—work that is accelerating today—a certain pattern of activity and mode of thought emerge. Technology alone, no matter how powerful, cannot bring about systemic change. It turns out that deliberately changing the way the world works requires a broader, longer-term approach, with the mastery of a few basic steps.

Looking at advances over the past century, Jeff uncovers a simple, intuitive and powerful model of progress. Today, that model is being renewed by our technology-powered capacity to see, map and understand vast amounts of new data about every dimension of both nature and society, opening up ways to make our world literally work better. And yet, these stories argue that acting—actually changing the complex systems of our planet in lasting ways—relies most fundamentally not on data but on belief. Our learning depends on a prior faith in our capacity to learn—as Thomas Watson Sr. often said, to *think*.

The lead actor through these narratives is a collective enterprise based on the power of ideas—their economic power, their galvanizing and structuring power, their transformational power. These are the ideas that drive progress—and by progress, I mean building a world that is not only more prosperous, more sustainable and fairer, but also better able to continually transform itself; a world that learns. When IBMers are at their best, the pursuit of this form of progress infuses everything they do.

Now, one way to explore and chronicle that idea is through science. We can also look at it within the framework of management theory. But the discipline that actually seems most appropriate is history—hence this volume and these writers.

On a personal note, let me say that this approach is encouraging for an old liberal arts major like me. More than once during my 38-year career here, I have jokingly apologized for my lack of scientific background. In truth, it can be intimidating to be surrounded by brilliant engineers, scientists, MBAs and other such thinkers. And without question, the amazing stories in these chapters do nothing to counter that feeling. On the contrary, they instill a deep sense of humility. I can't help being surprised to find myself in this position at this institution at this moment. I've been very lucky, indeed.

Still, it is gratifying to see what the lens of history reveals about our company, the world in which it has grown and the trajectories it has influenced. Without doubt, the perspective of history allows us to see IBM in a way that IBMers could not have done in earlier eras—

which seems appropriate on the occasion of our 100th birthday.

How is the world different because IBM existed? The stories in this volume provide a fascinating set of answers, and an even more intriguing set of yet-to-be-answered questions.

My fellow IBMers and I are proud to have been part of this journey during our own time here. We are inspired by the legacy of the pioneers who built this company. We are committed to serve as stewards of the collective enterprise they left in our care. And we are excited about the fundamental transformations that lie ahead, as the trajectories of the past converge and point us toward a very different future.

For IBM's clients, and for the communities of which we are a part, this convergence promises a smarter planet. For IBMers, it points toward a future that will be built by a new generation—the IBMers of tomorrow. It is these women and men for whom this book is intended, and to whom it is dedicated.

· · ·

Pioneering the Science of Information

Kevin Maney

DATACENTRE

On March 28, 1955, the cover of *Time* featured a drawing of IBM president Thomas Watson Jr. in front of a cartoonish robot, along with this caption: "Clink. Clank. Think." At the time, few but a small cadre of experts had ever seen—much less touched—a computer. The magazine story marveled at the machinery, built by IBM and operating inside a Monsanto office building.

"To IBM, it was the Model 702 Electronic Data Processing Machine," the story said. "To Monsanto and awed visitors, it was simply 'the giant brain.'"

We can't help considering computers this way. No matter the year—1911, 1955 or 2011—we continue to equate the functions of the hard, rigid, electric-powered computer with the squishy, pliable, biologically powered human brain. Computers have always been tools but function no more like a brain than a hammer works like a hand. Yet we mix the metaphors, with the idea that as computers advance, we can hand them more of the work of the mind, making them partners in our efforts to improve the world and manage its increasing complexity. IBM had thought of computing that way for much of its existence. As *Time* put it in that 1955 article:

> *IBM's new brain is a logical extension of the company's famed slogan, "THINK." In the age of giant electronic brains, IBM's President Thomas J. Watson Jr. is applying to machines the slogan which his father, IBM's Board Chairman Thomas J. Watson Sr., applied only to men. President Watson hopes to mechanize hundreds of processes which require the drab, repetitive "thought" of everyday business. Thus liberated from grinding routine, man can put his own brain to work on problems requiring a function beyond the capabilities of the machine: creative thought.*

Of course, the world's information scientists and technologists haven't spent the past 100 years trying to build a computer that can mimic the workings of the human brain. The goal has always been to augment the uniquely human capacity to think. Even though a computer beat the world chess champion and won against the two all-time champions on the TV quiz show *Jeopardy!*, a computer can't reason any more than a pitching machine can be a star baseball player. Still, the evolution of computing has done more than solve really hard math problems.

———

INFORMATION TECHNOLOGY LITERALLY CHANGES THE WAY WE THINK. It moves ahead, showing us what's possible and freeing our minds to dream of what we can do next. The dreams inspire us to build better technology, which in turn unleashes new ideas about what technology can do.

But there's a part of the information revolution that Watson Jr. missed. All of the pieces of computing—sensors, storage, processors, software, net works—have conspired to abstract information and thought processes from individual brains. What people know—even the decisions they know how to make—is captured and shared. It's combined with data about nature and human activity—information we've recently begun to capture in unprecedented volume and with unprecedented speed through sensors and electronic transactions. Technology is pumping the world's knowledge into a global pool, creating a higher plane—or, at least, a broader field—of consciousness. The quest to make machines think has delivered not a parody of individual human thought but a new kind of thinking. Many interconnected individuals can have access to the same wealth of information at nearly the same time and work on it together with the help of machines. We're creating a humming hive of knowledge, people and computers, all feeding one another.

Ultimately, the goal of this symbiotic relationship is to make the world work better. We are constantly creating systems that raise the level of existence on our planet.

The story of how we got here begins in 1911 with crude punched card machines and charges into the future with technology that can deliver supercomputer-like simulations to handheld devices through a cloud computer network and embed computing and networking into the very fabric of business and life. The details of that journey can be understood by examining the breakthroughs in six pillars of how information technology has evolved.

Sensing
The mechanisms for getting information from people and events into computers.

Memory
The way computers store and access information.

Processing
The core speed and capabilities of computers.

Logic
The software and languages that let computers do work.

Connecting
The ways computers talk to people and machines.

Architecture
The changing nature of computing and of the way we think about information.

Together, those pillars mesh and make up the modern computing environment. The stories behind the development of the pillars have heroes from all over the world. They worked at Bell Labs, Machines Bull, Cray Research, Intel, Xerox PARC, Sony, Apple and other companies and entities. IBM has played a significant role throughout the story of computing, through every decade of the past 100 years.

In 1911, financier Charles Flint merged three small technology companies: one making computing scales (which automatically figured out the total price of an item sold by weight); one making tabulating machines; and one making time-recording clocks that workers punched at factories. At first it was called the Computing-Tabulating-Recording-Company, or C-T-R, joined in 1914 by Thomas Watson Sr. In 1924, he changed the name to International Business Machines. The company has thrived for 100 years by building on those first simple information products and in every way continually making them better, faster, more efficient—smarter.

From his start in 1914, Watson introduced the iconic slogan "Think." And since then, his company has played a lead role in reinventing thought.

• • •

Sensing

To do anything with information, machines first have to bring it in; they need to sense the world. Over the past 100 years, computer sensing has gone from touching to hearing to seeing—and beyond.

For 60 years, punched cards—relying on a sense of touch in computers—reigned as the way to input information.

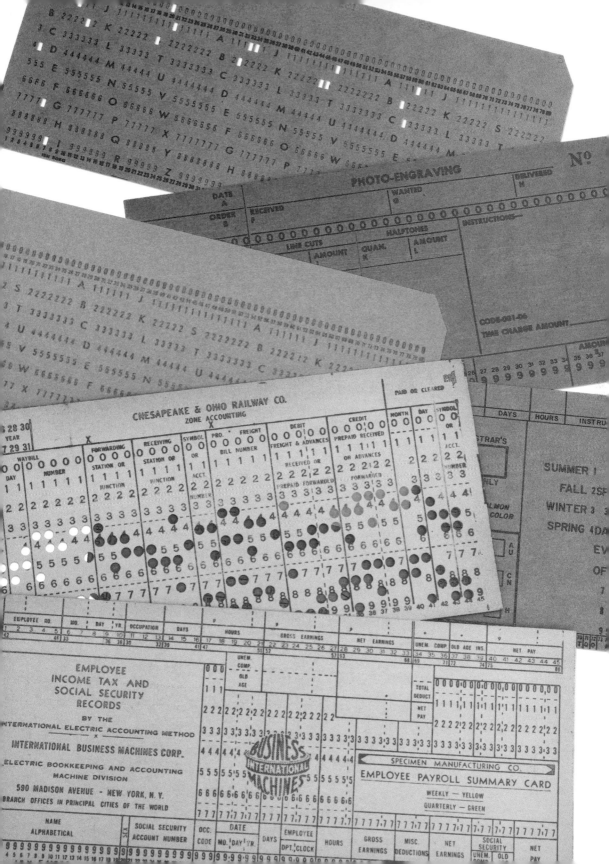

In the wilds of central Kenya, there are zebras that have become part of an exclusive, striped, peer-to-peer computer network. Scientists have fitted the animals with leather necklaces embedded with computerized sensing and transmitting devices. GPS chips in the devices allow the scientists to track each zebra's movements, from short ambles to the water hole to migrations across the plains. The gadgets monitor zebra eating habits, identifying how long and where the animals stop to dine, and follow zebra interactions with other species, including leopards and lions, whose own dining habits keep the zebras on high alert.[1]

Each zebra acts as a node on a network called ZebraNet. Each node wirelessly fires the information it has collected to a dozen other zebra nodes on the system whenever the ZebraNet devices get close enough. That makes each node a repository for everything that every node pulls in. A scientist need only drive past a single networked zebra to download all of the data onto a laptop.

With ZebraNet, scientists are able to collect details on zebra behavior never available before. What, for example, do zebras do at night? "Most of our knowledge about zebras had come from daytime observations. No one wanted to be out in the landscape after dark with the lions, trying to squint and figure out what the zebras were up to," said Margaret Martonosi, a professor at Princeton University, principal investigator on the ZebraNet project and former IBM Research staff member.

In the 2010s, computing and information science are benefiting from an explosion in sensing. In Ireland, nodes attached to yellow buoys in the chilly waters of Galway Bay detect pollution, scope out dangerous wave patterns, monitor seafood stocks and upload the information onto the Internet for the public. Medical specialists are experimenting with in-body sensor networks that will use pinhead-sized devices to track the health of patients, sending the data to computers wirelessly. Industrial robots rely on computer vision and touch sensors to assemble automobiles and look for defects. Chemical sensors can smell poison in the air. Cell phones can listen to search terms spoken into the handset.[2]

Humans use their senses—sight, hearing, touch, smell, taste—to gather information and pull it into their central processing unit, the brain. Computers—finally, after 100 years—are gaining a version of these senses. Sort of. Computer sensing is in some ways nowhere near as good as human sensing. Yet computers can sense in ways humans can't. With the addition of GPS they know their location. They can detect tiny differences in the molecular structure of the air in a room. They can do their jobs underwater, embedded in concrete or inside a diaper, and never, ever get tired.

In coming decades, sensing will change the way we think about computing and the data that computers can access. Yet until recently, computer sensing was horrifically bad. The journey to this moment—of computers starting to reach out and understand their environment—has been arduous and frustrating. Along the way, flashes of inventiveness have helped crack the darkness a little at a time.

For most of computing history, though, computers faced the challenge of experiencing the world only through touch.

———

HERMAN HOLLERITH got his graduate degree in engineering from Columbia University at age 19 and went to work for the US Census Bureau as a statistician, helping count the population for the 1880 census. The work of assessing the fast-growing country's population and breaking it down by age, gender, race and other factors was maddeningly slow and expensive. A manager at the bureau lamented that there wasn't a machine capable of counting the population more quickly. After all, this was the dawn of the age of machines—locomotives, steam-powered mills, computing scales, steam shovels. Why couldn't machines be designed to count? Hollerith agreed and set out to build a counting machine.[3]

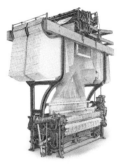

When developing the punched card, Herman Hollerith drew ideas from the Jacquard loom and by watching train conductors punch holes in tickets to mark traits of passengers.

As Hollerith worked, he often found it easier to get machines to count than to get them to comprehend *what* to count. Somehow, information from the outside world had to get into Hollerith's tabulating machines. The information written down by census takers or mailed in by the public had to be read by a machine that could neither see nor hear.

To solve the problem, Hollerith turned to history. More than 80 years before, in France, Joseph Marie Jacquard created a way to automate steam-powered looms, guiding them using a series of holes punched into cardboard cards. The cards contained columns and rows of holes arranged in different patterns. Hooks on gears would reach into the cards. If they found a hole, they'd pass through and engage with the thread; if they did not, the hooks were blocked and did nothing. Different patterns punched into the cards produced different textile designs.

A few decades later, English mathematician Charles Babbage picked up on the Jacquard design as he tried to build a steam-powered information processor. Although he never managed to get his Difference Engine (or the far more ambitious Analytical Engine) built, Babbage laid out detailed designs for what was intended as a polynomial calculating machine comprising gears and crankshafts. For data input, metal fingers would reach in to read a punched card's holes, much as the hooks did on Jacquard's loom.

Hollerith knew of Babbage and Jacquard. For that matter, in the late 1800s the first player pianos, which played music based on holes punched in rolls of thick paper, were becoming popular. Hollerith, though, had a new tool at his disposal. Electricity was becoming reliable and available, and it provided a way to improve on any previous concepts of punched cards.

In Hollerith's design, each card, roughly 3 inches by 7 inches, held one person's data. A clerk would read the census rolls and punch that person's details into the appropriate places on the card, with each punch representing a trait such as age, marital status or income. The machine operator would then place the card on a press attached to the tabulating machine and close the cover. This would push a field of pins down onto the card. The pins

Tabulating machines gathered bits of information by touching punched cards to find the holes, which represented data.

The Hollerith machine pressed rows of pins over a card. Pins that passed through holes touched metal on the other side, completing a circuit.

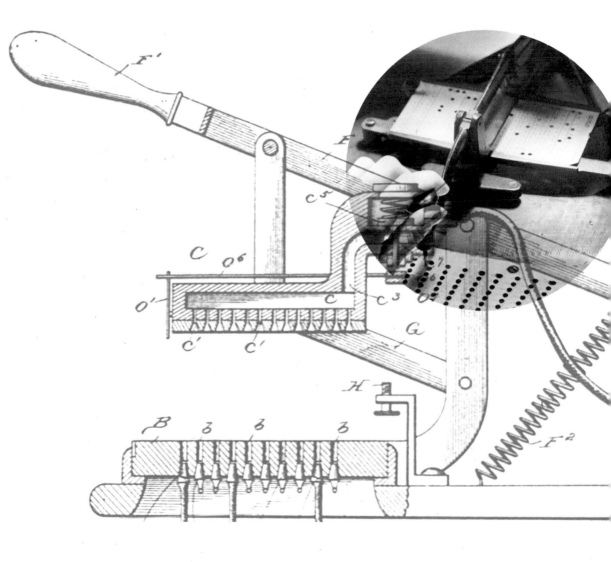

that made their way through the holes contacted small cups partly filled with mercury, completing an electrical circuit. This transmitted electrical impulses to the dial-like counters on the machine. How many single white females lived in Dover, Delaware, in 1890? Put a stack of cards representing Dover residents through the Hollerith card reader, and the results were registered on the counter board.

Hollerith gave computers a way to sense the world through a crude form of touch. Subsequent computing and tabulating machines would improve on the process, packing more information onto cards and developing methods for reading the cards much faster. Yet, amazingly, for six more decades computers would experience the outside world no other way.

But then an old contraption was adapted to give computers a better sense of what humans were trying to say.

——

TYPEWRITERS had been around since the mid-1800s. In the early twentieth century, a few small companies got the idea that electric motors could make typewriters faster and easier to use. One of those was a little Rochester, New York, outfit that became the Electromatic Typewriter Company. By the 1930s, electric typewriters were making their way into businesses, and secretaries were getting jobs based on how many words per minute they

IBM Selectric

IBM 1050 Data
Communications System

could type. At IBM, engineers began to wonder whether an electric type-writer could be hooked to an electric tabulating machine as a way to get information in and out. Other computer companies were considering the same. In 1933, after putting the pieces together and noticing the emergence of this new type of business machine, CEO Thomas Watson Sr. made an investment: he bought Electromatic.

In the early 1960s, electric typewriters veered off on their own path. The invention of the IBM Selectric typewriter created a sensation in offices around the world. The Selectric was fitted with a golf ball shaped typing head that replaced the conventional typewriter's basket of type bars. The bars tended to tangle, slowing a typist's speed. The silver-colored golf ball circumvented that problem: with no bars to jam, typists' speed and produc-tivity soared. The balls were interchangeable, so different typefaces could be used. The Selectric became the most successful electric typewriter ever made, utterly dominating the high-end office typewriter market for 25 years.

Yet to IBM computer scientist Bob Bemer, the Selectric represented one of the biggest professional failures of his life.[1]

Bemer had helped design planes at Douglas Aircraft in the 1940s and worked alongside computer legend Grace Murray Hopper on the program-ming of the UNIVAC in the 1950s before joining IBM in 1957. In 1960, Bemer was asked to create a standard for computers that would turn alpha-

Early time-sharing systems rigged typewriters such as the IBM Selectric to give operators a way to communicate with computers. In the late 1960s, operators relied on terminals like the IBM 1050. The ThinkPad 701, released in 1992, offered a keyboard that opened and expanded. Typing has been the dominant way humans have talked to computers for 50 years.

IBM ThinkPad 701

betic characters into code that any machine could understand. "We had over 60 different ways to represent characters in computers," Bemer told *Computerworld* magazine in 1999. "It was a real Tower of Babel." Bemer's effort produced the American Standard Code for Information Interchange, or ASCII, which even today defines the alphabet for computers. Bemer realized that computers needed some other keys and characters to help them understand human language, so he added, for instance, the Esc and Backslash keys. Bemer's wife, Bettie, used to drive around Texas in a Mercedes with the license plate ESC KEY. (Bemer died in 2004.)

In 1961, when prototypes of the Selectric were already being manufactured at IBM's typewriter plant in Lexington, Kentucky, Bemer reviewed the Selectric's specifications. Bemer knew that tapes and punched cards were still heavily used for input, and some computers employed teletype keyboards similar to those used by Western Union to send telegrams, but they were different from a typewriter. To Bemer, the Selectric would make a much more natural computer keyboard.

Bemer argued that the type ball should be designed to carry the 64 characters required for ASCII, rather than the standard 44 on the typewriter. That would make it relatively easy to convert the Selectric for computer input. But the Selectric never spoke ASCII—and that is what Bemer viewed as his failure.

And yet the Selectric seemed like such a natural connection between human thought and computer understanding that computer users—from engineers in corporate backrooms to researchers developing time-sharing at the Massachusetts Institute of Technology—jerry-rigged Selectrics so the typewriters could talk to computers. As the demand for a keyboard input grew, IBM "had to go through many contortions" to make the Selectric into a computer keyboard, Bemer said. In 1965, IBM introduced the 2741 terminal—basically a Selectric jammed with electronics inside a small cabinet—which allowed a user to type in words that then got translated into a language that could be understood by a System/360 machine. The type-writer's transition to a keyboard wasn't exactly smooth or well-planned, but computers got a new and extraordinarily successful way to directly sense the thoughts and commands of their human masters.

In fact, the keyboard and one other invention—Douglas Engelbart's mouse—remained the primary computer input devices for decades. Only in the 2010s has that begun to change.

———

LONG BEFORE TYPING—long before the written word, for that matter—humans communicated by speaking. One person talked, and the other understood by sensing the sound waves and translating them into words and ideas. So why has it been so hard to make computers do the same?

The desire to make machines understand speech goes back to at least the beginning of the twentieth century, though scientists had little success in this area for decades. At the 1962 Seattle World's Fair, IBM put on display the world's most advanced speech recognition machine, dubbed the Shoebox. It could understand 16 words: zero, one, two, three, four, five, six, seven, eight, nine, minus, plus, subtotal, total, false and off. Visitors to the IBM pavilion got a chance to speak through a microphone to the Shoebox, often looking on in amazement as the machine printed out answers to first-grade arithmetic.[5]

The Shoebox came out of work done by William Dersch and his team at IBM's Advanced Systems Division in San Jose, California. Like many other scientists, those on the IBM team were trying to get a computer to hear the way humans do, relying on sound frequency patterns. Machines,

William Dersch with the Shoebox, 1961.

Voice-activated automobile navigation, 2010.

Engineers have worked since the 1960s to get computers to decipher human speech. IBM's Shoebox could comprehend just 16 words. Now, computers can interpret natural spoken language. Many in-car computer navigation systems understand 10,000 words or more.

though, couldn't pick up where a word started and ended through these patterns. Then, in 1959, "one day serendipity occurred," Dersch wrote in an issue of *Datamation* magazine. While studying the wavy patterns of speech on an oscilloscope, researchers noted that the sound waveforms often went out of phase with one another. This phenomenon has no real impact on human hearing. But the phase differences could be translated in such a way that computers could begin to discriminate between sounds of human speech. Some scientists described it as adapting sound to the way machines hear, rather than forcing machines to hear like humans.

Getting the Shoebox to understand those 16 words for the World's Fair wowed the public. One radio reporter envisioned a time when "a business-man of the future may attach this machine to a typewriter and dictate his messages right into the typewriter"—although an IBM representative made clear to a reporter that speech recognition would "never replace a secretary."

After the Shoebox breakthrough, the development of speech recognition began to accelerate, aided by the exponential growth in computing power. (The Shoebox was fitted with 31 transistors; a Pentium chip holds more than 200 million.) Dersch said he hoped that speech recognition systems might one day understand as many as 1,000 to 10,000 words. By 1980, the 1,000-word milestone had been reached, with accuracy of 91 percent. By 1984, the best speech recognition systems could understand 5,000 words at 95 percent accuracy. By 1986, IBM was selling speech recognition software for its Personal Computer/AT, putting the technology in the hands of consumers. IBM's ViaVoice speech software ultimately was sold to a company called Nuance, which makes the Dragon Naturally-Speaking software.[6]

Today, speech recognition has become pervasive and astoundingly accurate with a broad vocabulary. Calls to a customer service help line often land in a speech recognition system. Smartphones allow users to speak search terms or input an address they want to find on a map. New automobiles come with speech recognition built in, so a driver can make calls, get navigation help or change the radio station without touching a

button. In another dimension of human speech, IBM's DeepQA system—
originally developed to allow a computer to compete on *Jeopardy!*—employs
sophisticated natural language processing that can dissect the nuances in a
tricky question.

Yet, despite how far speech recognition has come, real understanding
of human speech by machines remains a challenge. "Ten years ago, I claimed
that computers by now would beat human transcribers," said IBM Fellow
David Nahamoo, who leads IBM's speech recognition research. "We've set
that as a goal and come a long way, but we're not there yet. Ten years from
now? Possibly."

Nahamoo added: "The endgame in speech technology is deep conversational interaction. If I speak for three minutes, what did I say? That's
still hard."[7]

———

THE GROCERY STORE INDUSTRY in the 1970s saw an opportunity in an
enormous problem. At the time, inflation was raging, price fluctuations were
frequent and hiring workers to keep changing the sticky price tags on product after product was costly. Stores replenished their stock based on hunches
as much as anything else. At the same time, the grocery retail industry was
becoming more competitive as supermarket chains expanded. That made
customers more demanding. If a store were consistently out of, say, Cocoa
Krispies, consumers would switch to a competing supermarket chain with
better inventory control.

Technology coming to market in the 1970s offered a possible solution.
Mainframes and databases could store and sort enormous amounts of information on inventory and pricing. If there were a way to quickly enter data
about each product into computers at the cash register, stores would have
precise information about inventory. They could change prices by typing
on a keyboard.

The chief obstacle: no system existed that could read prices on thousands of products and move the data into those computers. Computers, after all, couldn't see.

Since the late 1940s, technologists had been exploring methods for recording product information at the cash register. In 1951, engineer Norman Woodland joined IBM and proposed a bull's-eye–shaped product code readable by a scanning laser beam. (He'd applied for a patent for both the linear and circular bar code concepts in 1949 and was granted one in 1952.) IBM executives were intrigued but deemed current technology too limited to make bar codes work reliably and later sold the patent for Woodland's code to RCA.

Over the years, the bull's-eye and other code styles were used experimentally to track railroad cars, delivery trucks, even vehicles on a New Jersey toll bridge. The equipment, however, remained too expensive and unreliable for wide deployment. By the late 1960s, transistors, lasers and other electronic components became small and cheap enough to make product scanners economically viable. The technology would be expensive, but retailers who could afford it would see rapid returns. The chains banded together and asked a dozen or so technology companies to submit proposals for a common product code technology. The concept would work only if all retailers and manufacturers accepted the same standard.

IBM was among the companies that worked on the standard. Top executives at IBM didn't care much which code was chosen, as long as a standard was established and the company could sell computers and other business equipment to retailers. IBM assigned George Laurer, an engineer at IBM's research center in Raleigh, North Carolina, to write a paper that supported RCA's bull's-eye–shaped code—the technology originally patented by Woodland years earlier, before he joined IBM. Higher-ups at IBM would review the paper the day after Laurer's manager, Paul McEnroe, got back from a vacation. Laurer was to have the paper done by then.[8]

The bar code was the first successful visual input for computers, allowing the machines to identify a product and its price.

Laurer never wrote the paper. McEnroe "wanted me to write something up that said the RCA proposal was the greatest thing," Laurer recalled. "But my nature and my training would not allow me to support something I didn't believe in." The specifications for the code were exacting. The multiple-digit code had to be readable at different angles with an error rate of less than 1 in 20,000. Laurer quickly concluded that the bull's-eye, coded using concentric circles, would not meet the requirements. The pattern was difficult to print without introducing errors, especially when compressed down to the small size the industry demanded. So "I simply went against my manager's instruction and set out to design a better system," Laurer said.

He'd already been working on optical codes, and the rectangular, zebra-stripe pattern he came up with was easy to print and worked well at any size. Laurer and his coworkers proposed a system of two mirrors placed in a bar code reader that created an X pattern of two lines. This pattern ensured an accurate reading of the code regardless of its orientation.

Laurer finished his presentation at home and watched for his boss, who lived across the street and three doors down, to return home from vacation. As soon as McEnroe arrived, Laurer marched over and showed him the plan.

McEnroe wasn't happy—IBM executives were expecting a proposal based on the RCA code. "He made it clear that if I was wrong... it would end my career, not his," Laurer said. "I was truly playing 'bet your job.'" Yet McEnroe supported him, and Laurer made the presentation. The IBM team bought in, agreeing to try Laurer's approach. An odd test sealed it for Laurer's system: the code was applied to the bottom of beanbag ashtrays, and the pitcher on IBM's local softball team tossed the ashtrays over a scanner at high speed. The code on every ashtray was read correctly.

The Universal Product Code (UPC) system turned into one of the most profound contributions to industrial technology. For retailers, the bar code meant savings, better customer service, precise inventory control and

Submissions for the Universal Product Code

Litton

Singer

Charecogn

Pitney-Bowes

RCA

IBM

rich stores of marketing data. The technology soon spread to other industries. Today the UPC system is ubiquitous and used to track everything from rental cars to dairy cows to airplane luggage to bags of blood. There is a UPC on just about every ticket, whether it's an airline boarding pass, a ski lift pass or a movie stub. The just-in-time inventory system that revolutionized manufacturing in the late twentieth century and launched the era of big-box stores and global supply chains would have been impossible to create if not for the UPC system.

The bar code gave computers a way to register data by seeing—not the way humans see, but in a way suited to computing. A computer could not look at a package of blueberries and recognize it, but it could read a series of lines on the package and know it contained blueberries—and how much it cost—as quickly as any human.

Computer researchers aren't stopping there. For decades, they've been trying to get computers to see. At first, computers could recognize boundaries in video. For instance, a robot could navigate across a room by processing the images it saw through a video camera. By the late 1990s, the first consumer software programs were able to scan a hard drive to find all the photos of a certain face. Today, facial recognition technology—a combination of 3-D sensors, skin texture analysis and template-matching techniques—can compare photos of suspects against a database of photos or videos, identifying the matching faces better than a human could.

Character recognition systems, such as those deployed in Singapore and Stockholm to monitor traffic, can read license plates, even if the plates are splattered with mud or snow. Video surveillance systems are beginning

Computing systems can rely on sensors to detect minute changes that humans wouldn't notice.

In Taiwan's high-speed rail system, sensors gather more than 320,000 data elements, from the rotation and temperature of wheels to the thickness of the overhead wire from which the train draws its power. If the system sees a problem, like excessive brake wear, it automatically sends a notification to the command center and generates the appropriate work order request.

to recognize shapes and movement, both of which give them the power to distinguish, for instance, whether an intruder is a dog or a person.

A peer-to-peer network of zebras in Kenya only hints at what's to come. In California's Napa Valley, sensors monitor water transpiration levels on individual grapevines and alert vintners to optimum watering times. Sensors mounted on bicycles in Copenhagen collect information about air quality, which riders can forward through their smartphones to other cyclists, who might want to choose a healthier route. Aggregate cell phone traffic is being monitored to determine which city buildings are crowded at what times, as a way to better manage energy consumption.

Machines once suffered from extremely limited ability to acquire information about the world around them, but they increasingly have the capacity to monitor the workings of the planet in intimate detail, deciphering and analyzing that information for humans. Working together, people and machines will sense and understand the planet in ways previously unfathomable.

In the meantime, the story of computer sensing has twisted back on itself. It began with tabulating machines touching cards. In 2011, humans are touching computers. Touch screen technology has been around since a Kentucky company called Elographics developed the first versions in 1977. Through the decades the technology has been used at kiosks and museums and shown up in the PalmPilot and a few other gadgets, but it hadn't become popular as a computer interface.

Apple changed that with the iPhone and then the iPad. In both cases, people primarily rely on intuitive, sophisticated multitouch technology to tell the devices what to do. The warmest, most emotional form of sensing is bonding people and machines, offering that physical connection—and letting people touch information—while everyone waits for machines to get better at seeing and hearing humans.

· · ·

Memory

Storing and accessing information—
the raw material of computation—has
become so efficient that we are now
approaching total recall.

Magnetic core memory was one of the first ways to store
information. The ferrite rings would be magnetized
in either a clockwise or counterclockwise direction by the
grid of wires, each ring representing a one or a zero.

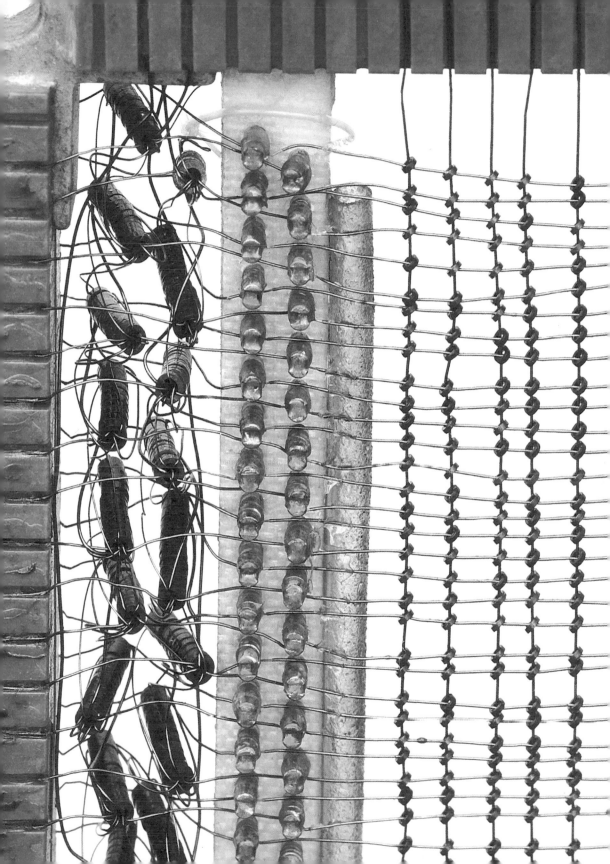

In the 1950s, Phil Fox was running the Tabulating Department for American Stores Company, which gave him a perspective on what it would be like to have a brain without accessible memory.

American Stores, formed in 1917 when the Acme Tea Company merged with four Philadelphia grocery stores, had grown into one of the biggest chains of supermarkets and drugstores in the United States. The only way it could manage more than 2,000 stores in the early 1950s and maintain some semblance of control was to rely on a roomful of electromechanical computing machines and another room jammed full of tubs of rectangular punched cards.[9]

This was very much like operating a brain in one room, with its memory in another. The computing machine was the processor, but it could store nothing. The cards held every bit of information relevant to American Stores: product orders, payroll, sales, expenses, inventory. The machine couldn't do anything unless a batch of carefully sorted cards was carried over to the machine and loaded in. When the machine finished sorting and counting the batch and reporting the results, the cards were removed—and the machine forgot everything.

"In our setup, this would mean that all orders for one brand of soap or one brand of cereal, or any other single item, would have to be put together first," Fox told an interviewer in 1960. "And with some 70,000 grocery item lines being processed each day, this could turn into quite a job." If a Coca-Cola order from a store came in two hours after the Coke batch of punched cards had been run, the order couldn't be recorded and filled until a day or two later, when the next Coke batch was run.

Similar problems affected much of global industry in the 1950s. Computing companies such as IBM and Sperry (later Sperry Univac) had invented electronic brains that could count, correlate and do math in a flash, automating what had been drudge work. But all the information— all the memory—was in those holes punched into stiff paper. The cards were manually sorted, stacked, loaded and filed by humans. The New York Central railway punched 175,000 cards a day.

And with the brain and the memory separate, there was no way to interact with the data—no way to use the computer to randomly find out how many Coca-Cola cases were sold in a given week or change the number of cars on a New York-to-Boston run any time of day.

As the 1950s unfolded, no one really knew what it would mean to have digital data readily stored and randomly accessed by a computer. No one knew how it could be done. No one understood that putting the brain and the memory together would completely alter the idea and power of computing.

——

FOR MORE THAN 60 YEARS, corporations and governments relied on punched cards to store and recall information. Punched cards represent one of the most remarkable success stories in information technology history.

Herman Hollerith turned punched cards into data storage devices when he took a practice used by train conductors to punch holes in passengers' tickets and applied it to identifying and counting people for the US Census Bureau. A hole in one place meant dark hair; in another place it meant male or female. Hollerith realized he could make a similar "punch photograph" of every US resident.

On July 6, 1911, Hollerith agreed to sell his Tabulating Machine Company to financier Charles Flint for $2,312,100, and the company became part of Flint's Computing-Tabulating-Recording-Company. In the 1920s, C-T-R evolved into IBM. Remington Rand emerged as the chief competitor in punched cards and tabulating machines. The cards evolved to hold more information. Early versions had 45 columns. An IBM breakthrough in 1928 created cards with 80 columns. Remington Rand countered with a 90-column card—which, interestingly, didn't dent IBM's business. The 90-column cards could store more data but were not as user-friendly as IBM's 80-column cards.

Institutional memory moved from files and handwritten ledgers to punched cards. Railroads were among the first to automate information about cars, freight and passengers. Retailers such as Marshall Field's shifted inventory tracking to cards. When the US government set up Social Security, the cards became the nation's financial memory, holding workers' wage information. By the late 1930s, punched card machines had spread across Europe, used by Nestlé in Switzerland, Gasworks of Budapest in Hungary, the Ministry of Finance in Greece and a host of other entities.[10] The memory of punched cards made the scale of the modern corporation possible. By 1937, IBM had 32 presses at work in Endicott, New York, printing, cutting and stacking 5 million to 10 million punched cards a day. The cards themselves accounted for one-third of IBM's revenue in the 1950s. While IBM surely was a technology company, a major factor in its financial success was making and selling paper cards.[11]

But as the punched cards made scale possible, ever-increasing scale required ever more punched cards. Corporations and governments were running headlong into problems with this form of memory. "You'd go into the MetLife building, and there'd be a whole floor filled with filing cabinets of cards," said James Birkenstock, a top IBM executive in the 1940s and '50s. "Customers wanted to do things that were beyond the capabilities of the punched card system. IBM moved in the nick of time—maybe even a little late."

Good thing Bing Crosby blazed a new path.[12]

———

AS WORLD WAR II ENDED, global industry boomed, driving a boom in demand for punched cards. While IBM's sales force milked that cash cow, some in management—including Thomas Watson Jr., who returned from the war to work with his father at the top of IBM—worried that customers were getting buried in cards. Another problem was developing: the newest computing machines, based on vacuum tube electronics, could process information far faster than cards could be fed into them. Memory was lagging processing, which was making it hard to develop faster computing machines and persuade customers to upgrade.

During the war, German company AEG developed magnetic tape and the tape recorder. An American Army Signal Corps radio specialist, John Mullin, had discovered the German invention near the end of the war and brought it back to the United States. About the same time, singer Bing Crosby started to look for ways to do his weekly radio show without having to perform live in the studio every time. Crosby hired Mullin to pre-record his shows. On October 1, 1947, the public heard the first radio show played back from magnetic tape, unleashing a new technology.

A group of engineers in IBM's Poughkeepsie, New York, lab picked up on Crosby's experiments and worked on ways to store data the same way. No one, anywhere, knew much of anything about the properties of magnetic tape, and it seemed risky to ask customers to trust their information to be safely stored in a form they couldn't physically see. Meanwhile, inside IBM, pursuing a successor to punched cards had become a political minefield. "Once, a white-haired IBM veteran in Poughkeepsie pulled a few of us aside," said Wayne Winger, a key member of that first tape-drive development team. "He said, 'You young fellows remember, IBM was built on punch cards, and our foundation will always be punch cards.'"[13]

Magnetic tape for the first time stored ones and zeros invisibly. The information from a single punched card could fit on a tiny sliver of a reel of tape.

The IBM 2401 magnetic tape unit.

Watson Jr., then just in his mid-thirties, was enough of a gambler to get behind the unproven technology. IBM scientist Nathaniel Rochester recalled that Watson assembled a meeting and "went all around the room asking people if this was the right thing to do or not, and some people said 'yes' and some people said other things. And then he told all those people who said other things that they should work on other problems."[14]

Minnesota Mining & Manufacturing (3M) developed the tape to IBM specifications while IBM's engineers designed tape drives with rapid start and stop times, moving the tape around reels at 100 to 200 inches per second. Again, nothing like it had ever been built. The engineers hit on the idea of using a vacuum column to suck in loops of tape to buffer the tape from jarring stops and starts. "We were in a hurry to try out the idea," recalled one of the engineers, Wayne Weidenhammer. "And we needed some very thin, flexible material in order to fabricate a sensitive pressure-sensing diaphragm. Nothing suitable being at hand, the quickest solution was to send one of the young engineers to the nearest drugstore for a pair of [rubber] baby pants. They worked."[15]

In 1952, IBM announced the industry's first magnetic tape unit, dubbed the IBM 726. It was paired with the 701, the company's first commercial electronic computer. IBM convinced customers that data would persist on tape, and the tape unit immediately relieved storage problems. A single reel of tape, 10½ inches in diameter, held the equivalent of 35,000 punched cards.

But a new problem soon emerged. The memory was still not married to processing. The processor had to locate data on tape, which had to be spun around, backward and forward. The processor sat in one machine, the memory in another. Tape took care of the storage and space problems, but it didn't take care of the batch processing problem. In a way, the batch problem got more harrowing because enterprises could use tape to store yet more information.

That's where the US Air Force came in. It wanted a new system for tracking inventory. And it wanted random access to that information—so that when a piece of equipment was checked out, clerks could instantly update that information and not be forced to wait until the next batch was processed. IBM had just built a lab in San Jose, run by a one-time high school science teacher who turned into a maverick researcher. The lab got the air force's job, with no idea how to pull it off.

———

THE NOTION OF SOME KIND OF MAGNETIC, quickly accessed memory had been around since the late 1940s. Small companies like Engineering Research Associates of St. Paul, Minnesota, developed magnetic drum storage. These rotating drums were reliable but slow. An Wang, a Chinese immigrant to the United States who later built the word processing giant Wang Laboratories, early on developed a technology that made magnetic core memory possible. These devices of wires and tiny magnets had quick access times but couldn't hold much information. They couldn't replace tape or punched cards, but they were used as short-term memory for early computers—the predecessors to the solid-state memory of DRAM chips.

In 1952, IBM sent Reynold Johnson to San Jose to start a new research lab. Johnson had been with the company since 1934, after teaching science in Ironwood, Michigan, where he and some students had developed an automatic test scoring machine that got IBM's attention. He was an unorthodox manager with dead-on instincts about technology. When the air force wanted a random access inventory system, Johnson set his 50-person lab in motion, trying everything—strips, rods, tapes, flat plates.[16]

The lab soon settled on using spinning horizontal disks coated with magnetic material. Spots on the disk would represent a character of data. The spots had a magnetic field, which meant that a magnetic arm, like a record needle, could hover over the spots and read them as the disks rotated at high speed. But the first challenge was finding material for the disks. The disks had to be perfectly flat, strong and light enough to be spun by a reasonably sized electric motor. A single aluminum disk, developed by Alcoa,

Disk drives allowed ones and zeros to be found
and rewritten randomly, without having to spin a tape reel
forward and back.

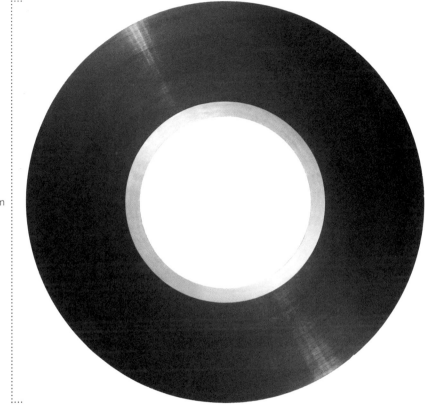

63.5 cm

RAMAC, out in 1956, was the
first disk drive and could store
about the amount of data in
a Manhattan phone book on
24 spinning platters.

13.4 cm

12 cm

14.7 cm

The work on RAMAC led to the
floppy disk, introduced in 1971,
which at first held data equal to
about eight encyclopedia pages.

Compact discs arrived in 1982
and greatly improved data
capacity, holding 700 megabytes,
or about 80 minutes of audio.

Hard disk drives, the most
direct descendants of
RAMAC, can now hold
as much as 3 terabytes
of data—more than all
the information in a major
university library.

warped at high speeds. After much trial and error, the researchers tried gluing two aluminum disks together. It worked.

Even more problematic was the arm. If it touched the disk, it would wipe out the data. Two researchers—William Goddard and John Lynott—came up with an arm that fired out compressed air to hover just above the disk. "When we concluded we could do that, we could see a fairly clear road to building a practical random access memory," said Louis Stevens, a senior engineer at the San Jose lab.[17]

It was a clear road, but still not an easy one. A lab accident nearly shut down the program. While testing the mechanism, one of the spinning disks split and rocketed out of the casing, fracturing one researcher's nose and severing another researcher's thumb tendon. Johnson had to promise IBM headquarters that all further tests would be run behind a stack of sandbags.

Because a single disk could not store enough data to be useful, the researchers built a machine that held 24 disks stacked horizontally, with a tiny space between each disk. "We called it a jukebox and a meat cutter and a lot of other things," Johnson said. To disbelieving executives at headquarters, it was known as the baloney slicer.

The jukebox setup left the San Jose team with one other challenge: how to get that arm to the right place on the right disk in the blink of an eye. Said Johnson: "That was our goal, to go from any track, which was 6 inches in on a disk, out, down, 2 feet to the bottom, and in 6 inches—in half a second. We achieved something like 800 milliseconds, and that's where the product came out. It was really an amazing achievement."

The product as it was introduced in May 1955 was the size of a couple of kitchen refrigerators side by side. Twenty-four disks inside spun at 1,200 revolutions per minute while the arm dashed in and out, accessing the data at about 100,000 bits per second. The whole thing could store 5 million binary decimal encoded characters at 7 bits per character—or about the contents of a Manhattan phone book. Each character could be read or changed randomly, in any order, at any time, making the machine a revelation.

IBM

IBM   **Prepare an Invention Disclosure promptly for something new or unexpected**   12953   **19**

Nov. R.H.D.

New Memory Scheme

The following idea was conceived in the evening of Wednesday, Oct. 7, 1966 and was disclosed to D. L. Critchlow by telephone. It utilizes the scheme for "reading" described on p.15. The state of the cell is stored in the gate of the output device T_{out} (which corresponds to T_6 in the nomenclature of p.15). See diagram:

The capacitance C_g which is inherent in the fabrication of the two devices (and can be supplemented if desired by, for example, adding a stub of aluminum line over the substrate) is used to store charge. When the C_g is shown as a stray capacitance to ground, but we realize that it is made up of several components, some of which may be at ground potential, but mainly the capacitance is between the gate and the substrate, which is at "a-c" ground in the sense that it does not change in time but may be actually at some negative potential, if (for example) NPN devices are being used. Using this example of NPN device the voltage, V_g, across the gate will be either at a positive level, greater than 6 volts, or at a lower level, less than 2 volts, corresponding to the logic states of a stored "1" or a stored "0" respectively. This charge can be placed on the gate in the following way:

Thus V_g can be changed only when the Write Word Line is energized; then V_g takes on (or remains at) the voltage level on the BIT IN line. Thus the data on the BIT IN line is entered into the cell. This data will remain at the same state for a certain period of time, say T_D. The charge on

Entered by: R. H. Dennard   Date: Nov. 10, 1966

Disclosed & Understood: P. W. Cook   November 10, 1966
Disclosed & Understood: D. L. Critchlow, Nov. 9, 1966,   Witnessed: D. L. Critchlow, Nov. 11, 1966

The morning after his epiphany about storing information by putting a charge on a capacitor, IBM scientist Robert Dennard sketched his idea on the notepad shown here. Like many new ideas, this one took Dennard a few more months to refine into the design for DRAM.

At the time, thanks to the success of the early UNIVAC computer, the suffix -AC was a popular tech branding construct—like the prefix in eBay or eToys in the dot-com era. The researchers called their machine Random Access Memory-AC, or RAMAC. The IBM marketers liked RAMAC but changed it to mean Random Access Method of Accounting and Control.

The day after RAMAC was announced, the *San Jose Mercury News* ran a story with the headline "A Machine With Super Memory!" The story described the machine, noting: "The information on the discs can be added to, altered or erased at will. Card-sorting, one of the most time consuming office-machine processes, is eliminated or greatly reduced."

More than that, enterprises could think about data in new ways— mixing and matching it on the fly. Random access made the relational data-base possible.

———

ROBERT DENNARD was sitting on the couch in his living room in Westchester County, New York, watching the sun set over the Croton River Gorge. And it just hit him.[18]

That morning, he'd gone to an all-day meeting of IBM researchers, where they all shared their projects. It was meant to stir ideas and cross-collaboration. Dennard had a doctorate in electrical engineering and had been assigned to work on MOS (metal-oxide semiconductor) transistor memories for computers. "Our goal was to replace magnetic core memory with semiconductor memory," Dennard said. Earlier in the day, though, he'd listened to the group trying to improve magnetic core memory and keep that technology alive.

IBM researcher Robert Dennard, inventor of DRAM, circa 1978.

Something about his work and what he saw at the meeting troubled Dennard. The magnetic memory being developed by his competing researchers had drawbacks, but it was extremely simple. His MOS project had promise but was pretty complicated, using six transistors for each bit of information.

"I thought, what could I do that would be really simple?" Dennard recalled. There on his couch he thought through the characteristics of MOS technology. It was capable of building capacitors, and storing a charge or no charge on the capacitor could represent the one and zero of a bit of information. A transistor could control writing the charge to the capacitor. The more Dennard thought, the more he knew he could make a simple memory out of this.

"I called my boss that night around 10 p.m.," Dennard said. "It's a rare event that I'd call him. He listened to me, then suggested we talk about it tomorrow. I joke that he basically told me to take two aspirin and call him in the morning."

Dennard still had to work on the six-transistor memory, so he worked on his new idea in his spare time, eventually figuring out the subtleties of writing a charge to the capacitor by way of an access transistor and then reading it back through the same transistor. In 1967, he and IBM filed for a patent for his single-transistor dynamic random access memory, or DRAM.

The patent was issued in 1968. In 1970, Intel built the first commercially successful dynamic random access memory chip, a three-transistor memory chip called the 1103. By the mid-1970s, several manufacturers had introduced single-transistor memory cells.

The simplicity and low power consumption of DRAM changed the computing industry. It allowed random access memory, or RAM, to become very dense and relatively inexpensive and yet require little power. As a result, mainframe computers could be outfitted with fast, reliable RAM to act as a buffer to the exploding amount of data stored on disk drives. This vastly sped up the process of accessing and using stored information.

Just as important, cheap, tiny DRAM, combined with the first low-cost microprocessors, made personal computers possible.

On his couch in his living room, Dennard envisioned how DRAM could work and how it would be important to the industry. But, he admitted, "we couldn't imagine how much it would change computing."

A HUMAN BRAIN is the greatest processor on earth, but it has nothing to process without memories. A brain, in fact, needs two kinds of memory—short term and long term—to work efficiently. Short-term memory keeps track of what's said in the current conversation, for instance, then files the most significant details into long-term memory and dumps the rest. It's the working memory, calling on stores of knowledge for the job at hand then shuffling in new knowledge for the next task. Long-term memory stores everything you've ever known—filed, cross-referenced and prioritized—keeping it in the background most of the time yet instantly making it available when you want it, and even when you don't.[19]

In computing, seamlessly marrying processing and memory was a long struggle. It finally became a reality in the 2000s, after the cost of disk drive and solid-state memory technology plummeted as its capacity skyrocketed. From the late 1950s to 2010, the amount of information that could be stored on a given area of a disk drive increased by a factor of 17 *million*. Over that same period, the speed at which data could be read from a disk increased 8,000 times, and the cost of storing data dropped a millionfold. The pace of improvement has picked up over the past 20 years. Storing a gigabyte of information—the equivalent of about an hour of standard-quality TV video—in the 1980s required a 500-pound, refrigerator-sized machine. By 2010, a gigabyte could be stored on a disk smaller than a coin.

In the lingo of computing, the terms *memory* and *storage* represent separate things. Storage is the data you save, like long-term memory in the brain. Computer memory is the working memory—the short-term memory—that keeps a laptop working smoothly.

The public has come to see memory and storage as commodities—especially storage. In 2000, a PC could easily run out of disk space, corporate IT departments put limits on e-mail storage, and cell phones could barely hold a few grainy photos. In 2010, an iPod the size of a few sticks of chewing gum held a music collection that on vinyl would fill a floor-to-ceiling bookcase. By 2010, the Library of Congress had downloaded and stored 167 terabytes' worth of websites and set up a facility to digitize audio and video at the rate of up to 5,000 terabytes per year. (A terabyte of DVD movies would run for 16 days.)

Technologists have made the work of memorizing trivial for machines, and they've married stored data to processing in ways that have made it possible to create commercial databases, simulations of nuclear explosions and computer-generated movies like *Avatar*.

And yet, any disk drive still needs an arm to move to find the data. A terabyte of data on a disk has a single access point, and it's all funneled through that read/write head. Meanwhile, processors have gotten so fast that they're often waiting for data from the disk. It harks back to the day when the first electronic computers had to wait for the data from punched cards.

Much like Bob Dennard in the 1960s, Stuart Parkin spent the early 2000s looking for a simple, solid-state solution. Parkin is an experimental physicist at Almaden Research Center in San Jose. He'd already forged a new path into spintronics, which uses the spin of electrons for memory instead of an electrical charge. His work is a significant reason for the increased density of disk drives over the past 20 years.

In solid-state storage, every bit can be read instantly—no waiting for the read/write arm. Boot-up times become a fraction of a second. Consumers can see how that works on an iPhone or any small device that uses a flash drive. The problem with solid-state storage, though, is cost. Each transistor

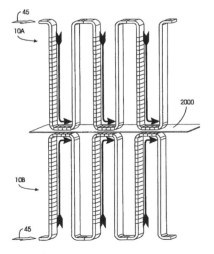

Racetrack memory stores ones and zeros in columns of subatomic particles. A device with racetrack memory could store thousands of movies and find a single image in a billionth of a second.

Diagram of racetrack memory
from US Patent 7,315,470, issued
to IBM's Stuart Parkin.

can store only one bit of information. The only way to pack more information into a flash drive is to pack together the latest tiny, costly transistors. In 2010, a flash drive cost about $2 a gigabyte. Disk drives cost about 10 cents per gigabyte.

Parkin figured out how to create a tall column (on an atomic scale) of magnetic material inside a transistor, with each floor of this little skyscraper representing a bit of data. The technique uses the spin of electrons to manipulate these bits, in effect shooting them around a racetrack up and down that tall column. "Each transistor could store not one bit, but 100 bits," Parkin said. "Then you can have the same low cost of disk drives but performance 10 million times better."

Racetrack memory works in the lab. Parkin estimates it will take a few years before it can be commercialized. By then, the kind of mass storage that now requires a disk drive could fit on a thumbnail-sized chip that barely uses any energy.

A handheld device could hold a few thousand movies, run for weeks at a time on a single battery and be practically unbreakable. A personal storage device could fit into a lapel pin and record every conversation its wearer has for years before filling up. In enterprises, massive storage could be dispersed, with terabytes of information built into every device, sensor, camera and doorknob.

Over the coming decade, businesses and government agencies will have to start thinking of information storage and access in a new way, much as they did after the arrival of RAMAC. What happens if storage becomes practically limitless, free and small enough to be built into anything? What happens when everything that happens can be recorded and stored?

The human brain has a mechanism for dealing with data overload. It forgets. If indeed we're on a path to building machines that think like us, how ironic if the next great invention in computer memory turns out to be forgetting.

· · ·

Processing

At its core, computation is about processing ones and zeros. Computing power is the art of doing so faster and faster.

These vacuum tubes, from a 1953 system, could multiply two 10-digit numbers 2,000 times per second.

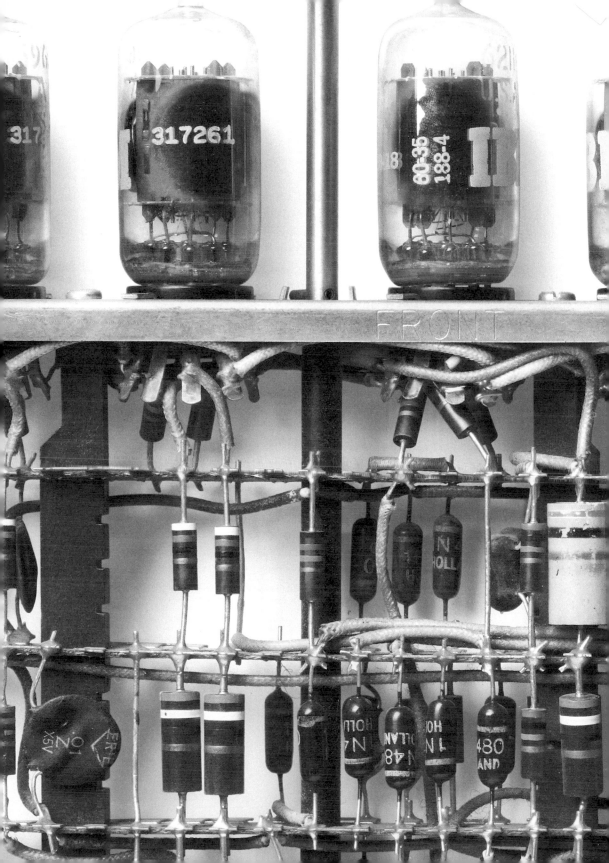

Just after World War II, on a gray March day on the campus of the University of Pennsylvania, two young men from the office of IBM's president—Charles Kirk and Thomas Watson Jr.—walked into a room made tropically hot by 18,000 lit vacuum tube switches. J. Presper Eckert, cocky and impetuous, explained how his invention, called ENIAC, worked and described how electronic computers were going to replace electromechanical machines like IBM's.

Eckert and his coinventor, John Mauchly, had contacted IBM to ask for help. The wartime development of ENIAC had been funded by the US Army, but Eckert and Mauchly needed peacetime funding and were looking to IBM, RCA and AT&T's Bell Laboratories for help. IBM agreed to design a custom-made card-reading device that would load numbers into ENIAC. The access allowed the IBM engineers doing the work to gather intelligence about the machine, particularly how Eckert and Mauchly had linked the tubes into arrays that could perform high-speed arithmetic. Other than peripherals such as the card reader, ENIAC had no mechanical parts, which was unlike any computing machine before it. Mauchly's proposal stated that if an electromechanical machine could solve a particular equation in 15–30 minutes, ENIAC could do it in 100 seconds. Yet ENIAC was still a risky lab experiment. At that first meeting, Watson Jr. and Kirk both dismissed the computer as too costly and unreliable. How could a business do critical work if tubes kept burning out and shutting down the machine? [20]

Still, there was a buzz in the air that couldn't be dismissed by anyone in the information business.

The demands of war had left the US government with an insatiable appetite for speed. The army and navy had rapidly developed new weapons, each of which required vast computation capabilities in order to create the ballistic tables needed to aim guns accurately. Intelligence agencies had captured and were struggling to analyze a flood of enemy communications, much of which was in code they had to decrypt. Unprecedented quantities of men and matériel had been tracked across oceans and continents.

There was an urgent need for machines that could produce results much faster. For more than 50 years, information had been processed by electromechanical punched card systems, a business dominated by IBM. But the machines' speed and the types of problems they could handle were limited, and the war effort spurred frantic research into purely electronic systems like ENIAC, which offered the promise of huge gains in speed. As ENIAC and electronics emerged from the war, the world economy boomed and a generation of soldiers returned home eager to reinvent life and business. Television, the electric guitar and Polaroid cameras were new technologies. Everything was going faster. Much like the military during the war, companies and other enterprises were being flooded with information. Business needed speed. The stage was set for an information revolution marked by orders of magnitude increases in computing speed and power, year after year, decade after decade.

In the middle of World War II, the military needed IBM to focus on products of the present, not the future, so IBM had shut down research on electronics—sort of. With the blessing of research chief James Bryce, a passionate young engineer named Arthur Halsey Dickinson continued to work on vacuum tube electronics in his basement at home. When the war ended, Bryce let Dickinson bring his work back into the lab. Weeks after Kirk and Watson Jr. snubbed ENIAC, the two men went to see Dickinson's prototype electronic calculator. Dickinson had linked a high-speed punched card reader to a black metal box about 4 feet tall. Watson Jr. asked what the box was doing. One of the engineers told him it was using radio tubes to multiply. The engineers explained that the device could multiply 10 times faster than a punched card machine. In fact, the box spent nine-tenths of its time waiting for the punched card mechanism to catch up. While Watson Jr. failed to see any good in the gigantic ENIAC, Dickinson's electronic black box excited him. "That impressed me as though somebody had hit me on the head with a hammer," Watson Jr. recalled.

IBM set out to make an electronic calculator that could be produced and sold—if anyone wanted to buy one. At the National Business Show in New York in September 1946, IBM unveiled the IBM 603 Electronic Multiplier—the first production electronic calculator, developed from Dickinson's work. It contained 300 vacuum tubes, as opposed to ENIAC's 18,000. It had no storage, so it couldn't handle complex equations. It couldn't do much more than multiply two six-digit numbers read from a punched card. But it could do that multiplication 10 times faster than anything else on the market.

To IBM's astonishment, customers liked the 603 and placed orders for it. IBM cut off production at 100, and the engineers built a more refined, versatile follow-up, the IBM 604 Electronic Calculating Punch. It used 1,400 tubes and could be programmed for simple equations. Over the next 10 years, IBM built and leased 5,600 of the 604 machines. No one at IBM had predicted such success.

Early tabulating machines relied on a mechanical device to turn circuits on and off.

The IBM-Harvard Mark 1 (left), and an engineer switching out an electromechanical relay.

For the first time, IBM got the message: *Customers will buy electronic products.* The hunger for speed had arrived in a way no one had anticipated.

——

VACUUM TUBE ELECTRONICS opened the door to speed, but as Thomas Watson Jr. discovered while watching the 603's processor run far ahead of the card reader, speed needed a whole system.

As the 1950s unfolded, 14 US companies were developing electronic computers with help from the government. The Cold War scared the Truman administration into pumping money into technology in hopes of maintaining an advantage over the Soviets. Some of that money went to university labs. Some went to start-up companies like Engineering Research Associates. And some went to Eckert and Mauchly, who found a backer for their business in Remington Rand. The duo built a commercial successor to their ENIAC, dubbed UNIVAC—the first electronic computer to win the hearts of the new generation of speed demons. Under pressure from the UNIVAC, IBM engineers felt that their reputations—and possibly an important part of IBM's future—were at stake. The culture responded in a surge of esprit de corps and created a systemic approach to speed, dubbed the 701.

The 701 design team couldn't wait for the space it needed inside IBM, so it started work on the third floor of a tie factory in Poughkeepsie, then moved to an empty supermarket building. "Tar leaked down from the roof on hot days," said Clarence Frizzell, one of the project managers. "We had to scrape it off the drawings to keep working." The team threw aside budgets and schedules, previously a fact of life in the labs. "Maybe that's why we did things so fast," said Jerrier Haddad, a managing engineer on the 701. "We didn't have schedules to slow us down."[21]

In a little less than two years, the team developed and began building the enormously complex Defense Calculator, which featured a number of breakthroughs in design. The Defense Calculator became the Model 701 Electronic Data Processing Machine, a scientific computer that could perform more than 2,000 multiplications per second, nearly 50 times faster than the 603. But the processor was only part of the speed equation. Memory—the ability to fetch and store information for the computer to work on—was the weak point in early computers. The 701's main memory, based on electrostatic devices called Williams tubes, could hold just over 20,000 digits, about one one-thousandth of a percent of the memory that in 2011 is standard in a $300 laptop. The main memory was supplemented by a bigger but slower magnetic drum—a sort of primitive disk drive—that held 82,000 digits and slower still magnetic tape units that held 8 million digits per reel.[22]

The combination of electronic processing and electronic memory made a machine that amazed the world. *Time* noted that a business-oriented version of the 701, the 702, could "remember enough information to fill a 1,836-page Manhattan telephone book… and work the information at the rate of 7,200 unerringly logical operations per second…. it can multiply a pair of 127-digit numbers and arrive at a 254-digit answer in one-third of a second." This kind of systemic speed spurred scientists to imagine what they could do with faster and more complex data. *Time* wrote that chemists at Monsanto felt the machine would "open up new horizons by rapidly working out complex equations to help discover new products, improve old ones, find out which of dozens of technically 'correct' answers to problems are the best."

The military kept driving for systemic speed. At MIT, computing pioneer Jay Forrester was funded to build a system called Whirlwind for the US Air Force. Other computers of the day handled problems in batches, loading one program and running it, then loading the next program. Whirlwind was to be the heart of a flight simulator, a role that would require it to

Vacuum tubes were the first "electronic" switches, using electricity that could turn on or off at the speed of light. But tubes were bulky, burned out and gave off a tremendous amount of heat.

———

Changing a vacuum tube on the ENIAC (left), and a close-up of a vacuum tube.

capture data from flight controls, instantly process it and feed it back continually in real time. This required a system an order of magnitude faster than anything that existed. The key was core memory, invented in the late 1940s. The technique used tiny doughnuts of iron-based material whose magnetic parity could be flipped and read by passing a current through wires strung through a matrix of cores.

Whirlwind never became a flight simulator and was reconceived as a digital computer. IBM picked up Forrester's use of core memory for the next version of the 701, the 704. Then IBM took the systems approach to speed a few steps further. The 704, released in 1954, featured three special memory locations called index registers that made programming easier and more flexible. Floating-point arithmetic, a variation on scientific notation, made it possible to store very large (or very small) numbers and to perform operations on them more quickly. The 704 ran at twice the speed of the 701, though the introduction of floating-point operations meant the actual leap in processing speed was considerably greater.[23]

For all the work by computer engineers of the 1950s to build ever faster computers, the machines still depended on vacuum tubes, and tubes guaranteed that computers would remain big, expensive, fitfully reliable and relatively slow. But a contraption that looked like a little arrowhead, with a tiny TV antenna stuck on top, changed that forever. At Bell Labs, they called their invention the transistor.

———

THREE BELL LABS RESEARCHERS—John Bardeen, Walter Brattain and William Shockley—first made a transistor work in 1947. The device replicated the switching characteristics of a tube in a solid piece of germanium. One big advantage of the transistor was its potentially unlimited lifetime; unlike the tube, it had no filament that would burn out. Even more important in the long run, transistors could be manufactured far more cheaply than tubes and shrink in size, allowing computers to pack more processing power into smaller spaces.

Transistors were a huge advance over tubes, but there was still a lot of room for performance improvement. As long as transistors came in discrete packages, there was a limit to how small they could get, and as computers got faster their size was becoming a factor in performance. Grace Murray Hopper used to demonstrate this at lectures. She would hand out pieces of wire about a foot long and point out that this was the farthest an electric signal could travel in a nanosecond, one-billionth of a second. "She offered that as a visual metaphor to say, 'This gives you an idea of why machines are shrinking,'" said John Backus, the inventor of Fortran. Smaller transistors, packed tightly together, would be able to zip information across shorter pieces of wire, accessing information faster.

The way to do this was discovered independently by Jack St. Clair Kilby of Texas Instruments and by Robert Noyce and Gordon Moore of Fairchild Semiconductor. They realized that the same techniques that were used to manufacture individual transistors could be used to place multiple transistors, along with the wires connecting them, into appropriate circuits on a single piece of silicon. The first integrated circuits combined just a few transistors, but the components on the chip rapidly got smaller and were more densely packed. By 1965, Moore came up with his famous formulation that the density of transistors would double roughly every 18 months, a forecast that has held up for 45 years. And the denser the circuits got, the faster they performed.[24]

In the 1960s, the quest for speed wasn't just about how fast a machine could do something. It was also about how fast it could do it in less and less space. Miniaturization took hold. The US government pumped billions of dollars into the space race, investing in anything that would shrink computing speed so it could fit in a rocket or satellite. In Japan, Masaru Ibuka and Akio Morita started Sony to make transistor radios and other miniature electronics. As the 1960s economy surged, companies were flooded with data about new customers, new products and new markets, and they needed faster, smaller and cheaper computers to track it all.

IBM gambled on integrated circuits in 1971 with the System/370 Model 145. The still-new technology was used not only for the computer's logic, but also for a new type of chip, which IBM called monolithic memory. It replaced the old core memory. The 370/145 came with up to 512 kilobytes of memory—puny by today's standards but twice the maximum amount of memory of the System/360 Model 40 that it replaced. And the solid state memory took up half as much space as core. With both memory and processor improvements, the 370/145 was five times faster than the 360/40—all thanks to integrated circuits.

The move to integrated circuits ignited the cycle of rocketing performance and plunging cost that continues today. Even in the integrated circuit-based 370, the processor was still a piece of equipment, often refrigerator-sized or bigger, crammed with circuit boards. But advances in chip design were about to put an end to that. In 1971, Intel Corporation, founded by Noyce and Moore when they left Fairchild, introduced the 4004, the first complete processor on a chip. The 4004 was a modest chip, better suited to a desktop calculator than a full-fledged computer, but Intel quickly followed it with a more capable microprocessor, the 8008. Other companies got into the business and produced the Zilog Z80 and the MOS Technology 6502, the processor in the Apple II. Computing speed was finally getting small enough to become personal.

———

AT IBM, THE DRIVE TO BUILD MICROPROCESSORS reshaped high-performance computing. In the late 1970s, IBM researcher John Cocke was working on a new type of microprocessor code-named America. He thought that processors would perform better if they used fewer, simpler instructions, an effort that became known as reduced instruction set computer, or RISC. The first RISC processor was the IBM 801. IBM considered, and rejected, the 801 for use in the IBM PC because the technology was unproven and expensive. But a version of Cocke's 801 made its way into the RS/6000, the

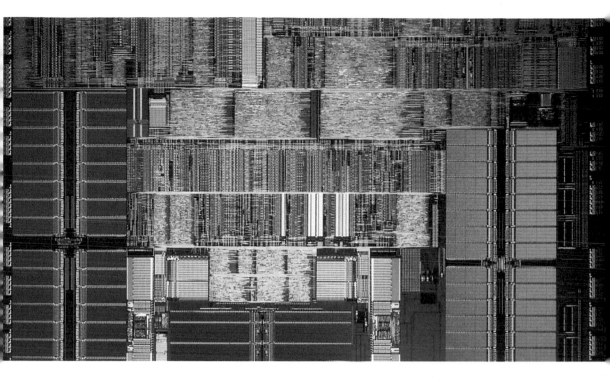

Transistors were solid state—there were no filaments to burn out,
plus they were much smaller and didn't get as hot as vacuum tubes.
Transistors could be packed together, allowing a computer
to do more calculations faster.

Power6 microprocessor (above), and microscopic view of transistors on a Power6 chip.
The transistors are the gold peaks.

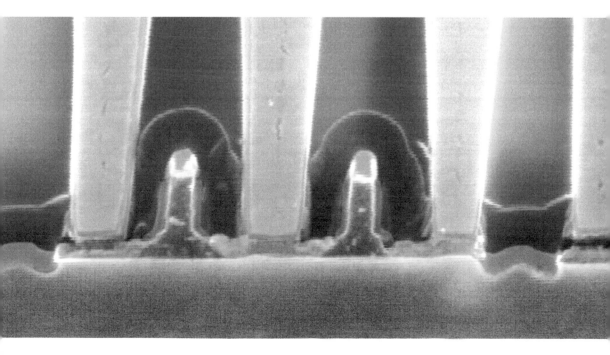

direct ancestor of today's immensely successful IBM Power Systems computers.[25] Sun Microsystems' SPARC chips were based on RISC technology, and RISC-based chips drove a number of popular video game consoles, including Sony's PlayStation series, Microsoft's Xbox and the Nintendo 64.

The transistor, integrated circuit and microprocessor brought miniaturization to speed. But a group of engineers was trying something else to gain speed. Maverick computer designer Seymour Cray led the charge to build elite, expensive machines optimized for nothing but the highest-speed computing anyone had ever encountered. The machines got the nickname supercomputers.[26]

By the 1970s, speed triggered a desire to know things that had been unknowable: What's at the farthest reaches of the universe? How does weather work? How does a protein form? Cray left computer maker Control Data to form Cray Research, a purely supercomputer company—a company dedicated to speed.

"Suddenly there was almost an infinite requirement for computing," Cray told an interviewer in 1995. "Modeling something like weather or, in the military applications, modeling a nuclear reaction, all these things required the solution of differential equations where you could divide it into as many small units as you could imagine, and you were limited by the computing power to do it at that level of sophistication." One of the most sophisticated weather-modeling agencies at the time, the European Centre for Medium-Range Weather Forecasts, often got forecasts wrong for the United States because its computers weren't powerful enough to account for the effects of the Rocky Mountains. "It gives you an idea of how far we have to go in sophistication before we can model the real environment, because the Rocky Mountains clearly have some effect on the weather here. You can't just flatten them out," Cray said.

The supercomputer race was on. Cray got most of the early attention, thanks not only to the speeds he achieved but also to the aesthetics of his semicircular machines. The Cray-1, delivered to the Los Alamos National

Lab in 1976, was designed to achieve unprecedented speed. It was optimized to perform vector arithmetic, a type of computation especially suited for parallel processing. No one would use a Cray or one of today's massively parallel supercomputers to run an accounting system, but that type of machine is ideal for complex computational tasks such as climate modeling.[27]

As Cray proved that there was a market for supercomputers, others jumped in, including NEC and Fujitsu in Japan. IBM got into the supercomputer business in the 1990s with a series of one-off machines built for the US Department of Energy's Advanced Strategic Computing Initiative. For the twenty-first century, it came up with a new design, called Blue Gene, to meet the high-performance processing needs of researchers in government, academia and industry. The first Blue Gene system was designed to do genetics research at the Lawrence Livermore National Lab, hence the name.[28]

The common factor in the design of the latest supercomputers is massively parallel architecture. The machines employ large numbers of relatively simple processors—often specialized units originally designed for graphics processing—to perform computations on great amounts of data simultaneously. The systems can be difficult to program, but for challenges requiring this approach (and that includes a wide range of problems, from image processing to quantum chemistry to business analytics), it can produce astonishingly fast results.

Today, it seems that the course of computing speed has cycled back on itself, transitioning from faster processors to systemic speed, smaller speed, super speed to what might be called smaller systemic super speed. For this new generation, IBM is working on a supercomputer on a chip. Monty Denneau, the original system architect for Blue Gene, has led the design of Cyclops64, which has 160 processor cores, all linked by an ultra-high-speed network on a chip less than an inch square. A complete Cyclops64 system will have more than 1 million processors and should be several times faster than the high-speed Roadrunner computers of the twenty-first century. A computer built around a single Cyclops64 chip could compute lunar ephemeris—something that IBM's 1950s-era machines labored at for years—in far less time than it would take to print the document.[29]

———

THERE ARE TWO WAYS to significantly boost speed in computers. One is to make all the components smaller, so that electrical signals moving at the speed of light need less time to traverse the machine; plus, more chips doing more work can be packed into one system. The other route to speed is through the discovery of new materials with which to build the components. Many times, a change in material has provided a way to carry pulses of information over thinner wires, in less space, with less energy—all contributing to greater overall system speed. In the 1990s, for instance, IBM built the first copper-based chips, which were essential to keeping up the pace of Moore's law just as older technologies were running out of steam.

Continued work with superconductors, which by the 1980s scientists had been experimenting with for decades, led to a significant materials science discovery. Superconductors are perfect conductors of electricity, offering no resistance. They also have unusual magnetic properties not found in other conductors. But scientists had encountered a problem—the materials they knew of would superconduct only near absolute zero, or minus-459 degrees Fahrenheit. Such temperatures are so cold that they could be reached only in lab experiments.

In 1986, at IBM's research lab near Zurich, Switzerland, scientists Georg Bednorz and Alex Müller were working with a class of metal oxides called perovskites and found that they would superconduct at temperatures

We're reaching a limit on how many transistors can be packed onto a computer chip. One option for making microprocessors more powerful is the optical chip, which uses light photons instead of electrons from electricity. Optical chips would give off almost no heat and would be much more efficient than chips with copper wiring.

———

An IBM experimental optical chip shown at actual size.

far warmer than all previous superconducting records: about minus-397 degrees Fahrenheit. Such a temperature could be achieved with relatively inexpensive and available liquid nitrogen—previous lower-temperature superconductors could be cooled enough only by using liquid helium. The difference was a breakthrough, opening a realm of more practical high-temperature superconductors that could be built into useful products. Superconductors have helped make MRI machines cheaper and faster, allowing them to be put to use in hospitals around the world. The Shanghai maglev train, which can hit 300 miles an hour, relies on superconductors. In 1987, Bednorz and Müller were awarded the Nobel Prize in Physics for their discovery.[30]

Superconductors have not yet been used in computers, but the conversation about speed in the coming decade will be moving to exascale computing. Such systems would perform a million trillion calculations per second—about 500 times the speed of the fastest supercomputers in 2010. One way to get there will be with the help of new materials, among them high-temperature superconductors.

The ever-increasing hunger for information has driven demand for speed, and speed keeps making us hungrier for information. The cycle shows no signs of ending, which leaves lots of interesting questions. If computers operate 30 billion times faster today than they did 50 years ago, could they possibly run another 30 billion times faster? Futurists such as Ray Kurzweil predict a day when machines are smarter than humans and begin running the world. Most computer scientists dismiss the idea, saying that speed does not equal thinking capability. Still, there's no doubt that seriously faster computers are coming, and they will be able to do the unimaginable. The question is: what's the unimaginable?

· · ·

Logic

Computers reveal patterns—if x, then y—
by translating the binary language of
machines into the languages of human
thought. As those languages have
become richer, so have the answers.

Fortran programmer's manual for
the IBM 704, printed in 1957.

Grace Murray Hopper and John Backus belonged to a very small group of people who in the 1950s knew how to talk to computers. Driven, headstrong and always ready to try unorthodox approaches, Hopper left her math professorship at Vassar College in 1943 to join the US Navy. She was dispatched to Harvard to help program the Mark I, a supercalculator co-developed by Harvard and IBM.

When the war ended, Hopper left active navy duty—temporarily anyway, since she would spend the bulk of her career in the military—and in 1949 joined John Mauchly and J. Presper Eckert, who had created the ENIAC during World War II. Hopper developed some of the early programming for UNIVAC I, the ENIAC's successor.

Backus, 20 years Hopper's junior, had just finished his master's in math at Columbia after an aimless early adulthood. He flunked out of the University of Virginia and discovered, when the army sent him for medical training, that he didn't want to be a doctor. Walking past IBM headquarters on New York's Madison Avenue, Backus was intrigued by the monster calculating machine running in the lobby behind the street-level display windows. It was IBM's Selective Sequence Electronic Calculator, or SSEC, the successor to the Mark I. "I just found this place, and I walked in and it looked so interesting," Backus said in a 2006 oral history. "I asked if they would give me a job, and they said, 'Yes, come up and see the boss.'" Backus went to work on the SSEC.[31]

Hopper and Backus, working for competitors and worlds apart in experience and personality, were the first to significantly alter the relationship between humans and computers. In the computing universe, they invented the equivalent of writing, creating a system of communication where there had been mostly grunts and frustration. They gave birth to computer programming.

———

ON THE EARLIEST COMPUTERS, programs consisted of plugboards with wires arranged to connect the switches that would perform calculations.

Programmers had to physically rearrange the wires to change what a computer would do. That evolved, and eventually programmers were inputting obscure alphanumeric codes to tell a machine what to do and where to store information. While working on the UNIVAC, Hopper considered a simple problem with such a method of programming: programmers made lots of mistakes when reentering code that had been used earlier. "I sure found out fast that programmers cannot copy things correctly," Hopper said in a 1980 oral history. "On UNIVAC, we used a delta for a space, and if [a programmer] wrote a careless delta, it could look like a 4. Any number of people used *B*s that looked like 13."

If programming was going to be practical for more than a tiny group of experts, programming language had to become easier and more human-friendly, Hopper surmised. Here's what the first few lines of a simple UNIVAC I program looked like:

```
B 0037L 0041    0
000000T 0003    1
500060B 0037    2
R 0031U 0019    3
500050500057    4
```

Hopper set out to write a program that could take the instructions comprehensible to humans and translate them into the code understood by computers. The program, which she called a compiler, let a programmer write $x = 5$ instead of the machine code to load 5 into a register and then send it to a memory location. Unfortunately, however, UNIVAC took a long time to run the translations. And the translator was inefficient, so the resulting code ran much slower than what a skilled human would have written. Still, Hopper's work on what was called automatic programming marked the start of real progress on software that would make the power of computers more and more accessible.

By then, Backus had moved on to programming the 700 series Electronic Data Processing Machines, IBM's first commercial computers. His

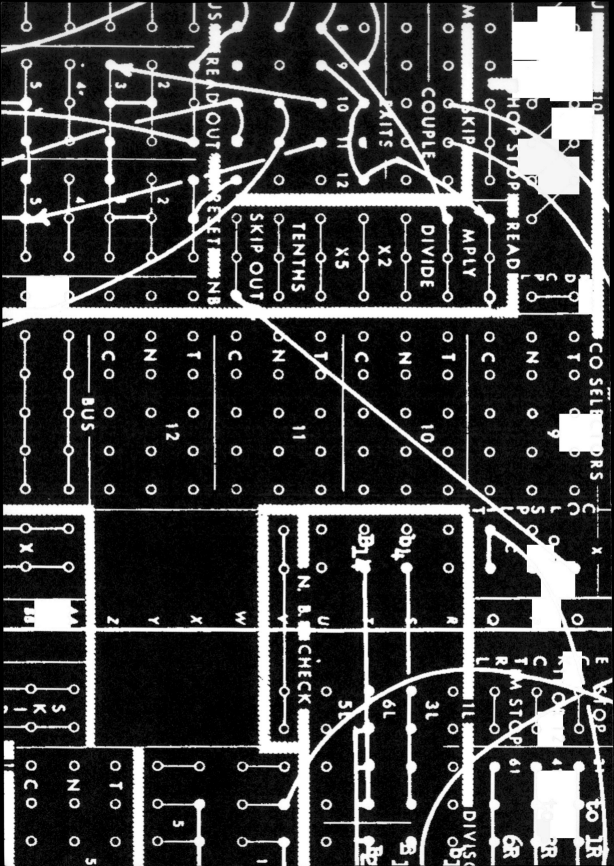

team—stuck "on the fifth floor of a little building" down Fifty-sixth Street from corporate headquarters, as he recalled—was also trying to help humans move beyond machine language. His first attempt was called speedcoding. Machine language provides for only very simple instructions, and many common mathematical operations require long sequences of instructions. Speedcoding created new instructions for these higher-level operations, such as taking the square root of a number, and allowed the programmer to enter the speed code instead of the underlying machine language. "Programming in machine code was a pretty lousy business," Backus said in 2006. "I figured, well, let's make it a little easier."[32]

In 1957, Backus and his team produced the first true high-level language, Fortran (for FORmula TRANslating System). The Fortran compiler was similar in principle to Hopper's earlier effort, but it produced machine code that was nearly as efficient as a good programmer's. Coders still had to know a fair amount about computers to write and run a Fortran program, but for the first time code was comprehensible to people whose expertise lay outside the field of computing, opening up programming to mathematicians and scientists. For example, someone who knew high school algebra but nothing about computers could probably figure out these Fortran statements:

R1 = (-B + SQRT(B**2 - 4*A*C)) / (2*A)
R2 = (-B - SQRT(B**2 - 4*A*C)) / (2*A)

They compute the roots of a quadratic equation.

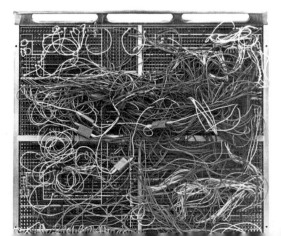

Early computers were programmed by plugging and unplugging wires. If one switch performed a calculation, then the switch at the other end of the cable would perform a related calculation. It was the computing language equivalent of caveman grunts.

Plugs on an IBM 407 control panel (right) and a diagram for programming a control panel.

Fortran began the process of abstracting software from the hardware it ran on. Machine language programs had to be written for a specific computer, but a Fortran program could run on any system with a Fortran compiler.

Two years after Backus's first version of Fortran, a new and improved version called Fortran II included a wonderful tool, the subroutine. Much of programming consists of doing things that have been done before and that will need to be done over and over again. A subroutine is a self-contained subprogram that is run from within another program. For example, a subroutine called ROOTS(A,B,C) might calculate the roots of $ax^2 + bx + c = 0$, and it will work for any such equation. A subroutine has two great advantages. One is that the programmer who uses it doesn't have to know much about how it works, just what values it expects and what it will return. Second, a prewritten subroutine can be dropped into a program with little effort. Today, programmers pick and choose from vast libraries of routines, but in the early days adding a subroutine often meant borrowing

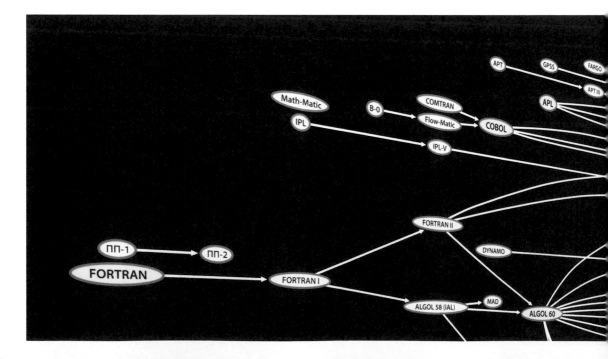

a pile of punched cards from someone else's program. Either way, though, the labor savings are tremendous.

"Fortran… was very similar to the algebraic formulas that scientists and engineers used in their daily work," the *New York Times* wrote in Backus's 2007 obituary. "With some training, they were no longer dependent on a programming priesthood to translate their science and engineering problems into a language a computer would understand…. Ken Thompson, who developed the Unix operating system at Bell Labs in 1969, observed that 95 percent of the people who programmed in the early years would never have done it without Fortran."

Still, the ability to write programs using mathematical symbols failed to impress the folks responsible for nuts-and-bolts data processing operations. "I decided there were two kinds of people in the world who were trying to use these things," Hopper said. "One was people who liked using symbols—mathematicians and people like that. There was another bunch of people who were in data processing who hated symbols and wanted words—

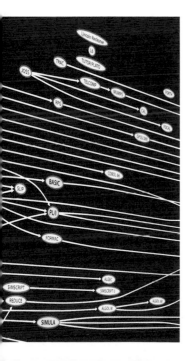

Grace Murray Hopper   John Backus

Grace Murray Hopper and John Backus developed early languages that let computers and humans talk to each other in code. Hundreds of other languages have since been developed, making more complex instructions possible.

A chart at the Computer History Museum in Palo Alto, California, showing languages that evolved from Fortran.

word-oriented people very definitely. And that was the reason I thought we needed two languages."

So Hopper created a language called FLOW-MATIC for UNIVAC, which evolved into the extremely successful COBOL (for COmmon Business-Oriented Language). True to Hopper's intentions, COBOL was verbose. An instruction for a simple calculation might look like this:

MULTIPLY HOURS BY WAGE-RATE GIVING STRAIGHT-TIME

"This provided a comforting illusion for administrators and managers that they could read and understand the programs their employees were writing, even if they could not write them themselves," Martin Campbell-Kelly and William Aspray wrote in their history of computing. COBOL's quirks also had expensive consequences decades later. Because memory was scarce, only two digits were allocated to the year part of dates, figuring that 19 could be assumed for the foreseeable future. At the end of the twentieth century, with most of the original authors long gone, a new generation of programmers had to puzzle through millions of lines of COBOL code to check for issues that could occur when the calendar clicked over to 2000—a situation the media dubbed Y2K.

Fortran was a proprietary IBM language, though it eventually became available for other systems. COBOL was developed by a US government-backed industry committee. When the committee was finished, the government, tired of having to rewrite programs every time it bought a new computer, decreed that all computers purchased by federal agencies must have a standard COBOL compiler available. This was another big step forward in the abstraction of programs from the machines they ran on.

———

UNTIL THE MID-1970S, most business transactions were recorded by clerks and passed on to experts who would enter them into a computer or card punch. The computers of the day used that information to produce daily, weekly and monthly reports, which were usually delivered in the form of a large stack of 14- by 17-inch fan-fold paper, perforated down the sides to feed through high-speed printers. If you wanted a new report, you would send a description to the data processing department and eventually the computer operators would have the report programmed and you would get the output. Even a minor change in an existing report could take weeks to process.

Three developments around the same time changed all that. Each became what might now be called middleware—a huge, profitable yet often overlooked category of software that keeps companies and governments running day to day.

In the late 1960s, IBM researcher E. F. "Ted" Codd looked at the way data was sorted and handled on computers and thought of a better way. Like Hopper and Backus, he had been trained as a mathematician and worked as a programmer on the earliest computers. Codd worked on a mathematically rigorous definition of a database. The goal was a generalized description of how to store, update and extract data so that the response to queries was accurate and that any changes to the data produced consistent results.[33]

In 1970, Codd completed his definition of the relational database. On one level, the idea seems completely obvious. The heart of the relational database is a table in which the rows represent entities of some sort, and the columns, usually called fields, represent attributes of those entities. In a library database table, each row might be a book and the columns would be title, author, publisher and so on. The real power of relational databases is revealed when tables are joined together, with each pair of tables linked by a common field—the relational aspect. In the library example, a second table might list all of the library's borrowers and the books they have borrowed, with the unique identifier of each book serving as the relational link. Simple links can create immensely complex structures. For a library, the connected tables would make it possible to discover patterns: for example, that people who liked author A also tended to read books by author B.

The relational database structured data in a common way, so information about different things could be matched, sorted or queried to find relationships.

The New York Police Department installed its CompStat database in 1994 so that officers could sort and match crime reports with other data to predict where crimes might occur. Credited with reducing crime in New York, it has since been adopted by Philadelphia, Vancouver and other major cities.

Codd's work spawned a generation of database companies, including Oracle and Sybase. Any given database could run on any computer—again, further pulling apart software and hardware.

Equally important was the development of the structured query language. After Codd published his paper, two other IBM researchers—Donald Chamberlin and Raymond Boyce—published a paper titled "SEQUEL: A Structured English Query Language." Because of trademark issues, the name of the language was later shortened to SQL. Chamberlin and Boyce made it possible to extract information from databases without either programming the computer directly or needing to know just how the data was stored. All anyone had to know was the structure of the database: what fields were in what tables and how the tables were linked together. Before long, applications were written that let users generate their own reports without actually knowing how to write a query in SQL. The user just selected the search criteria and the program constructed a query and submitted it to the database. Easy-to-use report-building software running on desktop computers let anyone query a database. The custom report that the data processing department once spent weeks creating could now be put together by the person who needed the information.

Of course, none of this could happen without a way to get the information into the system. In the late 1960s, IBM engineer Ben Riggins was working on implementing IBM computers for what was then called Virginia Electric Power Company. VEPCO and other utilities were interested in setting up customer service centers (where residential customers could go to pay bills or alter their accounts) that were tied electronically to the company's mainframe. Transactions would be entered and stored—except that no software existed to execute transactions from the field. Riggins had an idea about how to do it—a piece of software called CICS, for Customer Information Control System.

In 1968, Riggins moved to IBM's facilities in Des Plaines, Illinois, to develop CICS, which was introduced in 1969. In the mid-1970s, CICS development was moved to IBM in Hursley, United Kingdom, and the system blossomed into standard IT middleware that by the 2000s was processing hundreds of billions of transactions each day.[34] Today, most of the world's banking and retail transaction systems are based on CICS.

The relational database, SQL and CICS turned out to be some of the most important computer science breakthroughs of the twentieth century. Everyone deals with these systems every day: any time a person swipes a credit card, makes a reservation, sends an e-mail or even makes a phone call, these types of software systems are at work behind the scenes to make the transaction happen.

———

THE 1970S AND '80S brought two oddly contradictory trends in software. Computers became more standardized and much easier to program, but the average user had less reason to ever try to do any programming.

At AT&T Bell Labs, Ken Thompson and Dennis Ritchie created the Unix operating system and the C programming language. Unix got a foothold in academic computing and eventually became the standard operating system for midsize business computers. C and a later derivative, C++, became the lingua franca for most serious programming. In the 1960s, Niklaus Wirth of the Swiss Federal Institute of Technology wrote the Pascal language specifically as a tool to teach programming. About the same time, John Kemeny and Thomas Kurtz of Dartmouth College invented BASIC, a simple programming language designed to let nonspecialists program. As computer access became more available, BASIC instruction became a standard part of college and, eventually, high school and even elementary school curricula.

Meanwhile, experienced programmers in the burgeoning software industry created applications for personal computers, changing the way individuals thought about software and programming. The spreadsheet program VisiCalc, published for the Apple II in 1979, let analysts create sophisticated financial models without writing a single line of code. In short order, word processing programs such as WordStar, WordPerfect and eventually Microsoft Word rendered both the typewriter and the dedicated word processing system obsolete.

––––

THE CONCEPT OF ARTIFICIAL INTELLIGENCE, or AI, has haunted the field of computer science from the beginning. In 1950, Alan Turing, the British mathematician responsible for much of the theoretical work that led to the first computers, proposed a simple test: a computer would be deemed capable of human thought if a human conversing with it through a terminal was unable to tell whether it was a person or a machine at the other end. Yet no computer has come anywhere close to passing. Computer scientists and neuroscientists don't yet know enough about the brain to replicate its functions.

Computer scientists, though, realized that ever faster computers could equal or surpass humans in specific high-level cognitive activities. Chess has been particularly fascinating for AI researchers. The game is deep and complex but sufficiently finite in its possibilities.

In the mid-1980s, three doctoral students at Carnegie Mellon University, Murray Campbell, Thomas Anantharaman and Feng-hsiung Hsu, set out to build a chess machine that could beat the best human player. Taiwan-born Hsu, who had long been interested in computer chess, designed a dedicated chess processor called ChipTest. Murray was the provincial champion of Alberta as a teenager, and as an undergraduate he wrote a chess-playing program. Together, Hsu and Murray built Deep Thought, named after the computer in Douglas Adams's *The Hitchhiker's Guide to the Galaxy*. It was the best chess machine to date, beating all challengers at the World Computer Chess Championship in the spring of 1989. But that fall it played a two-game match against the reigning human world champion, who easily won.[35] IBM Research hired the Deep Thought team, and the group had the resources to build Deep Blue, a dedicated chess-playing supercomputer. In 1997, the reigning champ agreed to take on the latest version. Deep Blue II featured 30 Power processors and 480 specialized chess chips that let it run through as many as 330 million chess board positions in a second. The match was a heavily publicized, tense affair. The chess master won the first game, but Deep Blue came back with a victory the next day. The next three games were draws. In the decisive sixth meeting, Deep Blue won in 19 moves.

"In brisk and brutal fashion," the *New York Times* reported, "the I.B.M. computer Deep Blue unseated humanity, at least temporarily, as the finest chess playing entity on the planet yesterday."

Deep Blue approached the game like a machine, not a person. "Deep Blue operates in quite a different league than a human chess player," said Campbell, now a senior manager in the Business Analytics and Mathematical Sciences Group at IBM's T. J. Watson Research Center in Yorktown Heights, New York. "It does things that computers are good at. People rely on intuition. That is very effective but really hard to emulate on a computer." Deep Blue didn't play like a human because it didn't think like a human. Some of its moves baffled its own programmers, though they could later reconstruct the logic that led to them. And human handlers sometimes had to intervene to accept a draw to protect the human opponent from waiting a couple of agonizing hours as Deep Blue tried to eke out a win from a position known to be unwinnable.

Deep Blue had lasting consequences. It led the way for IBM's return to the supercomputing business. And it spurred ideas for how the impressive processing power of the newest computers could be used to go not simply faster but also deeper into a specific problem. Advanced business analytics—extracting multidimensional information from enormous databases—requires huge amounts of processing power and is making high-performance computing valuable to businesses.

———

FROM THE BEGINNING OF THE COMPUTER ERA, humans have had to learn specialized techniques to communicate with computers. The numerical codes of UNIVAC gave way to the art of constructing a good Google search. Machines have never been great at understanding human language. Closing that gap is one of the challenges for computer scientists. The TV quiz show *Jeopardy!* became the latest and most demanding test for a group at IBM Research.[36]

"Humans are elastic with language. They do not assume a word has a perfectly precise and unchanging meaning," said David Ferrucci, the IBM scientist who led a four-year quest to build a computer to compete live against humans on a televised *Jeopardy!* program. The team's computer, dubbed Watson, was set up in an IBM lab made to look and operate like the *Jeopardy!* studio. "When we read or hear a word, it is always in a context," Ferrucci said. "All that surrounding and related input profoundly influences what the word really means—how we interpret it. We face that kind of challenge in *Jeopardy!*"[37]

The questions on the show are full of subtlety, puns and wordplay—the sorts of things that delight humans but choke computers. In a category called "Before, During & After" this clue was given: "Poker hand of 3 aces

The DeepQA technology at Watson's core takes automated natural-language understanding to a new level, and the computer's architecture points to a new model of workload-specific systems.

———

Watson triumphed over all-time *Jeopardy!* champions Ken Jennings and Brad Rutter in their celebrated television tournament, televised in February 2011. In his Final Jeopardy answer, Jennings paraphrased a joke from *The Simpsons*: "I for one welcome our new computer overlords."

How Watson Won at *Jeopardy!*

Like all *Jeopardy!* contestants, Watson wasn't connected to the Internet. Instead, it drew from information in its own database—more than 200 million pages of content fed into it by IBM researchers.

Powered by 2,880 processor cores and 15 terabytes of RAM, Watson's algorithms quickly understand a question. Humans naturally understand puns; Watson runs complex analytics.

Hundreds of algorithms scour the database. The more closely their results match, the more confidence Watson has in its answer. If an answer is wrong, Watson adjusts its algorithms. Just like humans, Watson learns from its mistakes.

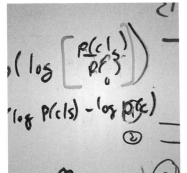

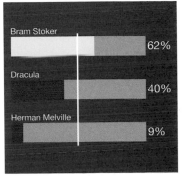

"We're going to demand that computers do a better job of understanding our natural language inquiries," said David Ferrucci, the principal investigator of IBM Research's DeepQA/Watson Project.

& 2 kings with a British royal family name adopted in 1917 that's a great way to tie a tie." The correct response: "What is a full house of Windsor knot?" That's not the sort of result that could be found in an ordinary computer search.

The serious purpose behind Ferrucci's work is a research effort called DeepQA (for question answering). It's designed to actually understand and answer questions, taking advantage of awesome computing power to look for answers from the growing store of human knowledge available in digital, searchable form. Web searches, in contrast, provide potential sources for answers rather than the answers themselves.

"We're going to demand that computers do a better job of understanding our natural language inquiries," said Ferrucci, who has spent the past 15 years at IBM Research working on natural language problems and finding answers amid unstructured information. "There's all this information in computers, but it's not organized in a way that enables the computer to relate to your questions. I want the computer to digest the information as humans express it, then give people the information they need on their terms."

That doesn't mean Watson thinks like a person, even if it produces humanlike answers. "The goal is not to model the human brain," said Ferrucci. "The goal is to build a computer that can be more effective in understanding and interacting in natural language, but not necessarily the same way a human does it."

Ferrucci said his team stopped adding to the data stored in Watson when it became clear that additional information was no longer improving the results. When a question is put to Watson, more than 100 algorithms analyze the question in different ways and find many different plausible answers—all at the same time. Yet another set of algorithms ranks the answers and gives them a score. For each possible answer, Watson finds evidence that may support or refute that answer. So for each of the hundreds of possible answers it finds, it searches out hundreds of bits of evidence, then uses hundreds of algorithms to score the degree to which the evidence supports the different answers. The answer with the best evidence assessment earns the most confidence. The highest-ranking answer on Watson's confidence scale is the one it chooses—unless its confidence doesn't cross a defined threshold. During *Jeopardy!*, if the highest-ranking answer isn't rated high enough to give Watson confidence, Watson will decide not to buzz in, thereby avoiding the risk of losing money. The computer also learns from its mistakes, refining its answers on the fly. The Watson computer does all of this in about three seconds.

By late 2010, in practice rounds at IBM Research in Yorktown Heights, Watson was good enough at finding the right answers to win more than 70 percent of the games against the former *Jeopardy!* champions who had come to play against it. Then in early 2011, Watson went up against *Jeopardy!* superstars Ken Jennings and Brad Rutter.

The matches aired over three days in February 2011, and they became an instant cultural milestone. Watson, represented by a swirling globe on a screen flanked by Jennings and Rutter, responded to clues in an even, unflappable tenor. At the end of the first day, Watson and Rutter were tied at $5,000 in winnings each, while Jennings had $2,000. On the second day, Watson pulled commandingly ahead. At the end of the third day, Watson won with $77,147 to Jennings's $24,000 and Rutter's $21,600. (As the winner, Watson was awarded $1 million, which IBM donated to charity. Jennings got $300,000 and Rutter $200,000. Both gave half their winnings to charity.) Jennings had the last word—one of ironic wit that delighted the audience—when he paraphrased a line from *The Simpsons* on his Final Jeopardy screen: "I for one welcome our new computer overlords."

The outcome of the contest made news around the world. In a front-page story, the *New York Times* declared: "For I.B.M., the showdown was not merely a well-publicized stunt and a $1 million prize, but proof that the company has taken a big step toward a world in which intelligent machines will understand and respond to humans, and perhaps inevitably, replace some of them."[38] Ray Kurzweil declared that Watson marked an important inflection point in the history of computation. "Watson is a stunning example of the growing ability of computers to successfully invade this supposedly unique attribute of human intelligence," Kurzweil wrote.[39]

Unlike Deep Blue, which influenced computer design but in the end could not do anything but play chess, Watson and its DeepQA technology have immediate and obvious implications. Databases now provide answers to deep analytical questions, provided that the queries involve information within the rigid structure of a relational database. DeepQA seeks to find answers from the great messy pile of unstructured information in the world and to make the results available to anyone who knows how to ask a question. One potential use of this kind of question-answering technology is smart diagnosis. No physician can personally stay abreast of the vast quantity of data and research published continually—so powerful question-answering software like Watson's, able to respond in real time to inquiries in the actual language of medicine, could be the difference between the right and wrong diagnosis and treatment. Just after Watson's *Jeopardy!* victory, IBM announced a partnership with the medical schools at the University of Maryland and Columbia University to explore such applications.

Another more prosaic use would be to deliver us from the voice menus of customer service help lines. Question-answering software could allow callers to speak in plain language to the system and actually get a useful answer. The legal industry expressed interest in using DeepQA to find information buried in thousands of pages of documents.

In many ways, the history of the increasing usefulness of computers is a story of helping humans and computers understand one another in ever more complex and subtle ways. "The holy grail for computer science is to get machines to fluently converse with us in our language rather than the other way around," Ferrucci said. "This can help people rapidly advance many fields since so much of human knowledge is captured and communicated in natural language." The sentient, self-aware computer remains the stuff of science fiction, but we are seeing the dawn of machines that will aid our thinking just by being asked.

• • •

Connecting

When people, computers and devices interconnect, computing's impact is multiplied exponentially.

In the 1980s—long before the spread of e-mail or instant messaging, web forums or social networks—IBM's Professional Office System, or PROFS, served as the business world's most advanced form of networked communications. It allowed IBMers (and the employees of many IBM clients) to chat, keep their calendars, send messages and manage everything from accounting to personnel records.

Communication Assist Window Help

OV/VM 1.2- Main Menu

of the following PF keys.

ss calendars   Time: 3:04

the mail

documents   1999   SEPTEMBER

ss notes and messages   S   M   T   W   T

re documents   1   2

ss the document log   5   6   7   8   9

il list processor   12   13   14   15   16

the status of outgoing mail   19   20   21   22   23

                                           26   27   28   29   30

an automatic reminder   Day of Y

main menu number 2

-084 (C) Copyright IBM Corp. 1983, 1997   PF9 Help

ype ISHELP/Call (607)770/8-853-HELP Highest Class=IBM Cor

In the 1930s, inventor Walter Lemmon put together a little company called Radio Industries Corporation. Lemmon was researching ways to connect two electric typewriters by shortwave radio, so that a message typed on one would automatically be typed on the other typewriter miles away. It was, in a sense, the first shot at e-mail.[40]

At IBM, Thomas Watson Sr.'s engineers had been exploring ways to use telephone lines to transmit the sequence of holes on a punched card to an automatic punch device in another location, so Lemmon's work caught Watson's attention. After seeing the prototype, Watson persuaded Lemmon and his associates to dissolve their company and join IBM, promising that IBM would fund all the research necessary to create a marketable product.

In 1941, Lemmon presented a working model—a Rube Goldberg kind of apparatus called a Radiotype. When a Radiotype operator typed a message, each keystroke sent a pulse to a tape-punching unit, which translated the pulse into a hole on the tape. The tape was then fed into a shortwave radio, which transmitted the holes using something like Morse code. On the other end, it worked backward—the radio punched a tape, and the tape was fed into a reader that told the electric typewriter which keys to activate.

As World War II escalated, the US Army installed Radiotypes in record-keeping offices around the world, allowing the military to quickly send routine information to remote areas. A lieutenant colonel called the Radiotype "one of the most impressive developments" of all the information products created for the war. Watson predicted that the Radiotype would someday eclipse IBM's mainstay accounting machines: "My horizon for that machine goes so far out I don't dare to stop to think about it."

The DeepQA technology at Watson's core takes automated natural-language understanding to a new level, and the computer's architecture points to a new model of workload-specific systems.

A production Radiotype was ready in 1941 and went to work sending communications for the US military during World War II.

Computing machines to that point had been isolated—unconnected in any way. The only way to move information from, say, a computing machine in London to another in Manchester would've been to load punched cards into a truck and drive them there. IBM seemed primed to create something new: a way to move data across geography over a communications network.

When the war ended, it seemed natural that IBM would develop the Radiotype for civilian use. That didn't happen. Watson realized that if IBM stayed in the business, it would have to compete against AT&T's teletype business, and AT&T was a major IBM customer. "Radiotype would never be a big deal" for IBM, recalled Richard Canning, an IBM data processing specialist who worked on the Radiotype. "So they got out."[41]

A cultural mindset took hold. Computer companies sold machines and services. Communications companies operated networks, and the two stayed out of each other's business.

It would be more than 20 years before computing machines started talking to each other again.

———

UCLA COMPUTER ENGINEER BOB BRADEN faced a task that was quite unusual in 1969. He had to write networking software for an IBM 360/91 that had been recently installed on campus in the Math Sciences Building. Few people knew what computer networking was. The computer's maker, IBM, didn't even seem very interested—at least not in the kind of network Braden was helping to build.[42]

The 360/91 was a coveted object. Its fast processors and extra memory had the US Defense Department's Advanced Research Projects Agency, or ARPA, salivating. With the United States hoping to gain an edge amid the Cold War and the space race with the Soviet Union, funds were being pumped into computer-based research. ARPA was eager to give as many scientists as possible access to the few existing computers as powerful as

Time-sharing allowed users in several locations
to take advantage of the resources of one computer,
connecting in a hub-and-spoke configuration.

the 360/91. The only reasonable strategy: tie the researchers and the scarce computers together in a network.

The problem was that the 360 series was terrible at communicating. It simply wasn't built for it. Starting in the 1960s, some computers were built for time-sharing, which allowed a number of users in different locations to access a single computer at the same time using a dumb terminal. The researchers at ARPA envisioned something more a flexible way for scientists to access any of a number of powerful machines, no matter who they were made by or where they were located. IBM was not opposed to computer communications per se and was even planning to add that capability to some of its own products. But the technology would be IBM's. In this regard, IBM wasn't different from any other computer company at the time. All sought to keep users loyal to their own complete, stem-to-stern proprietary systems. What IBM didn't like was letting hardware and software outside of its full control to link into its systems. Indeed, the whole premise of the System/360 was that it was complete—360 degrees of self-contained functionality. That was the tendency of the industry. (In those days, AT&T refused to allow any equipment that wasn't made by AT&T to connect to its network. Every phone and switch in the United States was made by AT&T.)

So Braden forged ahead, with the support of ARPA, adopting a radical new communications technology known as packet switching. Data would be broken up into many smaller electronic pieces called packets. Each packet would include an electronic address that could be read by computers and electronic switches. Unlike telephone conversations, packet data transfers between computers wouldn't have to hog an entire communications line. The packets could be split up, traveling through different lines and different intermediary computers before arriving at their destination, where the receiving computer would quickly assemble the packets back into the right order.

Users read a printout from a terminal on a TSS/360 time-sharing network designed exclusively for a special model of a System/360 computer.

It made efficient use of a network's resources, and it was resilient. If an enemy like the Soviet Union managed to disrupt part of the network, the packets could flow another way and still get to their destination. A packet-switched network might survive a nuclear strike in ways the telephone network would not.

In 1970, the network—dubbed ARPANET—went live. More institutions and mainframe computers were added. Scientists and engineers across the country had access to the most powerful computers on earth. It opened the idea that computing was not something to be owned but something to be shared.

————

IN 1973, ARPA ENGINEER Robert Kahn met up with Stanford University professor Vinton Cerf, who, like Kahn, had devoted himself to finding ways to make it easy for networks to share information. In other words, they pushed for inter-networking.

As computer networking developed, each network communicated using its own protocol. As computer companies such as IBM, Digital Equipment and Amdahl began to move into networking, each one established its own protocol sets, and these, of course, were incompatible with other companies' protocols. It was quickly becoming a mess for users.

Astrophysicist Larry Smarr recalled having a beer with a German colleague in Munich in 1982 and complaining about how he had to fly across the Atlantic to gain access to an American-built supercomputer so that he

ARPANET began to network computers, so many people could share the resources of many computers—a forerunner to the Internet.

————

A System/360, at the University of California, Santa Barbara, was among the first four computers to connect to ARPANET. The others were a Honeywell DDP-516 at UCLA, an SDS-940 at Stanford Research Institute and a DEC PDP-10 at the University of Utah.

could run his simulations of supernova explosions and colliding black holes. He couldn't get on ARPANET to do it. ARPANET, Smarr said, "had turned into something for the elite. It was for a few computer science departments and the military. Nobody in university physics departments or chemistry departments knew much about the ARPANET at all, much less had access to it."[43]

Kahn and Cerf campaigned to create a common protocol that would allow not just individual machines but all networks to communicate easily. With ARPA's support, they worked out a set of rules known as transmission control protocol/Internet protocol, or TCP/IP. In 1983, their work on TCP/IP allowed the ARPANET to connect with an academic network called CS/NET, and researchers on both networks began to swap information.

TCP/IP won a powerful backer in Washington: Senator Al Gore, who worked to provide government support and money. Gore talked up an idea he called the information superhighway, which he said would draw in more than just universities and corporations and eventually link all sorts of people in ways that would supercharge information exchange and economic expansion.[44]

The Reagan administration worked with Gore and the National Science Foundation to fund five supercomputer centers, one each at the University of Illinois at Urbana-Champaign, the University of California, San Diego, Cornell and Princeton, and one to be shared by Carnegie Mellon University and the University of Pittsburgh. The NSF would stock the centers with the latest supercomputers (some costing $20 million or more) from Cray Research, IBM, Thinking Machines and other companies. A network was needed to connect the centers with far-flung researchers— a network dubbed NSFNET, which ran on TCP/IP.[45]

That was the tipping point for inter-networking. Networks around the world began switching to TCP/IP, giving rise to the Internet.

But the Internet had adversaries. AT&T and other telecom companies, seeing computer networking as a competitive threat, fought government funding. IBM was also not quite on board with TCP/IP. In 1974, the company had introduced a proprietary networking technology called Systems Network Architecture, or SNA. Because of IBM's prominence in the data processing industry, SNA carried more data traffic than any other networking technology. SNA was the way IBM computers shared information for more than 15 years, until more open technologies like TCP/IP began arriving.

Al Weis at IBM Research was the company's hard-core fan of TCP/IP, and he believed the sooner a company got on board with it, the better. IBM made the routers for the new, improved NSFNET. "I started watching the traffic really carefully," Weis said. "You could see this thing was just going crazy. It opened up the floodgates."[46]

As more and more individuals came aboard the quickly developing Internet, they found ways to make it better. Tim Berners-Lee, a computer scientist at CERN, the European particle physics laboratory, created a way to access documents over the Internet through a linking method called hypertext, which connected pages in a World Wide Web. Marc Andreessen and fellow students at the supercomputer center at the University of Illinois assembled the first graphical browser, Mosaic. It allowed users to navigate the web by clicking on images rather than typing in strings of commands.

———

AS TCP/IP BEGAN linking big computers, the personal computing phenomenon was sweeping through companies. Oddly enough, although there had been reason to connect supercomputers in Munich to others in Illinois, no one had been driven to develop a way to connect a lot of little computers inside a single office building.

A small group of IBM researchers in Switzerland took on the task of creating local area networks, or LANs. Werner Bux and Hans Müller at

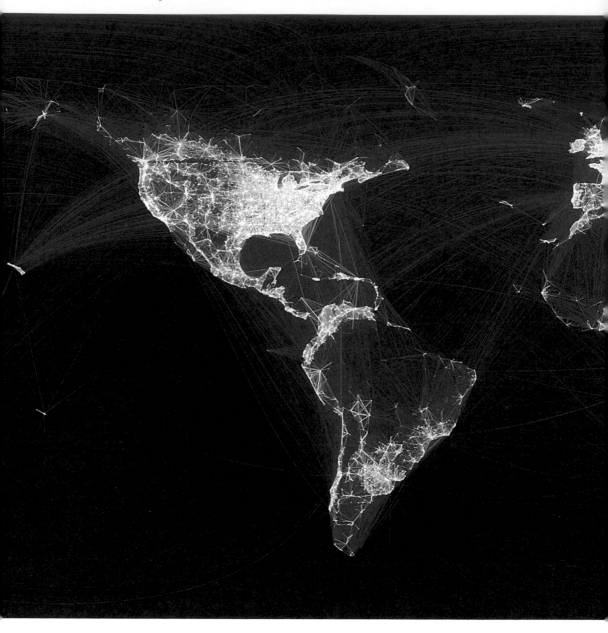

When interconnection infuses the
world's physical systems with intelligence,
the world's systems get smarter.

——

A visualization of all the connections
on Facebook in 2010.

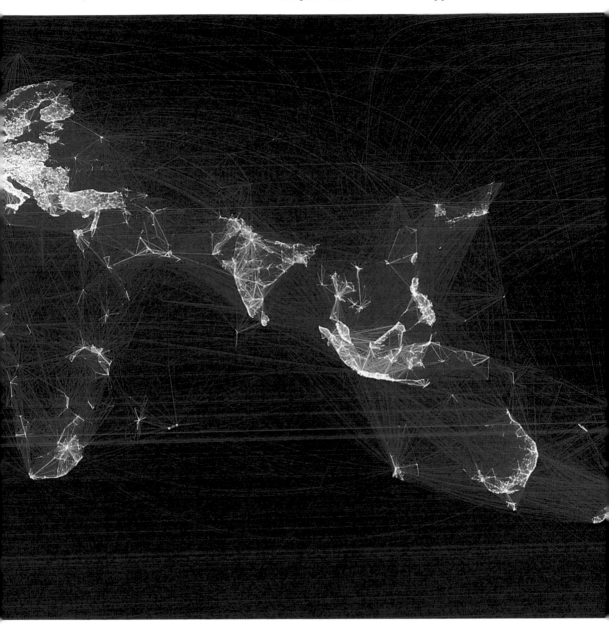

the IBM Zurich Research Laboratory developed technology they dubbed Token Ring. It was a way to direct traffic on a local area network so that messages wouldn't collide and send the system crashing.

Token Ring introduced LANs to the corporate world—the first intranets, before the word was known—but IBM's technology would not prevail. At Xerox's famed Palo Alto Research Center in California, engineer Robert Metcalfe perfected a LAN technology called Ethernet, which turned out to be cheaper and faster than Token Ring. Ethernet soon turned into the LAN standard. Important, though, was that LANs connected PCs inside companies to the Internet outside, bringing the communications network to every information worker's desk.

In 1995, demand exploded and the Internet began the process of changing the world. "The writing was on the wall, the Internet was going to start eating everybody's lunch," Weis said.

But it was also creating vast new possibilities. Through this network of networks, computers and the information inside them became socialized. A few decades before, machines had been islands. Now a curious user could type a single request into a search engine to ask computers around the world where to find data about the ozone layer or a photo of a supermodel, and that person would be pointed and connected to the right place. The Internet was the key to releasing information from physical limitations. You could be anywhere and find anything, and it happened automatically and instantaneously. Information belonged to the world, not to some entity that could hoard it. That simple idea is so powerful, it has reordered entire industries, from the media to retailing to banking and beyond. And its political and societal impact—potentially even greater—has just begun to play out.

Still, through the late 1990s, one physical limitation on the Internet remained: wires.

COMPUTING WAS DESTINED to become ubiquitous—always on, available anywhere on systems that could connect and communicate with any other system. As the century turned, wireless high-speed Internet access—Wi-Fi—turned up in homes, offices, airports, cafes and the occasional city park. Cell phone providers around the world—DoCoMo in Japan, SK Telecom in South Korea, Orange in Europe, Sprint and Verizon in the United States—built next-generation wireless cellular networks, able to transmit data at high speeds and low cost. This gave a boost to smartphones like the iPhone and BlackBerry, devices that are basically Internet-connected computers capable of making phone calls. By 2010, there were nearly 6 billion cell phones in distribution worldwide. And with that simple connection, a person had access to information, applications and computing power around the globe.[47]

Computing anytime, anywhere, by anybody has become more than just a vision realized. In 2011, it's an expectation. Networking technology has released computing into the air around us. This is the cloud in cloud computing.

These days, machines are increasingly talking to other machines—not humans—across the cloud. They might be two powerful systems exchanging financial information and making split-second trades, or a tiny sensor in a river wirelessly telling another computer how much water is flowing by. In the coming decade, machine-to-machine conversations will skyrocket, overtaking data communication that relies on having a human at one or both ends.

• • •

Architecture

Architecture is the story of technological advances coming together to create new systems, which in turn advance our thinking about technology.

A System/360 Model 91 console.

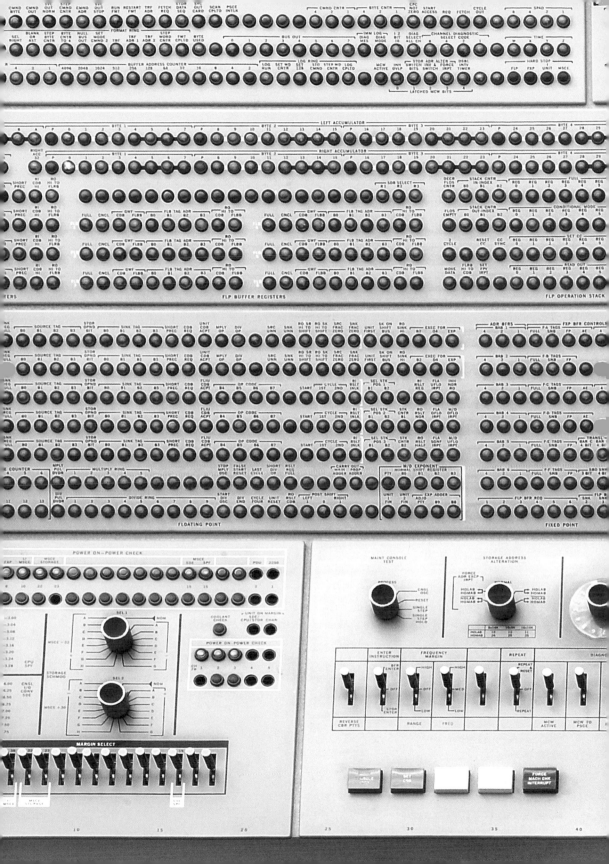

Ben Wood visibly trembled in front of IBM chief executive Thomas Watson Sr. The meeting had started out badly. Watson seemed only semi-interested in the idea that IBM's tabulating machines could efficiently score standardized tests. Wood, a professor at Columbia University, had pioneered the tests—a concept that would eventually become tests like the SAT. That led to the problem of scoring tens of thousands of tests at once. Wood found himself hiring hundreds of young women and packing them into Columbia's Hamilton Hall, where they'd mark the tests by hand at a cost of about $5 per test. Clearly, Wood thought, there had to be a better way.[48]

So Wood sent letters to the presidents of 10 corporations that made business machines. Nine did not reply. Wood recalled the curt phone call from his last remaining option, Watson:

"I'm Thomas Watson. I'm very busy and can spare only an hour. Be at the Century Club promptly at 12:00. I have an engagement at 1:00."

The Century Club was a stuffy businessman's establishment in New York, and Watson had reserved a private dining room for one hour. Watson brought along a young male secretary, whom he left outside the dining room door with instructions to interrupt in an hour, at 1 p.m.

The whole scene—the Century Club, Watson in his impeccable suit, a ticking clock—unnerved Wood. He began talking about test scoring but, seeing Watson's scornful face, decided to broaden his approach. This was 1928—an era of expansive ideas and big ambitions. Charles Lindbergh had flown the Atlantic the year before. Bell Labs had opened only a couple of years earlier. Individuals were feeling the power of new technology—two-thirds of homes now had electricity, one-third had radios and nearly half had telephones. Maybe, Wood considered, Watson wanted to dream a little. For nearly two decades, Watson had been selling IBM's tabulating machines as devices that could count and sort tangible quantities—money, inventory, troops and so on. As Wood saw it, that gave IBM a big potential market, but ultimately a limited one.

Columbia professor Ben Wood convinced Thomas Watson Sr. that computing could help scientific research, leading Columbia to open the first scientific computing lab—stocked with IBM machines.

Wood switched gears and began explaining how IBM machines could be used to measure intellect and psychology. Anything could be represented by mathematics, numbers and formulas. Biology, astronomy, physics or any other science could be aided by IBM machines. Never had Watson considered that numbers could be used to represent and simulate absolutely anything. All along he had measured IBM's potential market by its share of the accounting and record-keeping functions of business and government. This nervous professor was saying that IBM's potential market was almost limitless.

Watson's secretary stuck his head in at 1 p.m.; Watson shooed him away and grilled Wood until 5:30 p.m. Two days later, three trucks pulled up at Columbia to deliver all the tabulators, sorters and punches Wood might need.

Watson put Wood on the payroll as a consultant. At Columbia, Wood offered to let other professors use his computer center, as he called it, and Wallace Eckert of the astronomy department got hooked. He suggested modifications to IBM's machines so they could better perform astronomical calculations, which led to yet more computing machines being set up at Columbia. By 1937, Eckert's astronomical lab in Pupin Hall's Rutherford Observatory became the Thomas J. Watson Astronomical Computing Bureau, the world's first center for scientific computation.

In the evolution of computing—in the grand turns of the wheel that drive computing from one era into the next—the technology itself plays a leading role. The right pieces come together at the right time—advances in processing power or miniaturization, leaps in the ability to store and quickly access data, new programming languages and software—to give birth to a system that had been unthinkable just years before.

Yet these shifts in architecture always require an X factor to really matter. That variable is how we *think* about technology. The technology moves ahead and opens up ideas about what technology can do, then someone embraces an idea that makes the technology essential. Without that change in thinking, the great shifts in computing architecture happen in darkness, relevant only to those in computing. The grand *ideas* about computing, built on top of one another over 100 years—the successive appearance of new computing models and ultimately the revolutionary emergence of a new science of information itself—are the reasons computing has changed the world over and over again, and why it promises to do so in even more profound ways today.

In 1928, Ben Wood looked at machines that were made for business— they had always been made for business—and saw the future of science. The world of science and discovery was never the same. Computing had a new architecture.

———

IN THE 1960s, Bob Resnikoff was a low-ranking US Army techni- cian stationed at the Seventh Army headquarters in Stuttgart, West Germany, working with a computer that had been out for only a few years: IBM's 1401.

"We had a mobile 1401," Resnikoff recalled decades later. "It was in a big truck trailer. When we went out on maneuvers, it came with us. Once we were deployed in the woods or wherever, the sides of the trailer telescoped out and you had a fairly large machine room full of key punches, verifiers, the 1401, tape drives, desks. I had no idea what it was all used for, except that it was called a Command and Control Information System. Anyway, it did

The 1401—a.k.a. the mainframe— made computers practical for business use, spreading information processing to thousands of companies.

———

A 1401 (center) with tape drives, control consoles and a printer.

its job, whatever it was, for weeks on end in the depths of the Schwarzwald, no matter how much mud we tracked in."[49]

Resnikoff added something that just wasn't said about previous models of computers: "I always liked the 1401."

The very fact that liking a computer sounds ordinary to us today suggests what a big shift the 1401 represented. By the late 1950s, computers had gone through tremendous changes. During World War II, the military drove a desire for faster computing. Vacuum tube electronics replaced the electromechanical components of the tabulating machines that dominated information processing in the first half of the century. First came the experimental ENIAC, then Remington Rand's UNIVAC and IBM's 701, all built on electronics. Magnetic tape and then the first disk drives changed ideas about the accessibility of information. Grace Murray Hopper's compiler and John Backus's Fortran gave computer experts new ways to instruct machines to do ever more clever and complex tasks. Systems that arose out of those coalescing developments were a monumental leap in the capabilities of computing.

Still, the machines touched few lives directly. Installed and working computers numbered barely more than 1,000. The world, in fact, was ready for a more accessible computer. The IBM 1401 filled that need.

The first glimpse of that next generation of computing turned up in France. "In the mid-1950s, IBM got a wake-up call," said Chuck Branscomb, who ran one of IBM's lines of accounting machines at the time. French computer upstart Machines Bull came out with its Gamma computers, small

and fast compared with goliaths like those in IBM's 700 series. "It was a competitive threat," Branscomb recalled.[50]

Bull made IBM and others realize that entities with smaller budgets wanted computers. IBM scrambled resources to try to make a competing machine. "It was 1957 and IBM had no new machine in development," Branscomb said. "It was a real problem."[51]

Branscomb's group set a target rental cost of $2,500 a month, well below a 700 series machine. And the computer had to be simple to operate. "We knew it was time for a dramatic change, a discontinuity," Branscomb added.

IBM announced the result of that effort in October 1959. Dubbed the 1401, the new machine indeed rented for $2,500 a month and was touted as the first affordable general-purpose computer. The 1401 was one of the earliest computers to run completely on transistors—no vacuum tubes—and that made it smaller and more durable than preceding computers. Although the 1401 wasn't a great leap in power or speed, that was never the point. "It was a utilitarian device, but one that users had an irrational affection for," wrote Paul Ceruzzi in *A History of Modern Computing*. One key to the 1401's popularity: the 1401 was the easiest machine to program at the time. The system's software, wrote Dag Spicer, senior curator at the Computer History Museum, "was a big improvement in usability."

This more accessible computer unleashed pent-up demand for data processing. IBM was shocked to receive 5,200 orders for the 1401 in just the first five weeks after introducing it—more than was predicted for the entire life of the machine. Soon, business functions at companies that had been immune to automation were taken over by computers. By the mid-1960s more than 10,000 1401 systems were installed, making the 1401 by far the best-selling computer to date.

The 1401 as a whole marked a new generation of computing architecture, because it made executives and officials think differently about computing. A computer didn't have to be a monolithic machine for the elite. It could fit comfortably in a medium-size company or lab. In the world's top corporations, each department could have its own computer. A computer could even wind up operating on an army truck in the middle of a German forest.

"There was not a very good grasp or visualization of the potential impact of computers—certainly as we know them today—until the 1401 came along," Branscomb said. The 1401 made enterprises of all sizes believe a computer was useful, and even essential.

———

IN 1961, IBM was one of the most vibrant companies in the United States, bringing in $2.2 billion in revenue and $254 million in net income. It had 116,000 employees. Still, small innovative companies, plus well-financed and technically strong corporations like General Electric and RCA, were entering the computer business. IBM had good products and technological strength, but it lacked leadership, vision and a plan.[52]

Meanwhile, the computer industry and its customers were having difficulty training enough service people and providing adequate software support for the many different products created. There was little inter-changeability of hardware or software among competing products or even among IBM's own products.

This combination of fear and need for improvement spawned the System/360. It would ultimately cost $5 billion—about $34 billion in today's dollars—nearly destroying IBM. Thomas Watson Jr. gambled almost all of the company's development resources for more than two years, and it took another two years of engineering and manufacturing turmoil before confirmed orders and delivered products began to fulfill the 360's promise. In a 1966 *Fortune* story, one of the 360's architects, Bob Evans, was quoted as saying: "We called this project 'You bet your company.' "

It was also the defining event in the careers of many employees, including Watson and his younger brother, Arthur (Dick). It gave Thomas Watson Jr. the overarching success he sought, and it forced him to destroy his brother's career. To get the 360 done, Watson had to essentially start a civil war inside his own company. In the end, the 360 changed IBM and computers forever.

It was T. Vincent Learson on whom Watson placed his big bet. Learson, an imposing man at 6-foot-6, had a well-deserved reputation for being aggressive, insightful and decisive, and he had a strong track record, having helped Watson bring to market the company's first electronic computer, the IBM 701, in the 1950s.

His first decision was that computer products made in Endicott should be compatible with one another and with those made in Poughkeepsie, and vice versa. This would reduce costs and facilitate the migration of customers from small IBM systems to larger ones. However, the Poughkeepsie engineers had already begun to design what they called the 8000 series of computers to replace the successful 7000 series. Learson's plan was vigorously opposed by Frederick Brooks Jr., architecture manager of the 8000 series, and other executives, tearing IBM apart. Nevertheless, after considerable review, Learson accepted the recommendation of Bob Evans and terminated the 8000 series project in May 1961. Evans immediately asked Brooks to manage a project to create the "ultimate family of systems." "To my utter amazement, Bob asked me to take charge of that job after we had been fighting for six months," Brooks recalled. He accepted the job, and his knowledge and enthusiasm gained the support of many others.

Learson established a corporate-wide task group, code-named SPREAD, for Systems Programming, Research, Engineering and Development. It was to "establish an overall IBM plan for data processor products." Its 26-page report recommended strict compatibility among all processors, standard interfaces to permit interchangeability among all input-output devices, use of the 8-bit byte (first implemented on the IBM Stretch supercomputer) and construction of all processors with Solid Logic Technology, or SLT, then being developed by IBM's new Components Division.

On April 7, 1964, Watson unveiled the new product line. The word *system* was chosen to signify that the offering was not just a group of processors with peripheral equipment but rather an aggregation of interchangeable hardware units with program compatibility from top to bottom. The number *360* (the number of degrees in a circle) was chosen to represent the ability of each computer to handle all types of applications.

The initial response was as unprecedented as the announcement. The number of orders rapidly exceeded forecasts. More than a thousand orders were received during the first four weeks after the announcement. Another thousand were received during the next four months. Adding to production requirements, most orders specified more memory and storage capacity than IBM's product planners had anticipated.

The number of SLT modules manufactured in IBM's East Fishkill, New York, facility in 1963 was half a million. A 12-fold production increase in 1964 resulted in 6 million modules, and plans called for the production of 28 million modules in 1965. IBM's factories couldn't handle it. By September 1965, more than 25 percent of all SLT modules manufactured had been impounded by the Quality Control Department, and a decision was made to stop production. IBM was forced to announce an embarrassing two- to four-month delay in System/360 shipments.

Meanwhile, the magnitude of the programming task had been grossly underestimated. More than a thousand people were employed during the peak year, when more money was spent than had been budgeted for the entire project. Brooks wryly proclaimed what he called Brooks's law: "Adding manpower to a late software project makes it later."

Sensing disaster for IBM, Learson assembled a team to get the 360 back on track. One team member, Hank Cooley, recalled "a gray blur of 20-hour

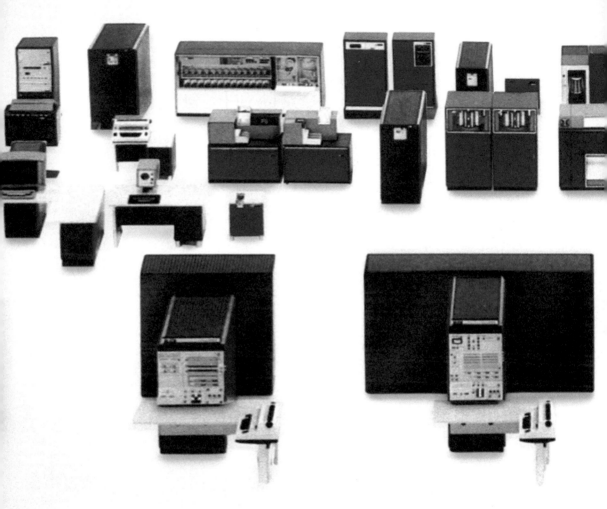

The System/360 was an end-to-end compatible system that could adapt to different uses and changing needs, bringing computing into the core infrastructure of business and society.

The 360 family included six processor models covering a 50-fold range in performance and 54 different peripheral devices, including several types of magnetic storage devices, visual display units, communication equipment, card readers and punches, printers, and an optical character reader. Monthly rentals at the time ranged from $2,700 for a basic configuration to $115,000 for a typical large multisystem configuration.

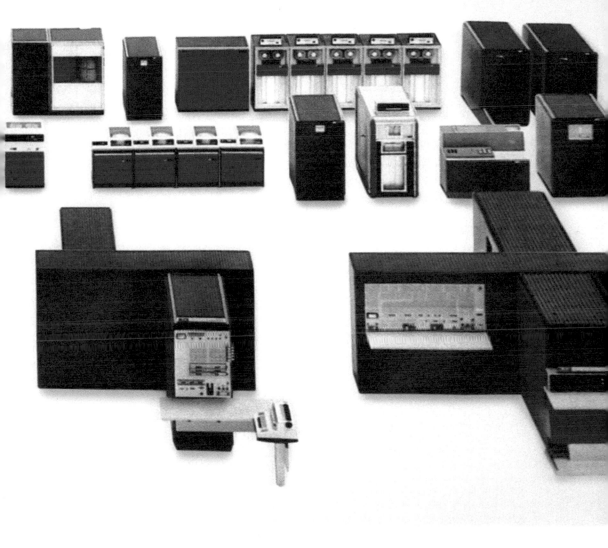

days, seven days a week—never being home." But in less than five months, they had System/360 shipments on schedule.

The 360 changed the industry's landscape. After the system was announced in 1964, the major companies in the computer industry were often referred to as Snow White (IBM) and the Seven Dwarfs—Burroughs, Control Data, General Electric, Honeywell, NCR, RCA and Sperry Rand. Of the estimated $10 billion worldwide inventory of installed computers in 1964, the seven companies had produced about 30 percent and IBM had produced the rest. Five years later, IBM's worldwide inventory had increased more than threefold to $24 billion and that of the other companies had increased by about the same ratio to $9 billion.

The popularity of the System/360 made it difficult for others to compete in the general-purpose computer market. RCA attempted to do this by creating the Spectra 70, a line of computers compatible with the System/360 but marketed at a lower price. Ultimately this was not successful, and RCA sold its computer division to Sperry Rand in 1971. General Electric did particularly well with systems for the banking industry and expanded its business in Europe by purchasing Machines Bull and the Olivetti computer division. Yet it failed to make a profit and sold its computer business to Honeywell in 1970.

The IBM System/360 had such a significant impact on the market because of its pioneering standard interface, which made it easy for others to attach their products to System/360 processors. Soon an entire industry of companies was making and supplying plug-compatible peripheral products. Led by Telex with tape drives in 1967 and Memorex with disk storage units in 1968, this industry enjoyed dramatic growth, partly because IBM's biggest profit margin was in storage products. IBM continued to succeed by investing in rapid improvements in technology.

But this success came at personal cost. To ensure successful introduction of the new product line, Thomas Watson Jr. had promoted Learson to senior vice president with responsibility for sales, and promoted his brother,

Dick, to senior vice president for research, development and manufacturing. However, Dick Watson was poorly prepared to handle the many problems of managing and coordinating the manufacturing of such a large and diverse product line. So Thomas Watson again turned to his strongest and most-trusted executive to take over the System/360 project and save it and IBM from disaster. By Watson's request but without a formal announcement, Learson returned from sales to replace Dick Watson as head of the development and manufacturing organizations. Dick Watson was put in charge of corporate staff with no line management responsibility. In 1970, he accepted the position of US ambassador to France. An assignment intended to prepare Dick Watson to become president of IBM had instead ended his IBM career.

Few products in American history have had as great an impact on the world—or on their creators—as the IBM System/360. Thomas Watson had bet the company, and he won in ways he never imagined. The 360 made IBM into something much more than a successful corporation or even an industry leader. The 360, and the act of creating it, turned IBM into a global icon and an essential part of the planet's infrastructure.

DESPITE THE SUCCESS of the 1401 and the launch of the S/360, for most of the population in the mid-1960s, a computer was still a mystery. It took almost a decade before computing spread out to people who had never before worked near a computer.

A film shot at MIT in 1963 features one of the first professors of computer science, MIT's Fernando Corbató, in a typical computer room of the era, full of big whirring machines and metal desks flooded in fluorescent light. An MIT colleague, John McCarthy, in the late 1950s had suggested that multiple users could access a single computer in a way that would make each of the users feel as if he or she were the only one tapping into the machine. Corbató and others at MIT set out to make it work. In the film about that project, Corbató, wearing a suit, bow tie and oversize plastic glasses, moves into his office and types on an ordinary-looking electric typewriter, spelling "Start." He explains that the typewriter is one of 21 connected by wires to a computer in another room at MIT. A few seconds later, the typewriter, untouched, writes: "Hello. I do square roots and compute hypotenuses. Please type either root or triangle."

It was a geeky, defining moment in what would later be called time-sharing—and time-sharing represented another change in the architecture of computing.

The 1401 pushed computing out to more enterprises, but the 1401 and every other computer created a bottleneck. Only one program, processing one set of data, could be run at a time. If 20 managers wanted 20 different reports, each would have to put in a request and get in line. The data for the first report would be loaded into the machine and the program to process it would run, generating the report. Only when it was done could the next set of data and the next program be loaded into the computer, processed and printed. No multitasking, no multiple users—just one task at a time. A manager might wait a day or two for his batch to be processed. The printed results would have to be delivered by hand or by mail. Information spent a lot of time lying idle.

But by the 1960s, electronics had ramped up the speed of computers, while disk drives made data and programs quickly and randomly accessible. The basic idea of time-sharing was to take advantage of the new speed and storage by inserting a supervising program in front of everything else that happened in the computer. The supervisor shuffled the requests coming in from various users sitting at terminals. One user might type a request for data, and the computer would spit it back to his terminal while another user elsewhere was typing her command. While the first user paused to read his data, the supervisor in the computer would grab the second user's request and process it. By the mid-1960s, computers worked fast enough to take advantage of pauses between user interaction, shuffling duties so quickly that each user rarely had to wait long for an answer. This capability was an early version of what's now commonly called virtualization—sharing a computer or system so it always seems like it belongs to whoever is using it at the time.[53]

Computers of the 1960s, though, weren't built for time-sharing. The major computer companies didn't foresee it. The project was driven by MIT—which got a $3 million grant for the work from the military's ARPA—and other university labs, and researchers there modified existing computers. McCarthy, reminiscing in 1983 about the dawn of time-sharing, said MIT's president proposed undertaking a market survey to establish demand for it among computer users. McCarthy realized this was futile. "I regarded this as analogous to trying to establish the need for steam shovels by market surveys among ditch diggers," he wrote. The people who would wind up using time-sharing weren't computer geeks of the day—they were mostly people who could not even dream of time-sharing on a computer.

So computer companies, listening to their existing customers, didn't see the opportunity. As IBM poured resources into developing the System/360, the company missed the emergence of time-sharing, and the 360 was built in a way that made time-sharing nearly impossible. Other companies began offering time-sharing computers, particularly General Electric and Control Data. Both built computers especially for time-sharing, and they set up computing bureaus that allowed companies to lease time on a distant machine. A November 12, 1965, story in *Time* proclaimed time-sharing "part of a growing trend to market the computer's abilities much as a utility sells light or gas." GE had 88 time-sharing customers by 1965. Control Data had opened the biggest center in the United States, in Los Angeles. IBM, which in 1965 had just unveiled the 360, had 50 customers time-sharing on older IBM machines. IBM eventually caught up by introducing the time-sharing–friendly System/370 in 1970.

As time-sharing improved and spread, typewriter-like terminals—most still relying on paper for communication between human and computer—

made computing more widely accessible. By late 1968, about 36 companies supplied time-sharing services, and they operated computer systems connected to 10,000 terminals at customers' sites, according to "Economic Perspectives on the History of the Computer Time-Sharing Industry," by Martin Campbell-Kelly and Daniel Garcia-Swartz. People who never touched an actual computer could now use one. The terminals popped up in factories, small companies, government agencies and even some schools.

In the early 1970s, the Mothers Club at Lakeside School in Seattle, Washington, used proceeds from a rummage sale to fund a terminal and buy a block of time for students to access a GE time-sharing system. A skinny eighth-grader with a mop of hair felt drawn to the terminal. He learned to program in BASIC, and before long Bill Gates used the machine to write his first computer program: a tic-tac-toe game.

The term *time-sharing* eventually gave way to *virtualization*, and in the 2000s the business of virtualization took off and became more sophisticated. It saved money because virtualization allowed a computer to operate at close to full capacity, so a company or organization could do more with fewer machines. Virtualization made cloud computing possible by allowing pools of computers to be shared by millions of users tapping in from all over the planet. The simple concept that floated out of MIT in the 1960s has become the present and future of computer use.

———

BILL LOWE wasn't in much of a glamour job at IBM in 1980. The company's glory was in its big, expensive machines that pushed the boundaries of technology and processing power. Revenue in 1980 passed $26 billion, and net income was $3.4 billion. IBM employed 341,000 people. The company poured money into research, producing four winners of the Nobel Prize in Physics.[54]

Lowe's title was manager of entry-level systems for IBM's General Systems Division in Boca Raton, Florida. He worked a thousand miles from headquarters on IBM's smallest, least-impressive products outside of typewriters. Yet in 1980, Lowe found himself in a meeting with CEO Frank Cary, who was looking at the personal computer uprising and wondering what to do about it. IBM had stayed on the sidelines.

In 1974, Intel had paved the way for miniaturization of computing with its 8080 microprocessor. In January 1975, *Popular Electronics* featured on its cover the MITS Altair 8800—the first viable personal computer—and that same year Bill Gates and Paul Allen formed Microsoft. In 1977, two break-through machines came on the market: RadioShack's TRS-80 and Apple's Apple II. VisiCalc, the first spreadsheet program, landed on the market in 1979, proving that personal computers could be useful to business. More than 700,000 copies were sold.

This made Cary act. PCs and VisiCalc were being purchased by IBM's business customers—that was clear by 1980. So Cary asked Lowe what to do.

Lowe recalled the conversation: "I said, 'Well, we think we know what we would like to do if we were going to proceed with our own product.' And he said, 'No, at IBM it would take four years and 300 people to do any-thing—it's just a fact of life.' And I said, 'No, sir—we can provide you with a product in a year.' And he abruptly ended the meeting. He said, 'You're on, Lowe—come back in two weeks and tell me what you need.' "

Lowe returned in two weeks and asked Cary to rethink IBM's culture—at least for this project. IBM had always built nearly all of the components for all of its computers. Lowe said he'd buy almost all the components from vendors and essentially assemble the computers. "The key decisions were to go with an open architecture, non-IBM technology, non-IBM software, non-IBM sales and non-IBM service," Lowe recalled. "And we probably spent a full half of the presentation (to Cary and other executives) carrying the corporate management committee into this concept."

Cary bought into the plan. Lowe started the project with 12 engineers in Boca Raton. Now the distance from headquarters seemed like a blessing—

it kept the old IBM culture out of the way. Philip "Don" Estridge was put in charge of the team, all the members of which had previously worked on only big computers. He told an interviewer that the hardest job was getting his engineers to think about how someone who knew little about computers would use one. "How people reacted to a personal computer emotionally was almost more important than what they did with it," Estridge said. "That was an entirely new lesson in computer design."

Lowe, Estridge and the team really did deliver a product in a year: the IBM Personal Computer. Estridge unveiled it August 12, 1981. It cost $1,565, including a keyboard and monitor, and was powered by Intel's 8088 microprocessor and—famously—Microsoft's MS-DOS operating system. It was the first IBM product sold in retail stores such as Sears and ComputerLand. Most significantly, because the IBM PC ran on technology made by outside vendors, other companies could create clones of IBM PCs that worked exactly the same way.

IBM, then at the height of its power in the corporate world, legitimized personal computing for business. Before IBM entered the fray, personal computers were a hobby. After the IBM PC, personal computers were an industry. Within two years of its introduction, the IBM PC overtook the Apple II as the best-selling PC. By 1985, IBM's PC division had grown to 10,000 people and was grossing $4.5 billion a year. Hundreds of software developers sprung up—Ashton-Tate, Lotus Development, Satellite Systems International (WordPerfect) and, of course, Microsoft. Clone makers, like Compaq Computer, flourished.

As the power of computing dispersed into the hands of individuals, computing changed profoundly. Computing kept moving inexorably outward, from the experts to the masses. In the early PC era, small businesses with a dozen people found they could do what-if planning on a spreadsheet. A writer could create, print and mail a professional-looking newsletter and make an impact without working for a media company. A small sales office could store customer information in a database. It was all new and

The PC spread computing to individuals, making it a part of daily life and small business.

empowering. These little machines couldn't perform the complex tasks of a mainframe—but the people who didn't need to perform mainframe-level tasks far outnumbered those who did. Once IBM entered the market, sales of PCs of all kinds soared. The public couldn't get enough.

———

A DECADE AFTER the IBM PC debuted, computing had become a part of everyday life in business for millions of people around the world. Computing was quickly becoming a part of personal life, too—a change as profound as the first wave of telephones, radios and televisions that had swept into homes. This architecture—this idea of computing for individuals—drove the industry for nearly 30 years. Personal computers kept getting more powerful. As the Internet emerged, they connected to the World Wide Web. People found personal and interesting things to do with computing, like video and music, requiring yet more power and capability from personal machines. Then converging trends brought on the cloud and an onslaught of motes: devices, sensors and gadgets.

As computing burrowed its way into just about every aspect of business and society, the concept of information took on new meaning and importance. Information was no longer something simply to be assembled and passed along, but a thing itself—to be studied, pulled apart and understood. Information contained value no one ever saw before, and a science evolved to find it. In information were ways to make the physical world operate better, save money in a business, build rockets, squeeze video down a tiny wire. Computing unlocked information's value because computers could make calculations at the high rates necessary to reveal information's hidden secrets. But in the end, this always came full circle, and the information became the main reason it was so valuable to own and operate a computer.[55]

Claude Shannon was the progenitor of the very idea that there might be a science of information. Shannon wrote a master's thesis in 1937, as a 21-year-old student at MIT, showing how electronic circuits could perform the formal logic known as Boolean algebra, a concept that underlies all electronic computers. The thesis showed how—as Ben Wood had earlier hinted—computers could do more than sort and tabulate. They could run algorithms that modeled almost anything. The faster a computer could run, the faster it could calculate a complex algorithm. More complex algorithms could represent more interesting problems, moving computing machines from, say, just keeping track of inventory to figuring out what inventory needed to be in which stores on which days.

Working in England around the same time as Shannon, mathematician Alan Turing formalized the concept of the algorithm, and then used the formulas to break German codes during World War II. Over the decades, mathematicians working at universities and at companies such as IBM, AT&T and SAS have continued to improve the algorithm. From the 1940s to the 1980s, there was only one kind of algorithm, called the simplex algorithm, for doing complex problems with lots of variables. It would, in a mathematical sense, move calculations from point to point along a zigzagging imaginary line until it found the optimal point—a process that took a long time. In 1985, Bell Labs researcher Narendra Karmarkar found a way to mathematically leap across boundaries instead of following that line.

A simplex algorithm is like driving an interstate from one city to another; a Karmarkar algorithm is like flying there.

That leap allowed algorithms to come to conclusions far faster, allowing computers to unlock yet more value in information. The advance, for instance, allowed American Airlines in the late 1980s to install the first yield management computer system in its industry. The system could take data about every seat on every route and manipulate it to see what would happen when variables were changed. The information helped American discover that it could charge high rates to business fliers and create a radical system to fill empty seats: Super Saver fares.

Other information science advances have taken the uses of computing in new directions. In 1975, IBM Research mathematician Benoît Mandelbrot conceived of fractal geometry. His concepts allowed computers to analyze and describe irregular, "rough" phenomena, like the shapes of clouds or patterns in music. Again, this made computing more valuable, and fractal geometry has been put to work to compress video so it can be transmitted over the Internet, make scenery in video games and make stronger metals.

When Benoît Mandelbrot conceived fractal geometry, he had no idea it would be used in such a wide range of ways, including compressing video on the Internet, creating scenery in video games and modeling neurological systems in medical research.

In the 2010s, math researchers at IBM and universities began looking for breakthroughs in nonlinear algorithms. Computers have always had to solve algorithms—even Karmarkar algorithms—from beginning to end, in order, much the way a sentence has to be read in order. Solving increasingly complex algorithms the traditional way will take too long. "We have to do something fundamentally different," said Brenda Dietrich, who runs the Mathematical Sciences Department at IBM's Thomas J. Watson Research Center. Information science needs a way to break up algorithms, solve the pieces in parallel and bring the pieces back together with an answer. "It's more like the human brain works, or if you give a problem to a group of people," Dietrich said.[56]

If researchers can come up with such a breakthrough, it will increase the speed of computing without relying on the microprocessors to get faster. That in turn will unlock information in ways as surprising as Super Saver fares in the 1980s.

———

IN THE FALL OF 2006, Amazon.com CEO Jeff Bezos plopped down on a couch in a hotel suite in San Francisco to talk about a service he was about to announce. He called it Elastic Compute Cloud. Bezos was famously sunny, and he quite cheerfully wrestled with a problem that few people in 2006 really understood—just what "cloud computing" might be about. "I haven't figured out a way to explain this very well yet," Bezos, grinning, said to a journalist in the room. "I was hoping you would."[57]

Amazon made its name as an online retailer, not as a technology provider, yet the company was about to rent out everything its technology did behind the scenes to anyone who wanted it, whether it was a big corporation or an entrepreneur in a yurt in Mongolia—as long as the yurt had a high-speed Internet connection. The pitch: rent space on Amazon's computers to run a business, or rent out its transaction capabilities to sell things and collect money. Anyone anywhere could become a global online retailer by using the public Internet to tap into computing somewhere in Amazon's system—computing that resided amorphously in the metaphorical clouds. "It's letting people create a business by remote control," Bezos said.

Bezos's timing turned out to be good. Amazon's move brought cloud computing into the public's consciousness just as an explosion of computing devices and sensors began making cloud computing essential to business and to daily life. The cloud and the motes have been feeding off one another since then, and in the 2010s will drive the next turn in the way the world thinks about computing. It is a new architecture being born.

Cloud computing originated well before Bezos jumped in. "It started to arrive before it arrived, but the market wasn't ready," said IBM's former Internet strategist, Irving Wladawsky-Berger. By 1995, with the advent of Netscape Communications' popular browser, the Internet and World Wide Web took flight. The power of connecting became as important as the power of processing, and the desire to connect drove the building of an infrastructure: broadband lines to homes, Wi-Fi wireless networks, 3G cellular data networks, long-haul fiber optic lines, server farms, data centers. All of these were set up to service the growing demand for connection, while storing and manipulating the burgeoning amount of data and content being generated by the masses.

The infrastructure became a platform—a way to create enterprises and services never before possible. As far back as 2002, major technology companies recognized that there ought to be a way to allow a corporation or an entrepreneur to tap into that platform without having to build or buy a piece of it. In 2002, IBM unveiled on-demand computing, selling the idea that computing would soon be like electricity—available anywhere and paid for in increments. For companies used to the security of private data networks, the idea seemed a bit scary. And individuals, used to keeping data on their laptops' hard drives, couldn't quite grasp the concept of relying on spreadsheets or sales automation software that resided somewhere in an unknowable cloud.

Then, in January 2007, Apple unveiled its first iPhone, touching off consumer desire for pocket-sized connected computing devices. "The explosion of smartphones around 2007 was when everyone saw we were in a different place," Wladawsky-Berger said.

The smartphones and the cloud together are repeating the pattern of previous architectural leaps by pushing computing out another level. This time, computing is reaching billions of people all around the globe, from preteens in Ohio to farmers in Namibia. People increasingly have access to inexpensive, low-powered devices that through the cloud can tap into the kind of computing power once reserved for giant corporations. Such users in turn will shape computing, just as new classes of users have done in the past.

At the same time, another class of user is joining the cloud. These machines, sensors and physical objects without people attached have been dubbed the Internet of Things. This Internet includes the smart electricity meters that are installed at homes and feed information to the utility company and the homeowners. It includes the sensors that are attached to zebras in the wild and collect and send data about where the animals go and what they do. Sensors embedded in asphalt can tell smartphone users which parking spaces on a street are empty. Some of these connected machines will be superintelligent devices that do things on behalf of humans. Microsoft Research scientist Eric Horvitz has a virtual personal assistant named Laura that can track his calendar, greet visitors to his office and offer them drinks.[58]

As devices drive computing outward, the systems that handle all of that data—the machines that make up the cloud—will need to become astoundingly sophisticated. In 2010, more than 1,200 exabytes of digital information were created. A single exabyte is equal to about 1 trillion books. Data generation will increase exponentially for the foreseeable future. It's coming from individuals posting on social networks, entertainers creating online movies, companies building massive databases, and more and more sensors detecting and transmitting everything from ocean tides to city traffic patterns to calories burned by people working out. The data deluge is challenging, yet the world relies on that data as never before, and that's driving new technologies such as racetrack memory. It's driving the development of stream computing—new software and algorithms such as real-time analytics that can look at data as it is produced and figure out what to retain and what to throw out. The cloud is becoming more industrialized and professional to allow the devices to become simpler and ubiquitous.

IBM's "smarter planet" is not just a clever tagline. The evolution of computing architecture is the story of moving computing power outward—from experts to scientists to smaller businesses on 1401s to terminals and then to PCs. Now it's being pushed out to every person and thing, with the cloud connecting it all and making sense of the data. Question-answering technology such as DeepQA and gesture technology like that on the iPad are increasingly making it seamless and natural for people and machines to collaborate. Algorithms, which once handled only the linear, deterministic paths of a simpler mathematics, are becoming sophisticated enough to take on the complex, probabilistic nature of reality. In the next decade, machines will begin to learn on their own. In so many ways, the planet is, in fact, becoming one massive computer—but not a computer in the old sense of stand-alone machines. The computing planet is one of machines, nature, us and information, all meshed together.

The world itself is becoming smart. It's a path we've been on since Ben Wood met with Thomas Watson in 1928.

• • •

A man in a suit is standing on a street corner in Shanghai, and he needs to get to an address across town. He has a simple question: would it be better at that moment to take a taxi or the subway?

Today that question can't be answered with certainty. Come 2021, the planet's computer network should be able to give an answer instantly—through a cell phone.

Over the course of 100 years, computing has changed our thinking, and our thinking has changed computing. Emerging from the science and technologies of the industrial era, computing helped spawn the new sciences and technologies of the postindustrial era. It let us abstract information, in order to analyze and manipulate it. And that pointed to a new science of information itself, underlying the disciplines of twenty-first-century scientific understanding—from physics to biology to chemistry to the social sciences. In many respects, pioneering the science of information has become pioneering science, period.

That's the trajectory of the past century. Where will the next century take us? It's hard to predict that far ahead, but it's already clear that in the span of just 10 years, computing and information science will take us to a new place, a new level of thought. When individuals' daily tasks can be optimized in ways now available only to major corporations, we'll rethink the way we live. When data from people, things and nature can be tapped, mixed, matched and analyzed, the world will speak to us in new ways. The challenge then for leaders will be to rethink conventional wisdom and existing institutions, corporations, cities and nations.

"A lot of societal issues and systemic problems can be solved," IBM CEO Sam Palmisano said. "Everybody says they're unsolvable—safe borders, clean water, energy. But the application of technology can solve a lot of these things we wrestle with."[59]

One hundred years of nonstop advances in the science of computing and information have landed us here in 2011, at the brink of profound transformation. Technology is liberating data from the world around us. The data has always been there—in the growth of crops, movement of people, billions of daily transactions, changing levels of a stream—but now we're beginning to capture, decipher and understand it. This new tide of intelligence is changing what we know and what we want to know. As the trend picks up speed over the coming decade, technology will once again change the way the world works.

At the same time, computing is continuing its 100-year drive to liberate human creativity and knowledge from the boxes that had contained it. Thought is no longer locked inside individual minds, corporations or countries. Punching data onto cards in the early 1900s was the first step in unmooring knowledge from people who had kept it in their heads. The Internet gave the process a rocket boost, allowing anyone to share information and collaborate over any distance, throughout companies or organizations. Smartphones, GPS, video and sensors are being deployed everywhere. Supercomputers can model the function of human organs at a molecular level. The boom in cloud computing and the explosion of mobile and personal computing devices around the planet bring more knowledge and creativity together in a global pool. Within a decade, automated language translation will knock down the last significant barrier. Nothing need keep our collective ideas apart.

What the world is about to experience is more than a new era of technology. It's a new era of thought. Technology just makes it possible.

The man on the Shanghai corner in 2021 should be able to speak into an app on his cell phone and ask, "Taxi or subway?" GPS will know where he is. His calendar will tell the app the address of his appointment. Taxis, armed with GPS and wireless communication, will tell the network where the cabs are, whether they have passengers and how fast they're moving. The taxis' movement will tell the network the condition of traffic. From all of those inputs, the network will know how long it will take for the man to get a cab, and how long it will take the cab to get to the man's destination. As for the subway, the system will know how far the man would have to walk to the nearest station, how long the ride would take and how long it would take to walk from the station at the other end to his meeting. The network will also know the weather and, thanks to a health monitor like the Fitbit, the man's physical condition. Is it so hot that a few blocks' walk would leave the guy out of breath and drenched in sweat?

So the man speaks into his mobile device, "Taxi or subway?" The answer returns: "Nice day, traffic's terrible, you could use the exercise—get on the subway, and here's the route."

Such a scenario is not a stretch. In fact, far more ambitious efforts are already under way in cities around the world. For example, IBM recently announced a "smarter city" agreement with Rio de Janeiro in which catastrophic mudslides that periodically hit its populous hillside favelas can be anticipated and their devastation averted. As *Fast Company* reported in December 2010, a newly established operations center will gather data from the city's various agencies, "running it through a battery of algorithms to monitor, predict, and visualize storm damage while deciding how best to respond. 'Which streets will require the most troops?' IBM materials suggest as one of the variables. 'Which hills are most prone to mud slides? Are there shelters that have vacancies? Which hospitals have beds available? What is the best way to exit from a soccer match at the Maracana? How should officials direct traffic coming from the Copacabana Beach?'"

This future is visible today, based on the technology of 2011 and knowing the technology rolling out or in the works through 2021.

Lawrence Livermore National Laboratory in 2011 is deploying its Sequoia supercomputer, based on IBM's Blue Gene/Q technology. It will exceed 20 petaflops—more processing power than the entire list of the top 500 supercomputers running in 2010. That's 20 quadrillion calculations per second. Roughly 120 billion people armed with calculators would have to do math for nearly 50 years to process what Sequoia will do in a day. The computer will be used to research astronomy, energy, human genome science and climate change. (Nearly all of the Sequoia research is classified.)

In storage, capacity is becoming essentially infinite, while its cost is plummeting. Whatever data we want to save can be saved. Often, the problem is not storing it but finding it, but that's changing. Technology called Scale Out Network Attached Storage, invented by IBM Research, provides access to billions of data files no matter where they reside in a system. SONAS can scan billions of files in minutes. The technology is necessary to sort through the unstructured data, from web-based video to e-mail, that's growing at a 47 percent annual rate.

In data centers, new systems are attacking a growing problem. Jumbles of disparate technologies have been acquired and deployed over time to run specific applications, all crammed under the same roof yet unable to talk to each other. In some cases, the different pieces require separate staffs. But instead of being made up of many disparate machines and software installations, the data center of 2021 should be able to operate more like one large machine, capable of mixing and matching components to fit different tasks. It could ultimately become almost self-aware, able to decide on its own how to reconfigure itself to meet the demand of certain tasks.

The Watson computer and DeepQA question-answering technology have proven themselves by beating human champions on *Jeopardy!*, showing that a computer can have conversational interaction with people.

Meanwhile, Apple, Research in Motion, Nokia and other companies are spreading powerful, handheld, connected computing devices deeper into the population. These increasingly are not just devices for consumer uses, but tap into enterprise-level applications available through the cloud.

Technology is making the planet smarter, but still only in pockets. And there are challenges. The kind of exponential increases in computing power described by Moore's law are slowing dramatically. The data deluge from the Internet and sensors threatens to outpace the ability of companies to buy and install the technology to handle it. The piecemeal data centers will be a reality for a while, creating in many cases a crisis of complexity.

And yet technology's 100-year trajectory won't falter. In every aspect of computing—speed, storage, software, sensing, networking, architecture—technology continues surging ahead, just as it has always done. Each generation inherits information technology that seems to stretch the bounds of human innovation, then that generation cracks through those boundaries, building on what's been done to go even further. There is no reason to think the cycle will end anytime soon.

Some key breakthroughs are expected in the next 10 to 15 years. Since their inception, computers have worked the same way, processing a series of "if this, then that" instructions at extremely high speeds. Scientists, though, are working on computing architectures that borrow from the human brain, processing many related ideas at once, applying logic that is a bit more abstract and fuzzy than the hard rules of today's computer programs. Such computers are expected to supplement the current architecture, and they will be able to do something current machines can't. They'll be able to learn from data, drawing out lessons and conclusions but throwing away details much as the human brain does. The computers won't be programmed—they'll be trained. In fact, they'll even be able to train themselves. Such systems would represent a radical break in the history of computing— the first step beyond the stored-program architecture pioneered by Eckert and Mauchly with ENIAC and commonly known as "von Neumann architecture," after a 1945 paper by John von Neumann. Scientists call this next generation "learning systems."

No one has yet built the computing mechanism that can work in such a brainlike manner—though IBM's Watson took some initial steps in that direction. But it's certain to come. One probable path is through quantum computing, which is a way to compute using the spin of atoms. A quantum computer would be able to process all the possible answers to a problem at the same instant, using very little energy. While quantum computers are only rough lab experiments in 2011, a working version is likely to be built before the end of the 2020s—a breakthrough that should be as important as the transistor.

In the meantime, much is developing. DeepQA-style natural language software and instantaneous language translation should allow anyone, not just database professionals, to query the data and get meaningful answers. Machine vision can help computers look through video cameras and understand what they see, storing data about the events, not just raw video that can't be searched. Analytics, running through real-time, streaming computers, are creating new ways to use data to model events and understand patterns. As the software gets smarter and the computing more powerful, simulations—the kind that not long ago could be done only on supercomputers—will perhaps get as inexpensive, easy and commonplace as spreadsheets.

Security—always an issue—should also advance in the 2021 world. As computing moves to the cloud, stronger and more professional security can be built into more computing activity—from the get-go, by design. New technologies like deep packet inspection are able to verify packets that flow through a system, helping block anything suspicious. While threats will certainly grow more sophisticated, technology should have an easier time staying ahead of the bad guys.

All of this technology will drive two key trends through 2021—both of which, not coincidentally, are the same trends that computing has driven for 100 years:

Computing at the top end will undertake more sophisticated analysis and make yet higher-level judgments, increasingly freeing humans from arcane thought processes. That will allow people to focus on uniquely human creativity, pattern recognition and innovation.

In the other direction, sophisticated computing will burrow further into everyday life. What used to be available only to corporations or government labs will be offered to individuals through laptops and mobile devices—and gadgets no one has yet dreamed up.

Throughout the past 100 years, this combination of computing-driven trends has caused us to rethink life, business and institutions. It's about to happen again.

For a century, society thought we were on a path to make computers that could think. In fact, that was never the case. We've been on a path to constantly re-create thought. That path continues.

. . .

Reinventing the Modern Corporation
Steve Hamm

Whinen Thomas Watson Sr. joined the Computing-Tabulating-Recording-Company as general manager in 1914, he stood at the epicenter of American capitalism at the dawn of a new era. The fledgling company, which he later renamed International Business Machines, had been formed three years earlier through the merger of three small manufacturing firms that sold mechanical accounting machines, scales and time recorders. Headquarters was a suite of offices in a newly built 20-story building at 50 Broad Street in New York City, 50 yards from the New York Stock Exchange and a short distance from the Lower East Side, the original home of New York's bustling garment industry.

To enter the building, Watson sometimes had to shoulder his way through an unruly crowd of traders who bought and sold securities at the so-called curb market on the cobblestones of Broad Street. Up on the 18th floor at C-T-R, the 40-year-old executive sat each day at a simple wooden desk dressed in a three-piece suit with a stiff Edwardian collar, poring over ledgers and correspondence. He could glance through the windows at the hubbub in the street far below—where the traders' derby hats and dark suits made them look like ants swarming at a picnic. His perch turned out to be a perfect spot from which to help invent the modern corporation.

New York was bursting with humanity in those days. Immigrants from Russia, Italy, Ireland, Germany and elsewhere poured off ships and into the city's narrow streets and warrens of rattletrap tenements. The human

Previous pages:
Broad Street in New York City, 1903 (left),
and Thomas Watson Sr., 1913.

torrent had nearly doubled the population over the previous two decades, to 4.8 million.[60] New York was both the nation's financial capital, home of the moneymen and traders who funded the industries of a burgeoning economy, and a manufacturing dynamo, jammed with clothing factories, printing plants, machine shops and gritty metal foundries. For more than a century, captains of industry had built empires by extracting value from natural resources or by building mammoth steel mills and continent-spanning railroads and harnessing the strong backs and nimble fingers of laborers. In 1920, the US census revealed that 30 percent of the working population was employed in manufacturing and 26 percent worked in farming, forestry and fishing. The other major categories were trade (10.2 percent), domestic and personal service (8.2 percent), clerical (7.5 percent) and transportation (7.4 percent).[61] Indeed, the leaders of heavy industry and commerce made up C-T-R's client base.[62]

Yet Watson fashioned C-T-R into a very different sort of company from those that surrounded him. He realized that his company's counting and calculating devices could help those railroads, steel companies, manufacturers and merchants manage their data. He saw that in the new century, a company's most valuable assets would be the information it amassed, the knowledge it created and the ideas of its employees—intellectual capital rather than money, muscle or raw material. "Tom Watson should be credited with the idea that information was going to be the big thing in the twentieth century," said Harvard Business School professor Richard Tedlow, author of *The Watson Dynasty*.[63]

When Watson took over C-T-R, the idea of the modern corporation was just beginning to form, and he played a significant role in laying its foundation. An outgrowth of the large industrial and financial organizations that had dominated commerce in Western societies, the modern corporation was also, in the United States, a reaction against the excesses of the Gilded Age, when market manipulators and anticompetitive trusts distorted the economy. In the new century, the form and function of the corporation were to undergo rapid change as the world's great commercial organizations mastered the science of applying new ways to extract and manage information to harness capital, natural resources and people and put them to work in increasingly effective, efficient and ambitious ways.

In 1914, this transformation was hardly clear—including in Watson's own mind. His belief in information and thinking was both fervent and unformed. It was clear to him that information would be the basis of economic value. It was also clear to him that commerce was destined to become global. He was convinced that businesses would have responsibilities not just to their shareholders but also to society at large. And he doggedly aimed to build an organization that self-consciously embodied his mantra, "Think." Over the next 40 years, he would start a process of discovery—with many missteps but with more successes—translating these gut impulses into policies and practices, scientific discoveries and the then-radical notion of an intentionally created corporate culture.

Today, we are again at a turning point in the history of the corporation. Faced with a potent mix of economic, environmental and political challenges, corporate leaders are reexamining basic assumptions. Just as diverse populations once poured into the commercial and societal melting pot of New York City, so, today, those who previously sat on the sidelines are becoming players in the global economy—as both consumers and producers. Business powerhouses are emerging from China, India, Korea, South Africa and elsewhere. They're inventing business models that give them the power to reshape established industries and leapfrog the twentieth century's giants. The Internet is disrupting traditional ways of doing business in one market after another, from media and music to manufacturing and retailing. It levels the playing field globally for businesses and individuals. Jobs that were once anchored in one place by tradition and convenience now can be done anywhere in the world. And the barriers to entry—once insuperable to all who could not amass large amounts of capital—are dramatically lower.

Individual citizens can become global capitalists. To combine two of the most widely used metaphors of our era, the global economy is becoming a long, flat tail.

How should businesses respond? As before, leaders are asking themselves fundamental questions about what their company should be and how it should operate—the kinds of questions that have shaped business thinking from ancient Greece to modern Silicon Valley. But today the answers are changing—and with neck-snapping speed. So it's time to reinvent the corporation once more. This essay lays out a point of view on the past and present of the modern corporation—and on what progress will look like in the twenty-first century. It is organized around four basic questions that leaders must ask and answer:

> **HOW DOES A COMPANY DEFINE AND MANAGE ITSELF?** Over the past 100 years, corporate management has shifted away from the nineteenth-century mode of centering a company around a single powerful leader, adopting a more networked, horizontal approach. Though, of course, there are exceptions, today more and more organizations are guided by deliberately created corporate cultures, often grounded in shared values, that survive even when a leader departs. IBM was a pioneer in this shift—not simply in inculcating ethics, but also in seeking differentiation, organizational identity and the definition of the company's raison d'être. In the future, the challenge will be to create ultra-flexible organizations made up of empowered professionals who can anticipate and prepare for change rather than merely sense and respond to it.

> **HOW DOES THE ORGANIZATION CREATE VALUE?** Through the lens of one company's evolution—but drawing broadly on modern business history—we can trace the shift from Industrial Age modes of value

creation to the twentieth century's monetization of knowledge and intellectual capital. This takes multiple forms and not just in product development but in every aspect of a company's operations. This progression suggests that organizations will increasingly create value by collaborating openly and deeply with other companies, and governments and even individuals, participating fully in a network economy.

HOW DOES THE ORGANIZATION OPERATE IN A GLOBAL ECONOMY? In the nineteenth century, being international meant having a presence all around the world. During the twentieth century, it came to mean something quite different: seeing the world holistically, both as a market and as a supply of resources and talent. As a result, the modern corporation has changed in form, from the international model of the nineteenth century to the multinational model of the twentieth to the globally integrated model of the twenty-first. Those companies that have succeeded, including IBM, have created new skills, processes and governance systems in order to manage the tensions inherent in being at once global and local.

HOW DOES THE ORGANIZATION ENGAGE WITH SOCIETY? Once, businesses answered only to their shareholders. Philanthropy was a personal matter for wealthy industrialists. Over the course of the twentieth century, the most enlightened corporations realized that how they defined themselves would hinge in part on developing responsible relationships with society—to the point that engaging with society has become woven into doing business, essential to nearly every decision an organization makes.

IBM's evolution over the past 100 years—including its near-death experience in the early 1990s—has made it a vastly different company from the one that Thomas Watson joined in 1914. Indeed, the company has changed enormously over the past decade. Throughout this journey, its leaders have asked those same fundamental questions, reaffirming some of the things the company once believed and coming up with some new answers. IBMers today know all too well what can happen if an organization loses sight of business fundamentals and fails to respond aggressively to satisfy its customers' deepest needs. And they understand that in today's business climate, what's required to last is nothing less than continuous transformation.

IBM is still reinventing itself—and it knows that the process will never be finished. Asked to name the most important lesson that IBM's history teaches us about leadership, chief executive Sam Palmisano didn't hesitate: "You have to be willing to change your core, and you have to be ahead of the shift." [64]

• • •

The Intentional Creation of Culture

When Soichiro Honda started the Honda Motor Company in 1948 to design and build motorcycles in war-ravaged Japan, his ambitions were audacious. A black-smith's son who usually wore the blue overalls of a mechanic, Honda stood on an orange crate in the company's factory four years later and declared his intention to make Honda not just the number one motorcycle company in Japan but number one in the world.

He didn't achieve his goal overnight, but right from the start he set out to build a corporate culture that would enable a tiny company to grow to greatness.[65] He did it by establishing a respectful rapport with the company's employees and by giving them clear direction about the company's values and ambitions. For instance, in 1956 he published a "company principle" in Honda's newsletter, distilling the company's purpose down to its essence: "Maintaining a global viewpoint, we are dedicated to supplying products of the highest quality, yet at a reasonable price, for worldwide customer satisfaction."

In classrooms and data centers, assembly lines and sales training facilities, Thomas Watson's mantra, "Think," gave visible form to the novel idea that a company could deliberately create its culture.

Systems Service Engineering Class for women, Endicott, New York, 1935.

1. IBM Service Bureau, Florence, Italy, 1953. **2.** Thomas Watson Sr., Seattle, Washington, 1947. **3.** Ruth Leach visit, San Jose, California, 1949. **4.** IBM schoolhouse, Endicott, New York, 1933. **5.** IBM seminar, New Delhi, India, 1956. **6.** Mechanical Services and Testing Department, Argentina, 1935. **7.** Electric typewriter demonstration, Brazil, 1958. **8.** IBM class, Saudi Arabia, 1951. **9.** Richard Whitcomb at IBM Honolulu, Hawaii, 1962. **10.** IBM office, Japan, 1966. **11.** IBM office staff, Ecuador, 1943. **12.** First Japanese sales representative, 1925. **13.** IBM employees, Philippines, 1939.

14. Hammersmith factory, London, England, 1960. **15.** First issue of *THINK,* June 1935. **16.** IBM office, Jakarta, Indonesia, 1964. **17.** "Think" signs, 1964. **18.** Singapore Constitution Expo, IBM exhibit, 1959. **19.** Thomas Watson Sr., 1914. **20.** IBM Service Bureau opening, Taipei, Taiwan, 1960. **21.** IBM sales class, Paris, France, 1937. **22.** Hundred Percent Club, Endicott, New York, 1940. **23.** IBM pavilion at World's Fair, Brussels, Belgium, 1958. **24.** North American Aviation, Rocketdyne Division, California, 1965. **25.** Walter Kneivel sending first IBM teletype message from New York City to Endicott, 1930.

The corporate culture that Honda created—called the Honda Way—has shaped the essential character of the organization ever since. It helped the company become the world's leading motorcycle maker and the sixth-largest car company, and guided it through the worldwide collapse in auto sales that began in 2008. While other auto companies laid off tens of thousands of employees, Honda fired nobody and instead cut production and salaries for non-production employees.[66] In a July 20, 2010, speech laying out the company's strategy and goals for the next decade, chief executive Takanobu Ito harkened back to Honda's vision. "Especially, as we are in the midst of a difficult business environment, nothing is more important than going back to Honda's basic principle; that is, to see things from the customer's point of view and continue offering products that please our customers."[67]

In Honda's example, we can see important dimensions of how the modern corporation has come to engage and manage people. Today, most major companies profess a formal set of beliefs and seek to establish a strong culture. Some values statements consist of a single sentence. The motto of Patagonia, the American outdoor clothing and equipment retailer, is: "Let my people go—surfing." The idea of Yvon Chouinard, its owner, is that unless employees feel happy and free they won't do their best work. The value statement of Whole Foods Market, the American food retailer, goes on for nearly a thousand words. The length of the document doesn't matter. The important thing is that leaders deliberately create corporate cultures grounded in values.

It was not always so. In fact, before the modern corporation came on the scene, the concept of corporate culture was unknown. Of course, every human community and organization has a culture—"It's the way we do things around here." But even today, many companies do not make a self-conscious effort to understand, much less establish and sustain, one. And even for those that do, the culture has widely varying goals, depending on the company or its circumstances. For instance, in a business whose value proposition is to deliver a mass-produced, low-price commodity, the culture may be aimed at enthusiasm for rote tasks and well-honed teamwork. Among organizations where creativity and discovery are vital—say, universities— very different cultural norms are appropriate.

Culture consciousness would have been inconceivable to most nineteenth-century businesses. But with the dawn of the modern, knowledge-based corporation, culture went from irrelevant to urgent. For these companies, the culture they intentionally set out to create became not merely a dimension of the enterprise, but its organizing principle.

Such a company was what Watson had in mind when he came to C-T-R. And from his managerial innovations over four decades, their extension by his son over two more, and the stewardship of their legacy by leaders and IBMers for generations since, we can extract some core principles of how the modern corporation engages and manages people. We can also see the tensions that inherently come with this new approach.

———

IF A CORPORATE LEADER'S AIM is to create a culture for a knowledge-based business, he doesn't start with a business model or a technology or a management system. He must start with *values*—not in the sense of ethics or morality, but of organizational identity and differentiation. How these values are established depends on the era and the organization. IBM did it first through declarations by its founder. But paradoxically, over the long term, the effect of basing an enterprise on values is actually to make the leader less important. In fact, that's the idea. If she or he were to be run over by a bus tomorrow, everybody else in the company would know how to behave and how to set priorities.

This is a crucial point. It's natural that the culture of a company would take on the personality and values of those dynamic individuals who created it. But unless the company culture is sustainable—meaning it can continue to thrive if products change, markets change, technologies change and the dominating leader isn't in command anymore—the company itself isn't sustainable. This is a dauntingly difficult task, and its success or failure shows up only over a long period of time.

Values really matter. Over the past 30 years there have been numerous studies showing that companies that establish well-defined and well-understood values and culture perform better than those that don't. For instance, in their 1992 book *Corporate Culture and Performance*, John Kotter and James Heskett documented the results of their landmark study of 207 large US companies, which they had tracked over an 11-year period. Companies that managed their cultures saw revenue increases of 682 percent versus 166 percent for companies that didn't manage their cultures well.[68]

Since its early days, IBM has been operated based on a set of core beliefs. IBM would distinguish itself with its respect for the individual, its pursuit of excellence in all things and its commitment to providing the best customer service. These values were baked into the corporate DNA by Thomas Watson Sr., who built the near-failing organization of 1914 into an industrial giant with staying power. And that DNA has taken hold in millions of employees over the course of 100 years.

In a lecture at Columbia University in the spring of 1962, Thomas Watson Jr. laid out his and his father's thesis of what it takes to make a business successful over the long haul. "I firmly believe that any organization, in order to survive and achieve success, must have a sound set of beliefs on which it premises all its policies and actions," he told students. "Next, I believe that the most important single factor in corporate success is faithful adherence to those beliefs. And, finally, I believe that if an organization is to meet the challenges of a changing world, it must be prepared to change everything about itself except those beliefs as it moves through corporate life."[69]

Basing an organization on core beliefs lies at the root of IBM's approach to corporate culture. Of course, when Watson's father introduced IBM's Basic Beliefs a century ago, no one would have used that term. But with the benefit of hindsight, we can understand why Watson Sr. is credited as the first business leader to so consciously and pervasively create a culture for a company.[70]

Many of the policies that Watson created to shape IBM grew out of his respect for employees. He considered all employees to be equals, laying out what he called "the Man Proposition" in a speech to IBM executives, salespeople and factory workers in Endicott, New York, in 1915. On a large sheet of paper, Watson wrote out a list of roles in the company, including "sales manager," "sales man," "factory manager" and "factory man." Then he crossed off everything but the word *man*. He told the crowd: "We should keep in mind at all times regardless of what our occupations or duties are; we are just men—men standing together, shoulder to shoulder, all working for one common good; we have one common interest, and the good of each of us as individuals affects the greater good of the company." [71]

This attitude was anything but typical of the captains of industry during Watson's era. "He struck his contemporaries as a nut and a crank with his personnel policy that 'People who perform are my partners.' Radical. No class war!" said the late management consultant and author Peter Drucker, who worked with both Watsons over a period of two decades.[72]

The Man Proposition applied to women, too. In the early 1930s, Watson launched a program that sent sales executives into the field to visit customers and instructed their secretaries to fill in for them. He advised the women to keep their letters brief, eliminate red tape and use the opportunity to show they were capable of taking on more demanding jobs.[73] In 1935, long before the demands of World War II required the entry of millions of women into the American workforce, IBM began hiring women to help

"Men and women will do the same kind of work for equal pay.
They will have the same treatment, the same responsibilities
and the same opportunities for advancement."
—Thomas Watson Sr., 1935

customers learn to use their machines and as personnel professionals. "Men and women will do the same kind of work for equal pay. They will have the same treatment, the same responsibilities and the same opportunities for advancement," Watson told the *New York Sun* that year.[74] Ruth Leach, who joined IBM to demonstrate machines at the San Francisco Golden Gate International Exposition in 1939, was promoted in 1943 to be the company's first female vice president, becoming one of the first women at that executive level in a major industrial company.[75] This willingness to pioneer social progress within the workforce became an essential part of IBM's culture. Today, 29 percent of IBM's employees worldwide are female and 25 percent of the company's managers are women.[76] C.L. Reeser, a longtime IBM manager at one of the Endicott plants, jotted down a record of Watson's advances. They included:

Ruth Leach was IBM's first female vice president.

> *1916: The workweek reduced from 54 to 48 hours;*
> *1924: A study club set up for employees where they could learn new skills;*
> *1934: All employees shifted from piecework pay to salaries;*
> *1937: Vacation pay for hourly workers;*
> *1945: Pensions for all workers.*[77]

Patrick Toole, a former IBM executive who at one point was in charge of IBM's manufacturing, said Watson's legacy lived on long after he left the company. "You knew that if you tried hard, you wouldn't be fired," Toole recalled. "But if you were dishonest, you'd be fired, or if you cut corners and somebody got injured, you'd be fired. It was clear that the highest standards of safety were part of 'respect for the individual.'"[78]

Tom Laster was IBM's first black salesman.

One of Watson's management innovations was the so-called open-door policy, which he introduced in the early 1920s. Any employee who felt that she or he wasn't being treated properly or fairly was encouraged to send a letter to the president, and the complaint would be investigated. John Opel,

In 1942, IBM hired psychologist Michael Supa, who was blind, to recruit and train people with disabilities.

IBM's chief executive from 1981 to 1985, recalls that the policy made a strong impression on him when he joined the company in 1949. "It said that the individual had a right to say what they wanted to say, and the manager should damn well listen," he said.[79]

Not only did Watson respect his employees, but he also wanted IBMers to be well regarded by outsiders. He insisted that people dress formally so they would make a good impression. "He always dressed as if he was going to call on the president of a company," recalled longtime IBM executive James Birkenstock.[80] Watson rewarded outstanding performance richly, setting up the Hundred Percent Club for salesmen who reached their annual sales quota, and treating club members to special parties and golf outings. IBM trained new hires in the company culture and reinforced its values in essays penned by Watson in internal publications.

———

SOMETIMES, OF COURSE, culture is shaped not through pre-planning but through an organization's response to crisis. If that response is successful, it can become a formative experience in the evolution of the organization's character. For IBM, one such event was Watson's undaunted optimism about the future in the face of the Great Depression. On November 18, 1929, just three weeks after the stock market crash, he called IBM's executives together for a pep talk. The men had been preoccupied with stock market losses and, in his mind, were shirking their duties. "I have run a stockbrokers' office for three weeks, but that office is closed," he told them. "I have now opened up the IBM company with a vengeance, and I want all of you to get your heads up and tails over the dashboard." He announced that starting in a few days he would appoint an advisory board of executives to hold weekly meetings that would focus primarily on the future. "We are going into the future, and we are not going to wait until some other company gets ahead of us," he said. "There are greater prospects for our machines in the future than any of you have dreamed of."[81]

Rather than hunkering down like many other business leaders, Watson bet that IBM could beat the Great Depression by being aggressive. He kept his factories running, didn't lay off people and increased spending on product development. The company nearly went bust—but then events proved Watson's instincts prophetic.[82] In 1935, President Franklin D. Roosevelt signed the Social Security Act, a national system that required workers to pay into a fund so they could receive payments when they were retired. It was an immense and complex information processing job on a societal scale, and because IBM had been building, improving and warehousing its tabulating machines, it was far ahead of any competitor in its ability to respond quickly. IBM bid on and won the contract.[83] This was the first embodiment of the company's impulse to take on huge, seemingly impossible tasks, which has become an essential element of its culture.

In managing the company, Watson certainly got help from those around him. But make no mistake, Watson *was* IBM. He made all of the important decisions and many of the unimportant ones, too. For instance, he'd order changes in the way IBM machines were displayed in the windows of sales offices. It was another corporate giant of the time, Alfred Sloan, the longtime president of General Motors, who pioneered the art of managing large and diverse operations and empowering lower-level managers. In 1931, Sloan was the first to create a university-based executive education program, which later grew up to be MIT's Alfred P. Sloan School of Management.

After Thomas Watson Jr. became president in 1952, he vowed to reshape IBM into an organization modeled on GM and others like it that could handle the challenges of a fast-changing industry. Specifically, he had gotten a wake-up call in 1950, when competitor Remington Rand had purchased the tiny company that designed UNIVAC, the first commercial electronic computer. IBM's engineers scrambled to respond and came out quickly with the IBM 701 computer, but Watson Jr. believed that the company needed to be reorganized so it could better anticipate the changing technologies and needs of the market and get out in front of them. The son

was domineering in his own way, but he realized that the company could no longer be run by one man, or even a handful.

In November 1955, when 50 IBM executives gathered at the sprawling stone Skytop Lodge in Pennsylvania's Pocono Mountains for a four-day "executive school," the occasion marked the end of one era and the beginning of another. Seven months later the elder Watson would die. In what turned out to be something of a farewell address to his executives, he recounted the early years of the company and the many difficult decisions he'd had to make. He praised the men who had been with him at the beginning, and he urged IBM's current leaders to be brave and to set ambitious goals. He told them: "You can't get anywhere without vision and courage." [84]

While the old man's mood was valedictory, Watson Jr. was preoccupied with retooling the organization for the future. The purpose of this meeting, he said, was to lay the groundwork for a new IBM, beginning the process of setting up better management systems, improving internal communications and distributing power and responsibility deep into the organization. "It's the total salvation of this business if we can delegate—picking the right men and delegating authority to them," he said. [85]

Just a few months after his father died, Watson held a three-day management meeting in Williamsburg, Virginia, that he called "a kind of constitutional convention for IBM." By the time the conference ended, the executives had adopted a staff-and-line structure that was already commonplace at companies like GM and General Electric. The managers of the operating divisions were given the authority and responsibility to run their businesses, and corporate staff would set overall policies and strategies and serve as advisers to the line managers.[86] The changes made at Williamsburg created the stalwart organization that would stand atop the computer industry for decades.

Watson Jr. came into his own when he was no longer operating in the shadow of his father. In fact, he took many of the ideas about how a modern corporation should run that his father had merely sketched out and transformed them into the muscle and sinew of the midcentury IBM.

One of those was to launch an executive development program. In this, he followed closely in the footsteps of GE. In 1956, the electrical equipment company had set up the corporate world's first major in-house management school, along the Hudson River just north of New York City, in Crotonville. A year later, Watson inaugurated IBM's first management training class—a group of 12 people who spent a month in temporary facilities at the Sleepy Hollow Country Club. His father had established IBM employee training programs shortly after he joined the company and for years had sponsored top-management retreats, including the four-day session at Skytop. But this was to be the company's first formal management education program.

Like GE, IBM hired university professors to teach some of the courses. But IBM also put its own stamp on the institution. It introduced a computer simulation program, Top Management Decision Gaming, based on war-gaming concepts, which it developed in conjunction with the American Management Association. Speaking to the first class of 12, Watson urged them to be argumentative and creative. "Be nothing like the safe company man. There is no place in this school for that kind of man," he told them.[87] Since then, IBM has trained hundreds of thousands of managers (18,000 in 2010 alone), many of whom have gone on to be top executives at IBM and other companies. Indeed, *Fortune* magazine named IBM the top global corporation for developing leaders in 2009.[88]

To give IBM's top technical talent the same kind of recognition they would have earned by staying in academia, in 1963 Watson established the IBM Fellows program, an initiative aimed at honoring the contributions of the company's engineers and scientists. The company's inventors no longer had to forego their technical pursuits and switch to management-track careers to gain recognition and financial rewards. At the first technical achievement awards dinner, he commented, "When you look around this room and think of the creativity that all of you have shown and how it affects the IBM company, I think it's the difference between having an ordinary company and one of the great companies in the world."[89] The technical fellow innovation has since been adopted by other leading corporations.

Under Watson's leadership, IBM also became one of the first companies to institute a formal code of business conduct. And it had teeth. To this day, employees must certify every year that they have read and understand it.[90]

For all of this new structure and management rigor, however, IBM under Watson Jr. retained the daring of the father's company. IBM was one of the most successful companies in the world at a time when the US economy was thriving, but Watson wasn't satisfied. He saw that by maintaining five separate computer product lines, IBM was wasting a lot of effort. At the same time, customers couldn't easily switch from one product to another as their computing needs changed and grew.

Rather than waiting around to see if a competitor would come up with a better business model and customer proposition, in 1962 Watson decided to reinvent the company's product strategy, replacing the existing products with a new family of computers, all of which used the same software and peripherals. The family of machines was called System/360.[91] Launched in 1964, it was a game changer. Its performance in the marketplace led to IBM's pre-eminence in the computer industry for the next two decades. At the time, many people referred to IBM and its competitors as Snow White and the Seven Dwarfs. "Before that, the Seven Dwarfs were tough competition. After that, they weren't," said Frederick Brooks Jr., who headed S/360 product development.[92]

The technological innovations of the S/360 were considerable, but in some ways they were the least of the challenges the wildly ambitious project faced. The S/360 cannibalized the company's existing products. Perhaps most daunting of all, it required that the company persuade its customers to change the way they managed themselves. For the S/360 to succeed as a product, the large enterprises of the world needed to commit a lot of money to a radically new approach. And they even had to create a new function within their companies, the management information services department, and a new kind of corporate officer, the chief information officer. The S/360 drained about $5 billion—$34 billion in today's dollars—from the coffers of a company whose net income in 1961 was $254 million. In his autobiography, *Father, Son & Co.*, Watson called it "the riskiest decision I ever made."

Watson's big bet on the S/360—like his father's response to the Great Depression—illustrates one of the key factors in IBM's ability to survive for a century and an essential piece of its corporate culture. The company always thought big. As Watson Jr. put it at Columbia in 1962, "We believe an organization will stand out only if it is willing to take on seemingly impossible tasks. The men who set out to do what others say cannot be done are the ones who make the discoveries, produce the inventions and move the world ahead." [93] In this regard, IBM's culture was one of its greatest research assets, enabling it to spot sea changes in customers' needs, technology advances and industry dynamics.

It also usually enabled the company to respond quickly, before a looming threat or opportunity turned into a crisis. In the early 1980s, for instance, then chief executive Frank Cary saw the potential of personal computers in the workplace and launched a crash effort to establish IBM as the leading maker of PCs for businesses. In the late 1990s, IBM caught the Internet wave with its e-business strategy, bringing the benefits of the Net to the enterprise.

There was one notable exception. In the late 1980s, IBM had become complacent about its position in the computer industry and rapidly lost business. Why did that happen? It's arguable that the company's leaders lost sight of some of the core elements of IBM's culture—namely, the willingness to make big, risky bets and the dedication to serving customers.

Even though IBM made a fast start in PCs in 1981 with the launch of the IBM Personal Computer, it failed to press its advantage. The bureaucracy that had built up around the mainframe business asserted itself. The company commissioned months-long studies to evaluate the business challenges it faced but responded slowly or in the wrong ways. Some senior executives were so busy competing with one another that they didn't focus on external threats. They slowed their peers' initiatives by "non-concurring"—

a deadly maneuver in a company that had come to depend on consensus-based decision making. IBM's long war of attrition with the Justice Department over antitrust issues also sapped its competitive juices. The government sued IBM in 1969, claiming that it was dominating the computer industry. The case dragged on for 13 years, requiring IBM to retain 200 attorneys at the peak. The government dropped its case in 1982—on the same day that a judge ordered the breakup of AT&T.[94] But by then, long-lasting damage had been done. "The culture was: Be careful what you're doing. Be careful what you're saying. Be careful what you're writing. People are watching," recalled former executive vice president Nicholas Donofrio, who witnessed IBM's post-S/360 rise, fall and revival during his 41-year IBM career.[95]

In the early 1990s, IBM's problems became acute, and it nearly ran out of cash. In stepped Lou Gerstner, a former McKinsey consultant and CEO of RJR Nabisco. Contrary to expectations, he wasn't mainly a cost cutter. He was a rebuilder—and his leadership is widely credited with catalyzing one of the great turnarounds in modern business history. But almost as interesting as what Gerstner did to IBM is what IBM did to him, changing his view of what matters most in business. "The thing that came out very clearly to me was that simply setting a strategic direction or pointing to the fences is nowhere near sufficient to drive change in an organization," Gerstner said. "Change doesn't happen unless you understand the culture of the organization. What do people value? What do they think is right for the company? These things are terribly important."[96]

At the time Gerstner arrived, IBM's culture seemed to have become dysfunctional—and much of his and successor Sam Palmisano's leadership has been devoted to reexamining and reviving the company's cultural assumptions. Indeed, with hindsight, we can now see the role that culture played both in the company's near collapse and in its persistence and eventual revival. As much as any organization in the history of business, IBM is a testament to the tensile strength—for good and for ill—of a deeply embedded organizational culture.

Even when some aspects of IBM's culture were atrophying, other elements weren't failing. For example, Bernard Meyerson, an IBM Research Fellow and vice president of innovation who joined the company in 1980, said one of the main reasons IBM has survived so long is its willingness not only to tolerate but also to encourage radical thinking. In the early 1990s, he proposed a technology for transforming the mainframe. Another approach was chosen, but instead of giving up on his idea, he kept working on it on his own and figured out how to use this technology, called silicon germanium, in semiconductor chips for wireless communications such as Wi-Fi networking. Other IBM scientists and managers were skeptical, but he gathered overwhelming scientific evidence to back up his proposal. Finally, his idea was approved. That technology now forms the basis for about half of the output of IBM's chip fabrication plant in Burlington, Vermont. "Most places have a history of shooting disruptive people like me," Meyerson said. "IBM isn't perfect, but if you're willing to have the battle and you base your argument on data, you can win." [97]

Meyerson is one of IBM's so-called wild ducks, rebels who sometimes buck the organization. Watson introduced the concept in a memo in 1959. The original memo has been lost, but Watson wrote in his book, *A Business and Its Beliefs*, that it was a reference to a story told by Danish philosopher Søren Kierkegaard, who wrote about a man who fed migrating ducks year after year until they no longer flew south for the winter. After a few years they became so lazy that it became difficult for them to fly at all. "We are convinced that any business needs wild ducks, and in IBM we try not to tame them," Watson wrote.

THE WATSONS' BASIC BELIEFS stood IBM in good stead for decades. Nevertheless, major changes in a company's business environment—not to mention a near collapse—can necessitate deep self-examination. Within months of taking over as IBM's chief executive in 2002, Sam Palmisano decided it was time to ask the question: what are our actual beliefs today? He did so for three reasons. First, he, like Gerstner, realized that the Basic Beliefs had in many respects devolved into something very different from their original intent. "Respect for the individual" had, over the decades, morphed into a sense of entitlement. "Excellence in all things" had become a decision-inhibiting perfectionism. And "the best customer service" had often come to mean "give customers whatever they say they want."

Second, IBM was expanding globally, adding thousands of employees in emerging markets. Palmisano wanted to create a cultural fabric that would knit together the sprawling organization.

Most important, Palmisano believed that IBM needed to reengage at the level of *values* if it were to become a great company once again. Jon Iwata, IBM's senior vice president of marketing and communications, recalled the mobile phone call he got from Palmisano around that time: "My phone rings, and it's Sam. He says, 'I have been thinking about what it means to be a great company. We used to know: be admired, be the role model. Then we became a very troubled company. And now we're back, and we're a pretty good company. But what does it mean to be a *great* company in our time? Because it's not the same thing it was in Watson's time.'"

Palmisano wasn't asking himself whether values were still important for IBM. He was thinking about whether the values should be updated to reflect the shifting realities of a new century. It was a risky move. But after much reflection, he decided that it was time for a change, and he invited IBM's entire global workforce of more than 300,000 people to have a say. "This was a way to get everybody to understand what IBM stood for," Palmisano said.[98]

During ValuesJam, a 72-hour brainstorming session on the company's internal network in July 2003, IBMers hashed out ideas. The jam got off to a rough start. Some veteran employees were resentful over layoffs and changes in the pension plan that came as a result of the company's need to be more efficient and competitive. Others complained about gaps between the company's espoused values and its behavior. "The only value in IBM today is the stock price," wrote one participant. Another wrote: "I feel we talk a lot about trust and taking risks, but at the same time we have endless audits, mistakes are punished and not seen as a welcome part of learning, and managers (and others) are consistently checked." [99] The critics deluged the forum with negative comments. Things got so bad that one senior executive wanted to pull the plug. But Palmisano wouldn't go along with that, and over time the tone changed and became constructive.[100] After the jam, the discussion was analyzed and three new values emerged:

> *Dedication to every client's success*
> *Innovation that matters—for our company and for the world*
> *Trust and personal responsibility in all relationships*

Without question, there is a family resemblance between the new, employee-created values and the Watsons' Basic Beliefs. But some of the differences are instructive: for example, the change from "excellence in all things" (appropriate for an institution seeking to establish its reputation) to "innovation that matters" (reflecting technologies and work that have

"You just can't impose command-and-control mechanisms on a large, highly professional workforce. I'm not only talking about our scientists, engineers and consultants. More than 200,000 of our employees have college degrees."
—Sam Palmisano, 2004

More than 1,700 IBMers gathered outside IBM's Silicon Valley lab for a photo that appeared in the company's *2004 Annual Report*.

assumed a far greater impact on the world). The most emotionally fraught of the Basic Beliefs—"respect for the individual"—has been succeeded by a value more explicitly rooted in a culture of mutuality and shared empowerment: "trust and personal responsibility."

But apart from the particulars, the biggest change has been that the company's employees, rather than just the CEO, have defined the values. Indeed, the company makes it clear that these are not IBM's values, but *IBMers'* values. That shift, more than anything else, reflects the new spirit of the company in the twenty-first century.

Palmisano explained this shift to the *Harvard Business Review* in 2004: "How do you channel this diverse and constantly changing array of talent and experience into a common purpose? How do you get people to *passionately* pursue that purpose? You could employ all kinds of traditional, top-down management processes. But they wouldn't work at IBM—or, I would argue, at an increasing number of twenty-first-century companies. You just can't impose command-and-control mechanisms on a large, highly professional workforce....The CEO can't say to them, 'Get in line and follow me.' Or '*I've* decided what *your* values are.' They're too smart for that. And as you know, smarter people tend to be, well, a little more challenging; you might even say cynical."

It remains to be seen whether these new values will have the staying power and impact of the Basic Beliefs. Establishing a company culture is a difficult task; redefining one may be even tougher. Look at how hard it is for big successful companies to change the way they see themselves and operate. General Electric under legendary CEO Jack Welch was known for its relentless dedication to efficiency and quality improvements. If a business unit couldn't be hammered into shape, Welch would sell it. But times have changed, and his successor, Jeffrey Immelt, faces major challenges in transforming a hard-driving, process-oriented company into one where creativity and risk taking flourish.[101]

This challenge of continual reinvention is one that IBM has faced over and over again. Indeed, the reality is that it is never-ending—not just because the world never stops changing, but because the promise of change is the key to attracting the smartest and most forward-looking people. As former IBM CEO John Akers put it: "The environment is so dynamic. The competition for people is so intense. What worked yesterday won't work tomorrow. In order to attract the best people, they need to have confidence in your future successes, so they'll be willing to take a crack at it with you." [102] Palmisano, who early in his career was Akers's executive assistant, agrees. One of the keys to managing change during his tenure as CEO has been to focus on employees' desires to contribute to progress. Through his years as CEO, Palmisano has sold off one commodity business after another and replaced them with products and services that are higher on the technology food chain, focusing less on hardware and more on software and business expertise. In doing so, he has pulled IBM out of product categories, such as disk drives and PCs, that IBM engineers and scientists pioneered in earlier days. In one meeting and memo after another, Palmisano laid out the rationale for the changes and urged employees to turn away from their past glories and help invent the future. "There's an incredible acceptance in the workforce for change," he said. "They want to go invent something that transforms the industry." [103] This element of IBM's culture, the drive to innovate and make the world work better, to keep moving to the future, is a key factor in success during the good years and survival in the bad.

———

WHAT DOES IBM'S EXPERIENCE SUGGEST for corporate culture in the future? If anything, it will become even more important. Whether a leader is managing a giant, global operation or a 10-person start-up, the stresses of functioning in a fast-changing, highly competitive, complex and global business environment simply cannot be managed by traditional processes. As Palmisano put it to *HBR*:

> *Think of our organizational matrix. Remember, we operate in 170 countries. To keep it simple, let's say we have 60 or 70 major product lines. We have more than a dozen customer segments. Well, if you mapped out the entire 3-D matrix, you'd get more than 100,000 cells— cells in which you have to close out P&Ls every day, make decisions, allocate resources, make trade-offs. You'll drive people crazy trying to centrally manage every one of those intersections.*
>
> *So if there's no way to optimize IBM through organizational structure or by management dictate, you have to empower people while ensuring that they're making the right calls the right way....You've got to create a management system that empowers people and provides a basis for decision making that is consistent with who we are at IBM.*

Clearly, this applies not just to companies like IBM. In the years ahead, it seems likely that the culture at more and more companies will be based on collectively developed and clearly articulated values and behaviors, rather than on supervision and uniform processes. And this has a direct impact on the role of the most visible embodiment of the old hierarchy—the manager. Managers are increasingly seen as orchestrators and catalysts rather than overseers. "The world of management as we know it will change radically over the next 10 years," predicted Randy MacDonald, senior vice president for human resources at IBM. "Managers will be less needed. A lot of what they do will be replaced by management systems using the network to enable a collaborative diversity of thought." He believes that at some point IBM will develop sophisticated decision-management software that in many cases will enable employees to make decisions that they formerly depended on managers to make.[104]

IBM has learned over a century that culture isn't just one of the tools of management; it is the purpose of management. The company also understands that words in corporate values statements, as powerfully as they may be expressed, are empty platitudes unless they're acted on rigorously and consistently in day-to-day business activities. In that way, organizational culture—embodied in everything from making decisions the right way to projecting the company's values in word and deed—can become as natural to employees as walking, breathing...and thinking.

• • •

Creating Economic Value from Knowledge

Thomas Watson Sr. had adopted "Think" as a slogan before he took the helm at C-T-R. It happened in 1911—the same year that financier Charles Flint was stitching together Herman Hollerith's Tabulating Machine Company, the Computing Scale Company of America and the International Time Recording Company. In Dayton, Ohio, Watson was the sales manager of the National Cash Register Corporation. The company's sales executives met every day at 8 a.m. to talk about new developments and ideas.

One gloomy winter day, they couldn't come up with a discussion topic. Frustrated, Watson strode to the podium at the front of the room and urged them to think more deeply. "The trouble with every one of us is that we don't think enough," he boomed, according to an account published in IBM's *Business Machines* magazine in 1954. "We don't get paid for working with our feet. We get paid for working with our heads. Feet can never compete with brains."

IBM Research pioneered advances in operations research.
From left: Benoît Mandelbrot, Richard Levitan, Paul Gillmore, Ralph Gomory
and Te Hu explore a complex transportation problem in 1961.

Watson then softened his tone, intent on turning the awkward situation into a learning experience. He spent 10 minutes lecturing on the usefulness of thinking. "Knowledge is the result of thought, and thought is the keynote of success in this business or any business," he told them. He decided on the spot that henceforth "Think" would be the company's slogan and ordered a subordinate to post a placard with the word printed on it in bold letters on the wall of the room the following morning.

When Watson moved to C-T-R, he took the slogan with him, and there, after C-T-R became IBM, "Think" ran amok. At the peak of the slogan's popularity, "Think" signs cluttered the desks and walls of countless IBM offices; the company published a magazine called *THINK*; and many IBMers carried pocket-sized notebooks with "Think" embossed on the cover. (Those little notebooks—the original ThinkPads—were handier than you might guess. IBMer Oliver Collins, a Marine private fighting on Okinawa in 1945, credited his leather-covered notepad, which he had tucked into his knapsack, with deflecting a bullet and saving his life.)[105]

Gradually, Watson's once-radical point of view became conventional wisdom. In the 1973 book *The Coming of the Post-Industrial Society*, Harvard University sociologist Daniel Bell extrapolated the social and economic trends of his day to predict a society shaped by the dominance of service industries, the rise of technical and professional employment, and innovation driven by scientific research. His target date was 2000, but the postindustrial society arrived early. By the mid-1990s, the United States and other Western countries were rapidly shedding smokestack industries and embracing digital technologies as the source of economic growth and competitive advantage. Manufacturing employment in the United States was 30 percent of the nonfarm workforce in 1950 and had shrunk to just 10 percent in 2008. Meanwhile, service employment had grown to 68 percent.[106] And in both the service and manufacturing industries, knowledge has become the fuel of the modern economy. One estimate from the US Bureau of Economic Analysis valued the world's human capital—based on such factors as school enrollment rate, average yearly earnings and hours worked per person—at about $750 trillion, compared with $150 trillion for proven reserves of oil and natural gas.[107]

In recent decades, advances in information technology have contributed mightily to productivity growth. Nonfarm labor productivity in the United States grew an average of 1.6 percent between 1981 and 1995 but accelerated to an average of 2.6 percent between 1995 and 2007.[108] Erik Brynjolfsson, a professor at MIT Sloan School of Management, credits aggressive investments in technology for much of this growth.[109]

We have also come to understand that knowledge drives much more than product innovation. Indeed, numerous studies have shown that there's no simple correlation between financial performance and the level of R&D spending by a company. Rather, what matters is the combination of the knowledge, talent, tools and ways of working that companies bring to bear.[110] Northeastern University professor Michael Zack wrote that a knowledge-based organization "takes knowledge into account in every aspect of its operation and treats every activity as a potentially knowledge-enhancing act. It uses knowledge and learning as its primary criteria for evaluating how it organizes, what it makes, where it locates, whom it hires, how it relates to its customers, the image it projects and the nature of its competition."[111]

No matter what you call it—postindustrial society, the knowledge organization or something else—the fundamental shift is clear. However, underneath this megatrend, the question remains as to how organizations actually capture the value they create. IBM's history reveals a broad pattern in how information and knowledge have been turned into money over the course of the past century—and this pattern suggests a trajectory that will govern the continuing evolution of the modern corporation.

In the early stages of the Information Age, capturing value from information and ideas worked very much the same as it had when productivity was based on natural resources, labor and capital. It was a matter of proprietary discovery, acquisition and sale. A company created intellectual property by establishing the capacity to explore, produce and distribute—whether in the form of research labs or printing presses or movie stars under contract or broadcast centers. The company sold that valuable intellectual property in the market. And since an idea cannot be controlled, the company protected its source of income by controlling the right to reproduce it via patents and copyrights.

As the century proceeded, however, the kinds of value that information could create expanded beyond the scope of individual firms—or, indeed, entire industries. For one thing, it became increasingly clear that the discoveries of academic science and research had economic value and needed to find a way into the marketplace. In addition, the expense of exploration on a societal or global level—from military research to the application of information science to social welfare programs—was often beyond the means or motivations of individual firms. So governments entered the game as major funders of research and hubs of cross-disciplinary collaboration.

In the early twentieth century, businesses, academia and governments operated like three solar systems, with very little overlap. Only the necessities of war brought them close. The most notable such collaboration, involving the government, university researchers and corporations (including IBM), was the Manhattan Project, conducted by the United States to develop the first atomic bomb. But by midcentury, the increasing use of advanced technologies in warfare created bonds in other fields, particularly in scientific spheres. The United States' funding of computer science research in universities increased from $10 million in 1960 to nearly $1 billion in 1995 and helped bring about a host of advances, including the personal computer and the Internet.[112] And the emergence of a whole new category of investment—venture capital—further expanded the ways in which ideas and knowledge could be monetized and dramatically increased the speed and scale of return to investors.

To the increasingly overlapping circles of government, industry and academia, we can now add a fourth, thanks to the Internet—the far wider circle of individual creators and communities of collaborators. Indeed, we have come to understand that a global information economy works not like a hierarchical structure, but like a network. Some even call the phase we're now entering the network economy, capturing the idea that the elements of financial capital, labor, knowledge and natural resources are, in essence, a huge web of relationships. From this perspective, the network economy is governed by the same rules as the Internet, principally Metcalfe's law, which posits that the value of a network is proportional to the square of the number of people connected to it. These days, economic value arises less from ownership of things than from interconnectedness of information and ideas. And so we have seen a further expansion of the arena of value creation—with phenomena such as open source, co-creation between firms and their customers, Web 2.0 and social media.

As these new forms of value creation have emerged, the old forms haven't disappeared—and different organizations have chosen to focus on different ones, depending on their business models, strategies and cultures. We're beginning to see that a mastery of information can drive value beyond efficiency and productivity. It also sparks innovation, market expansion and transformation of organizations' business models. This occurs not simply because companies adopt new technology, but because they engage with other companies, governments and individuals across an open, dynamic arena of shared ideas, information and effort.

To understand this progression, consider the modern corporation's major forms of intellectual capital creation through the lens of IBM's history of innovation—how the forms emerged and how they function today.

———

RESEARCH: The most straightforward and intuitive source of creating economic value through knowledge is in technological and scientific research, which began to make its way into business in the late nineteenth century. Innovations typically came from individual inventors like Herman

Hollerith, but it was electronics pioneer Thomas Edison who transformed inventing into an industrial process. He set up a development laboratory in Menlo Park, New Jersey, and staffed it with engineers, draftsmen and other technicians who worked in teams to turn scientific discoveries into products.[113]

When Watson joined C-T-R he was already acquainted with the company's most important product, the Hollerith tabulating machine. The world's first commercial mechanical tabulator, it was used for all sorts of number-crunching tasks, including recording the US census. Watson caught his first glimpse of the machine when he worked for National Cash Register and was in upstate New York on a visit to his mother. He stopped to see an old friend in Rochester who worked at Eastman Kodak Company, and the man showed him a chart covered with detailed sales records for all of the company's salesmen. Watson was taken with the data and asked how it had been gathered. His friend showed him a Hollerith machine. It was Watson's first encounter with paper punched cards, which would later become the source of his wealth and IBM's good fortune.[114]

After Watson took the reins at C-T-R, he realized that the company would have to improve the Hollerith machine and invent other devices if it hoped to stay ahead in the fast-changing world of business machines. C-T-R didn't have a single engineer on its payroll when Watson joined, so he quickly hired engineers and set up a product development department in a brownstone across from the old Penn Station in New York City.[115] A key hire was James Bryce, an engineering consultant whom Watson named IBM's chief engineer. Bryce's job was to dream up new ways of doing things and then patent them. He established a patent development department in 1932 and hired Arthur Halsey Dickinson,[116] (who went on to pioneer vacuum tube electronics). Dickinson later described his boss's style: "If he had an idea or was thinking about something, he would discuss it. Usually he would make a sketch or a drawing, which was sufficient to establish what he was thinking about or what he wanted to do." Bryce and Dickinson turned IBM into a patent-filing phenomenon—between them racking up more than 440 US patents. By 1935, the company had a staff of 300 engineers, and, by Watson's own estimate, 95 percent of its profits came from innovations introduced since 1917.[117]

In the 1940s, Watson broke ground when he established the country's first corporate scientific research lab connected to a university. His eyes had already been opened to the business and societal potential of research. In 1928, Ben Wood, head of Columbia University's Bureau of Collegiate Educational Research, had convinced Watson that everything in the universe could be understood as information and that IBM's calculating machines would enable scientific discovery. As a result, IBM began supplying Columbia with machines and collaborating with its scientists. The IBM laboratory at Columbia, established in 1945, was a major advance. Watson hired a handful of respected scientists, led by astronomer Wallace Eckert, and placed the lab in a former fraternity house adjacent to the campus. The idea was to develop advanced calculating machines and use them to solve some of science's most daunting challenges. One of the first machines the researchers built, referred to as the SSEC, was a major breakthrough in information science—a mixture of mechanical calculator and electronic computer.[118] It didn't matter to Watson that the initial discoveries at the lab might not have a direct application to IBM's current business. "Watson looked on IBM as a sort of supernal force for good in the whole universe," recalled the late Herbert Grosch, one of those first IBM researchers.[119]

However, for all of Watson's pioneering vision, what we know today as IBM Research was not truly his creation, but that of his son. In the 1950s, under the leadership of Thomas Watson Jr., IBM's research initiative grew quickly from a tiny laboratory tucked away near Columbia into an institution capable of keeping the company at or near the top of the computer industry for generations to come.

The first step was deciding whether to set up a true research division. In this, as in many other areas of IBM's organizational evolution, Watson's

A Long Legacy of Innovation

——

Since its founding, IBM has maintained a balance between two kinds of R&D investment. Some inventions come to market within a few years. Other more exploratory research might not bear fruit for decades. Both span multiple disciplines and fields of science—from semiconductors, software and computer hardware to e-commerce and life sciences. Many innovations find use not only in the company's own products and services but in those of other companies.

This strategy has yielded a large body of intellectual property, with the company's patent awards increasing exponentially over the years. It took 53 years for IBM to receive its first 5,000 US patents, but in 2010 alone it earned 5,896. Since 1993 IBM has landed on top of the US patent list for 18 consecutive years.

IBM US Patent Totals:
1911–2010

Patents from IBM's frequently licensed portfolio:

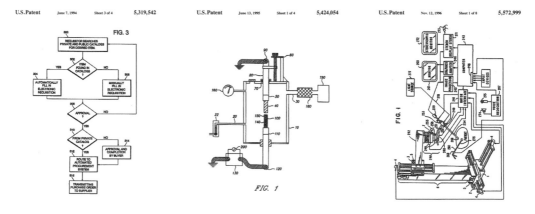

US Patent 5,319,542 (1994)

Organizing online catalogues and creating orders— a foundation for web commerce.

US Patent 5,424,054 (1995)

Production of carbon nanotubes; expected to enable a new class of smaller, faster and lower-power computer chips.

US Patent 5,572,999 (1996)

Robotic surgical instrument positioning, relative to a patient's body.

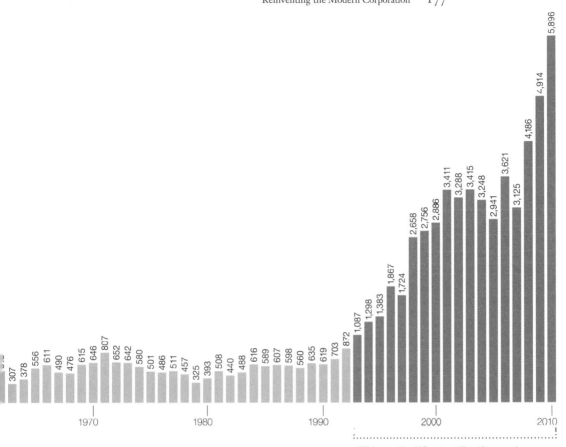

IBM tops the US patent list 18 years in a row.

U.S. Patent	Feb. 29, 2000	6,031,910

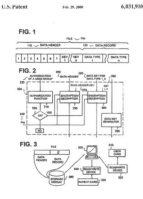

U.S. Patent	Feb. 28, 2006	Sheet 1 of 14	US 7,006,793 B2

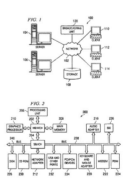

U.S. Patent	Mar. 23, 2010	Sheet 1 of 8	US 7,684,673 B2

US Patent 6,031,910 (2000)

Secure transmission of electronic medical records and other sensitive information.

US Patent 7,006,793 (2006)

Linking and operating a mobile electronic device, such as a cell phone, using an onboard car computer.

US Patent 7,684,673 (2010)

Describes a method for programming and managing a digital video recorder over the Internet.

Leo Esaki was awarded a Nobel Prize in Physics in 1973 for his invention of the electron tunneling effect in semiconductors.

Heinrich Rohrer (left) and Gerd Binnig received the Nobel Prize in Physics in 1986 for their invention of the scanning tunneling microscope.

instinct was to institutionalize and expand what had been a comparatively informal organization, dominated by the outsized personality of his father. And here, IBM had a model: AT&T's Bell Laboratories. Established in 1925, the labs provided fundamental scientific research for the telephone company's business units.

In 1956, Watson hired Emanuel Piore, the former chief scientist at the US Office of Naval Research, as research director, and Piore assigned three senior IBM scientists, whom he called the Three Wise Men, to study the alternatives. After touring IBM's product development facilities and speaking to leaders in the research community, they recommended setting up an independent research organization that would focus on long-range projects rather than incremental advances that would be immediately useful for product development. Piore and Watson agreed and set the wheels in motion. "Some of these projects led to blind alleys, but others led to discoveries that put IBM in the lead," said Gardiner Tucker, one of the Three Wise Men and who later headed up IBM Research.[120]

One such notable discovery came in 1981 at IBM's laboratory in Zurich, Switzerland. Working together, physicists Gerd Binnig and Heinrich Rohrer invented the scanning tunneling microscope, which for the first

Alex Müller (left) and Georg Bednorz were awarded a
Nobel Prize in 1987 for their discovery of high-temperature
superconductivity in a new class of materials.

time allowed scientists to see individual atoms. The STM became an
essential tool in the emerging science of nanotechnology. Rohrer had
hired Binnig right out of graduate school and asked him to study materials
at a near-atomic level, but Binnig found that no existing microscopes were
up to the job. So they decided to invent one. Binnig broke the lab rules
and worked at night, when nobody else was around, to avoid sounds and
vibrations that might disrupt his experiments. After months of trial and
error, they invented a powerful tool that had an even higher resolution than
they had expected. What made this discovery possible, according to Binnig,
was a culture that gave scientists the freedom to pursue lines of inquiry
wherever they led. "IBM was a place where you could go very deep
and invent something completely new," said Binnig, who now works at
Definiens, an imaging equipment company. For their work on the scanning
tunneling microscope, the two scientists received the Nobel Prize in
Physics in 1986.[121]

The results of this freedom were palpable. IBM scientists and engineers
helped invent the Information Age, producing breakthroughs in information storage, semiconductor technology, database software, programming
languages and computer systems. Along the way, researchers won nearly

IBM Research Labs

Thomas J. Watson
Columbia University,
New York, 1945–1970

Yorktown Heights,
New York, 1961

Hawthorne,
New York, 1984

Cambridge,
Massachusetts, 1995

Almaden
San Jose,
California, 1955

Zurich
Rüschlikon,
Switzerland, 1956

Haifa
Haifa, Israel, 1972

Tokyo
Yamato, Japan, 1982

Austin
Austin, Texas, 1995

China
Beijing, 1995
Shanghai, 2008

India
New Delhi, 1998
Bengaluru, 2005

Brazil
Rio de Janiero, 2010
Sao Paolo, 2010

Australia*
Melbourne, 2010

*Research & development

every major honor in technology, including five Nobel Prizes. Among IBM's star researchers was the late Benoît Mandelbrot, who in the 1970s created a whole new branch of mathematics called fractal geometry. IBM Research is now a global powerhouse with 3,000 researchers, making it the world's largest corporate research department. It also houses what amounts to the world's largest non-academic mathematics department, with 200 researchers working on advanced analytics. Also, thanks in good measure to IBM Research, the company is the world's largest patent creator, having been the number one recipient of US patents for 18 years in a row—contributing to the approximately $1 billion it receives annually in intellectual property-related income.

———

CONNECTING RESEARCH TO PRODUCT DEVELOPMENT: IBM Research has remained focused on long-term challenges, but one main way it has continued to thrive is through aligning itself with the company's strategy. Other once-mighty corporate research organizations haven't done so and are in decline or have disappeared. The executives who ran IBM Research early on understood that they had to feed product development, which had emerged as a discipline among manufacturing giants like General Electric, DuPont and General Motors. IBM's success with research "was due to management's willingness to rethink and reposition the role of the research division in the company—to make it more relevant to customer and company needs as times dictated that—and then the ability to sell that to both employees and management," said Robert Buderi, author of *Engines of Tomorrow*, a book about the evolution of corporate research in America.[122]

Ralph Gomory, the fourth IBM Research director, recalls a meeting with then president Cary not long after he took the director job in 1970. Gomory asked Cary what he wanted from research, and Cary replied that, as a starting point, he wanted to be sure that IBM was not surprised by new technologies. Gomory hoped the division would have a far greater impact.

"I told him I didn't think we'd survive in the long run without a strategy and a structure to make continuing contributions to IBM," he recalled.

Cary accepted Gomory's advice, and over the coming years IBM's researchers tried many approaches aimed at putting their work at the center of the company's future. For example, James McGroddy, one of Gomory's deputies and later director of IBM Research, suggested trying projects manned by both research scientists and product developers—so-called joint programs. The first of these, launched in 1980, was the Advanced Silicon Technology Lab, an effort that paired research scientists with engineers from the semiconductor products division to advance microchip technologies. The program was a success for both groups. Eventually, IBM Research formed more than a dozen other joint programs. Through the joint programs and similar efforts, IBM Research steadily evolved into an essential part of IBM's product development engine and became the heart of its pure research activities.

These days, IBM not only has nine research labs around the world, including the newest ones in Brazil, India and China, but also operates dozens of hardware and software development centers. The software group alone has more than 40 development labs housing 26,000 programmers in 25 countries. The company's scientific researchers often toggle between assignments in research and positions in IBM's product groups, infusing innovation into the product teams and business realities into the labs. R&D at many companies leaves research out of the equation. But for others—today's pharmaceutical giants, chipmaker Intel and IBM among them—the integration of basic research and product development is the key to producing wave upon wave of innovations that both advance science and create powerful effects on the world.

——

ACADEMIC AND GOVERNMENT COLLABORATION: It's well known that in the 1970s and '80s, Silicon Valley in California emerged as America's high-tech incubator. But how it emerged—through cross-sector collaboration— isn't often recognized. The US government, Stanford University and the University of California, Berkeley, combined forces informally with the R&D departments at IBM, Sun Microsystems, Hewlett-Packard and other companies to create a fertile ecosystem of innovation.

In fact, with Silicon Valley as an inspiration, similar collaborations have provided some of the most important advances in electronics and information technology over the past four decades. For instance, in 1987, the National Science Foundation awarded a grant to a consortium of IBM, MCI and a research group at the University of Michigan to create some of the core technology that led up to the modern Internet.[123] Investment in R&D by US corporations, universities and government agencies grew from $63 billion in 1980 to $368 billion in 2007.[124] Other countries have invested even more aggressively in R&D. Japan's government increased investment in non-military research from 1.8 percent of GDP in 1978 to 2.6 percent in 1985, a period that corresponded with its emergence as a global power in industry after industry. During the same period, in comparison, the United States boosted its investment from 1.6 percent to 1.8 percent.[125]

IBM's collaboration with universities was born in the same epiphany that launched its journey toward scientific research—the alliance with Columbia University. These collaborations expanded under Gomory's leadership of IBM Research. His goal was to create multiple pathways for bringing new discoveries and bright young scientists into the IBM fold. Since then, working with the world's leading research universities has remained a key

Transforming national or societal infrastructure requires collaboration among government, business and academia. IBM has played a major role in many of the most consequential of these efforts—from Social Security to the Manhattan Project to the US space program to the foundations of the Internet. It continues with IBM's Smarter Planet work today.

———

In the 1960s, IBM researchers helped build the information infrastructure of the Saturn rocket and many other elements of America's manned space program.

element of IBM's innovation strategy. Today, IBM works with 6,000 colleges and universities and 30,000 faculty members around the globe, providing them with opportunities for grants and collaborative research. The company has invested more than $500 million in academic programs over the past five years. And it remains deeply involved in government-sponsored research projects. For instance, in 2008, the Defense Advanced Research Projects Agency, or DARPA, issued an audacious challenge to IBM and its research collaborators at Stanford, Columbia, Cornell and other universities to create compact computing systems that can emulate the human brain's ability to sense and understand.[126]

———

COLLABORATION WITHIN: Although it may surprise young people raised on MySpace and Facebook, social networking and online brainstorming were not born in 2004. The ARPANET, the precursor of the Internet, was launched in 1969 to link university researchers.[127] And IBM played a seminal role in initiating office collaboration: its Professional Office System software program, introduced internally in 1981 and eventually used by many of IBM's large customers, included an early form of e-mail, shared calendars, shared document storage and systems for managing back-office processes, from accounts payable to inventory to personnel. And while newsgroups were proliferating on the pre-web Internet, PROFS also housed hundreds of chat rooms to encourage free-form discussions among IBMers. It was the world's first corporate intranet.

During the 1990s, business gurus heralded the emergence of so-called knowledge management systems that could gather, store and conveniently serve up the knowledge capital of an organization. But the promise was never fulfilled. Employees tended to guard their knowledge or didn't want to spend time typing it into a big complex system. On the receiving end, they found it difficult to locate just the pieces of information they were searching for when they needed them.

The situation is finally changing, though. After seeing the information-sharing experiences afforded by Wikipedia, Facebook and YouTube, business leaders have begun adopting web-based collaboration tools internally. The attraction: they're easier to use than traditional knowledge-sharing software programs—so much so that employees actually want to use them. A 2010 survey of corporate chief information officers by the market research firm Gartner ranked Web 2.0 technologies as their number three priority, ahead of networking, business intelligence and mobile technologies.[128] Gartner later predicted that by 2014, social networking services will replace e-mail as the primary vehicle for interpersonal communications for 20 percent of business users.[129] Andrew McAfee, the MIT Sloan School research scientist who coined the term Enterprise 2.0 to describe this phenomenon, wrote, "It allows good new business ideas to emerge from anywhere and spread organically, rather than being developed at the center and imposed from the top down."[130]

To get a sense of this new way of working, consider Cognizant Technology Solutions, a Teaneck, New Jersey-based consulting and IT outsourcing firm with more than 100,000 employees around the world. Cognizant performed better than most of its competitors during the 2008–'09 recession, which its executives credit, in part, to a knowledge-sharing and work-management system called Cognizant 2.0. The system manages each step in the process of developing large and complex software programs with Web 2.0 collaboration tools. It mines nuggets of information from employees' blogs, online forums and instant messages so no one has to spend a lot of time feeding their knowledge into the system. When Cognizant's engineers are writing software programs, suggestions and relevant information are fed to them on their computer screens, based on what they're doing. If they don't see what they need, they can perform Google-like searches or ask for online help from a list of in-house experts.[131]

It's too early to measure the value created by such connectedness and collaboration, but two studies published together in 2010 suggest that the once-theoretical belief in "collective intelligence" is gathering empirical support.[132] In one architectural design problem, the collective intelligence was nearly three times as great as the maximum member intelligence, as measured by performance scores on a diverse set of cognitive tasks. "This work really calls into question our whole notion of what intelligence is," said Anita Williams Woolley, the paper's main author and an assistant professor at Carnegie Mellon University's Tepper School of Business. "What individuals can do all by themselves is becoming less important; what matters more is what they can do with others and by using technology." [133]

The next big challenge for managers is blending collaboration tools with policies that free employees' minds. "If we're going to keep the bright folks, we have to manage in a different way. We don't want to inhibit our people. We want to unleash them," said Linda Sanford, the senior vice president in charge of IBM's continual transformation initiative. In some cases, that means doing things that seem antithetical to the very idea of management. Rather than accumulating control, she said, the successful IBM manager is learning to succeed by giving it up—allowing the people around her or him to make decisions and take initiative with the minimum amount of supervision. "Now we find power in our shared effort," Sanford said.[134]

IBM itself has pushed the concept in new directions with its online jams—global, radically open, three-day brainstorming events. For InnovationJam in 2006 the company brought together more than 150,000 IBMers, clients and business partners from 104 countries to suggest ideas for how some of IBM Research's technologies could be turned into new businesses.[135] As a result of the jam, 10 IBM businesses were launched with a seed investment of $100 million. While some ideas fizzled, others have become important initiatives for the company, including core elements of its Smarter Planet strategy in healthcare, transportation and environmentally sustainable data centers.

As promising and profitable as those new businesses have become, however, in Palmisano's mind creating them wasn't the primary goal. The primary goal was about a new kind of collaborative thinking: "The point wasn't to come up with a new product idea if we do this. It was more about how I could excite…engineers and scientists at IBM about how they're going to create the future."[136]

All of the investment in human capital by governments, individuals and businesses has resulted in highly capable workforces. This makes it possible for companies to hand more authority and responsibility to employees at all levels of the organization, in what MIT professor Thomas Malone calls loose hierarchies. "For the first time in history, technologies allow us to gain the economic benefits of large organizations, like economies of scale and knowledge, without giving up the human benefits of small ones, like freedom, creativity, motivation and flexibility," Malone wrote.[137] Indeed, some corporations are taking on some of the distinctive characteristics of the university. They see the purpose of the organization as discovering knowledge and putting it to good use. The means is free thinking and open debate. An employee's success in this model is determined not by whom they know and how well they follow orders, but by what they know and how well they're able to act on it. Malone cited Merck's research division, where individual scientists have a lot to say about which projects they work on. Project leaders don't have budgets or command authority. They have to recruit people, who bring their equipment and resources to the team.[138]

At today's IBM, "Think" signs and notebooks are no longer mandated from above, but the company's appreciation for the intelligence and expertise of its employees is undiminished. In fact, a culture of thinking is more important than either Watson contemplated.

———

COLLABORATION WITH CLIENTS: Businesses have been catering to customers in one way or another since the dawn of commerce, so one wonders why it took until the late twentieth century for companies to see the value in collaborating with their customers to create new products and services. The concept of co-creation was memorably framed by authors C.K. Prahalad and Venkat Ramaswamy in their 2004 book, *The Future of Competition*. Citing examples like dot-com upstart Napster, the original music-sharing web service, and Netflix, the movie-renting site, the two argued that customers would no longer be satisfied with the choice of either accepting a company's offering or walking away; they wanted to help companies craft their products and services. The authors urged business leaders to embrace the new model—not just as a way of improving customer satisfaction but also as a means of improving their ability to innovate. They praised Lego, for instance, for allowing customers to customize Mindstorms, a science project kit integrated with a PC that allows people to design and build their own robots using Lego building blocks. One customer even wrote his own software operating system for the kit and shares it with others. In this way, Lego has created a community of customers who help improve its product.[139]

Today, IBM's scientists and developers frequently collaborate with clients, engaging in so-called First-of-a-Kind projects that bring inventions more quickly to market. For instance, working with Denmark's Thy-Mors Hospital, IBM researchers in 2009 embedded information about individual patients in on-screen 3-D models of the human body, making it possible for the medical staff to get an up-to-date and holistic view of each patient's condition at a glance.[140] The impact on IBM's business strategy is material. "It was through these kinds of engagements that we realized a few years ago that something was missing from our plans, something that clients needed to solve their problems," Palmisano said.[141] That "something missing" was a recognition of the marketplace potential for business analytics technologies—leading to an investment of $12 billion in acquisitions and internal developments to beef up IBM's capabilities.[142]

The economic benefit of collaboration with other organizations is also one of the driving principles behind IBM's collaboratories initiative. In 2007, when John Kelly III took over as IBM Research chief, he began looking for ways to expand research activities without spending more money. He saw that by collaborating deeply with other organizations, IBM could do more than its own budget would permit and, at the same time, tap into a formidable diversity of thought at a global scale. "The world is our lab now," he said.[143]

IBM so far has collaboratories in the United States, Saudi Arabia, Switzerland, China, Ireland, Taiwan, Australia and India. In one notable example, IBM researchers have linked with the government of Taiwan and four leading research universities there to help develop technologies aimed at improving the health of the Taiwanese people and, eventually, people worldwide. Henry Chang, a veteran of IBM's labs, returned to his native Taiwan and coauthored with a professor at National Taiwan University a proposal for redeveloping the country's economy. The idea was to suggest a way to shift from electronics manufacturing, where mainland China had distinct cost advantages, to an economy based on higher-value technology services. "Like IBM, Taiwan has to change from hardware to services," Chang said. Ultimately, government leaders embraced the idea and made it a national quest.[144]

––––––

INNOVATION BY ACQUISITION: One of the most important sources of value creation these days is the phenomenon of established companies buying innovative young companies and amplifying their impact on the world. The fact that entrepreneurship flourished in the United States in recent decades is significantly attributable to the emergence of a new industry, venture capital. The industry got its start when a handful of government and investment leaders in 1946 recruited a former US Army general, Georges Doriot, to set up the first venture capital firm, American Research and Development, to help foster economic development in New England. Over the next

25 years ARD backed more than 100 start-ups, most notably Digital Equipment Corporation. ARD's $70,000 investment in DEC ultimately yielded $400 million[145]—which demonstrated the astonishing returns available to venture capitalists and set off a VC gold rush. In the United States, the VC industry peaked in 2000 with $94.8 billion in financings and more than 200 initial public offerings of stock.[146] Now, in the wake of the dot-com bust, acquisitions of high-tech start-ups by established companies have essentially replaced IPOs as the primary means of cashing out for entrepreneurs.

IBM was late to the mergers and acquisitions game. For most of its existence, it had shunned acquisitions. But a shift in thinking began in 1995 when John Thompson, who then led IBM's newly independent software group, persuaded Lou Gerstner to buy Lotus Development Corporation, one of the leaders in PC software with its spreadsheet and collaboration programs. Thompson saw that software collaboration would be vital to the future of business and that by buying the market leader, IBM could instantly be the major player in a huge growth market. Lotus CEO Jim Manzi at first rebuffed IBM's advances, which led to something that was culturally unprecedented for IBM—a hostile takeover bid. Ultimately, Manzi and the Lotus board gave in and accepted a $3.2 billion offer.

Under Palmisano, IBM has opened the floodgates on acquisitions. The company saw that the sources of value in a post-PC era were shifting, and acquisitions were a means to remix the company's portfolio rapidly. The impact of the strategy switch has been profound. Since 1995, IBM has spent $40 billion–plus on more than 160 acquisitions. While a handful were large, including PricewaterhouseCoopers's consulting arm in 2003 and Cognos business intelligence software in 2007, most have been small to medium-size. The strategy isn't about industry consolidation; it's about innovation. IBM's goal isn't to buy revenue or market share; it maps its strategy against the technology it needs to fulfill its goals. When executives see that they can acquire vital technologies or service capabilities and expertise for a reasonable price faster than by developing it internally, they go the M&A route. The capacity to do this—and to capture this tactic's potential for creating new value—is emerging as one of the newer and so far less-studied skill sets of collaborative innovation.

But, of course, the purchase of a company is only a small step in capturing and leveraging its value. One of the most striking elements of IBM's ongoing transformation is its growing skill at integrating other operations and cultures into its own. The history of corporate mergers is not one of consistent success, to put it mildly. But IBM seems to have made a science out of integrating acquired companies, syncing up operations, melding workforces, capturing innovation synergies and leveraging the acquired intellectual property through its global sales and distribution system. In February 2003, the company used an online jam to help introduce the 30,000 consultants from PricewaterhouseCoopers to IBM's 30,000 consultants.

The success of acquisitions depends in part on convincing leaders at these companies that there will be a business benefit to the acquired, as well as to the acquirer. When IBM bought French software company ILOG in 2008, founder and chief executive Pierre Haren saw that ILOG's business-rules management products were attracting customers who before would not have considered buying from a small company. IBM amplified ILOG's ability to bring innovative technology to market. "As a small company, you may have great technology, but the real meat of the market is out of reach," Haren said. "By being part of IBM you gain instant credibility and access with business leaders. You see the impact." In the two years after the deal closed, sales of ILOG's main product tripled.[147]

———

OPEN INNOVATION: A century of research, development, public-private sector collaborations, venture capital and M&A has firmly ingrained the concept of the knowledge-based organization into the minds of progressive corporations. But the concept took on a new dimension with the introduction of the World Wide Web in the mid-1990s. And now, a decade into a new millennium, it's becoming clear that organizations that think of themselves in isolation may miss out on an important new model for value creation: open innovation in a network economy.

Consider Procter & Gamble. The 165-year-old merchandiser's journey from insular to open illustrates the dramatic changes that are under way. When A. G. Lafley was appointed chief executive of the American consumer products giant in 2000, he was faced with flat sales, lackluster product introductions and a swooning stock price. By the time Lafley retired in 2009, P&G's sales had doubled, its profits had quadrupled and the company's market value had increased by more than $100 billion. Observers credit Lafley's adoption of a new open innovation strategy for helping to deliver those stellar results. These days, more than half of all new product ideas come from outside parties, and about 40 percent of them come from outside the United States. Meanwhile, P&G has increased its hit rate—the percentage of new products that succeed—from 15 percent to 50 percent.[148]

Gone are the days when corporations were vertically integrated behemoths, handling everything from prospecting for natural resources to delivering finished products to customers. These days, companies leverage distributed supply chains, business ecosystems and their partners' diverse skills and concentrate their own resources on what they do best. A dramatic example is Bharti Airtel, India's leading mobile communications provider, which outsources all of its IT operations and network management to other companies (including IBM) and focuses on market development. At the same time, many companies are shifting their mindset from hoarding intellectual property to investing in intellectual capital that they create with others via open source software and other shared-effort strategies. Such approaches can produce large-scale efficiencies. For instance, by joining forces, individuals, universities and companies were able to produce and share the core Linux computer operating system, an effort that required an estimated 145,000 person-months of work and would have cost an individual company more than $1 billion to produce, according to a 2006 report prepared for the European Commission.[149]

"The firms that can harness outside ideas to advance their own businesses while leveraging their internal ideas outside their current operations will likely thrive in this new era of open innovation," wrote Henry Chesbrough, executive director of the Center for Open Innovation at UC Berkeley's Haas School of Business.[150] While much of the information about the level of open innovation that is going on is anecdotal, a survey by the National Science Foundation released in 2010 showed that 11.5 percent of the $330 billion in R&D conducted worldwide by US corporations in 1988 was performed by other firms. In the pharmaceutical industry, the number was 25 percent. Of the $330 billion total, 18.8 percent was performed outside the United States.[151]

Chesbrough's thinking was heavily influenced by the aforementioned phenomenon of open source software. With roots in the early days of personal computing when hackers shared simple programs with one another, open source software emerged as a force to be reckoned with for corporations in the late 1990s. Web browser pioneer Netscape Communications got things rolling by allowing some of its programs to be used and modified by others free of charge.

An even bigger breakthrough for open source software came in 2000, when IBM announced that it would invest $1 billion in the Linux ecosystem. That sent a strong signal to corporations that Linux was going mainstream. Within a few years, Linux had become the operating system on more than 20 percent of server computers, according to tech market researcher IDC. "There's no doubt that IBM was Linux's biggest coup," wrote Linus Torvalds, the program's creator.[152]

This represented a huge cultural shift for IBM. In the 1960s and '70s, the company had built a leadership position in business computing based on proprietary technology. In the late 1990s, some IBM executives worried

The Linux computer operating system is an example of a new way to develop software called open source. Taking advantage of global connectivity, thousands of independent programmers built on Linus Torvalds's original software kernel to create an open, high-quality operating system. IBM was an early and substantial supporter of the movement. "There's no doubt that IBM was Linux's biggest coup," Torvalds wrote.

that Linux would eat into the company's server business. But the company's leaders had learned the lesson of the near-death experience. They concluded that Linux was going to succeed sooner or later, and rather than trying to resist it, IBM should build a business around it. "At the time, IBM was still viewed by some as old and stodgy. This gave us the opportunity to differentiate ourselves and be seen as forward thinking," recalled Robert LeBlanc, a senior vice president at IBM Software Group who was one of those advocating for embrace.[153] IBM's investments paid off quickly through sales of software and computing systems.

IBM has also contributed significantly to other open source projects, including Eclipse, a framework for developing complex software applications quickly, which IBM created and then handed to the open source community. IBM's involvement in open source software continues to pay rich dividends. "Open source will only grow," said Robert Sutor, IBM's vice president for open systems and Linux. "More and more of the core infrastructure of corporate computing will be open source. Proprietary innovation will come at the top."[154] Indeed, the success of networked, collaborative innovation has led IBM to develop a dual strategy for intellectual property—participating in open source efforts for building-block technologies and differentiating itself from the competition with homegrown proprietary technologies built on top of them.

———

COLLABORATION ACROSS GLOBAL SYSTEMS: New methods for creating value are not just more abundant today, but also more necessary, as challenges and opportunities have become vastly more complex. The explosion of data from both natural and human-made systems is revealing what complexity theorists call "systems of systems." This new world is a vast network of interdependencies, and the only way to address it successfully is through multidisciplinary approaches, which can generate innovations that no single industry or scientific discipline could produce by itself. Already, this kind of knowledge sharing is having an impact on the economy. Multifactor productivity, which includes the use of technology, organizational improvements and globalization of work, accounted for roughly one-half of productivity growth in the United States from 1995 to 2007.[155] This is the foundation of the twenty-first-century knowledge economy.

As IBM engages with clients as part of its Smarter Planet agenda, it is finding that it has to build new bridges among existing fields and even invent new disciplines. One example is service science, an emerging field of study that IBM pioneered in 2005 with seven universities. There are now service science programs at more than 450 universities in 54 countries.[156]

"The big payoff will be an acceleration of innovation as we develop the ability to combine different areas of R&D—IT with biotech, biosciences with energy, energy with nanotechnology," said Michael Mandel, an economist and innovation expert at Visible Economy. One example of this is a collaboration between IBM and pharmaceutical giant Roche to develop a process for reading and sequencing human DNA quickly and efficiently. The process combines nanotechnology, data analysis and genetics. If successful, it could make it possible to inexpensively sequence the entire genomes of large numbers of individuals, greatly improving doctors' abilities to treat diseases.[157]

The organizations that evolve to meet these challenges will create value differently from the empire builders of the railroad age, the Big Three Detroit automakers of the mid-twentieth century and even the fast-moving Silicon Valley outfits of the personal computer era. It's likely that they'll readily form alliances and share technologies. They'll compete some days and in some ways, and collaborate in others. In form, they may be amalgamations of a variety of enterprises: public and private, for-profit and nonprofit, small entrepreneurial outfits and giant corporations, established organizations and ad hoc communities that take shape to capture an opportunity and then dissipate. The iconic next-generation organization may, in fact, be a network of alliances rather than a mighty monolithic corporation like those that ruled in the middle of the twentieth century.

In the past century, companies created value through mass production. In the twenty-first century, it will be vital for companies to draw value from the phenomenon of mass collaboration.

———

THE FUTURE OF VALUE CREATION: Where will the knowledge-based organization go from here? It's hard to predict with precision, but scientists at IBM Research have some definite ideas. When they peer out into the distant future, they foresee advances in three areas—computing power, the understanding of human cognition and analytics software. Together, these will help shape a "conscious organization" made up of humans and computer programs that will collaborate much as humans do with other humans today.

In this organization of the future, computing tools will adapt to their human masters rather than the other way around. Sophisticated analytic engines will understand how an organization works and know the capabilities of the humans and the software programs, or conscious artifacts, which will think almost like humans. In all likelihood, they will lack our capacity for creativity. But the software programs will create models of the organization that can anticipate changes and improve decision making, and they'll learn from successes and mistakes. "The end result will be more efficient, productive organizations that serve the needs of all of their stakeholders," predicted Charles "Chad" Peck, manager of Biometaphorical Computing at IBM Research.[158]

This vision may seem overly ambitious to some and frightening to others. As with other technological advances, it's hard to predict when something will be possible. And as with other advances, it will be up to people to assert their mastery of machines and to use them profitably, ethically and for the benefit of humanity. IBM is optimistic on all counts. If we look back and recognize how far the modern, knowledge-based corporation has come over the past 100 years—or even the past 20—nothing should surprise us about the future.

• • •

Becoming Global

The idea of a global economy is hardly new—but *being* global as a business organization has meant different things over the course of the modern era.

For Europe's empires in the seventeenth century, it meant the establishment of new arms of the state: "corporations" such as the British East India Company and the Dutch East India Company carried out their governments' colonial ambitions. Their employees roamed the world by ship and horseback, importing raw materials to feed their countries' industries and exporting finished products to their colonies. This work was not simply trade. The great mercantile corporations of the seventeenth and eighteenth centuries settled down where they did business and, for a time, governed large swaths of India and North America.[159]

Globalizing the organization means you need to do as the locals do.

———

An IBM salesman on his way to visit a client in Venice, Italy, in 1966.

1. IBM 6400 Machine Class, Taiwan, 1963. **2.** Leningrad fair, Russia, 1971. **3.** IBM customer engineering classes, Paris, France, 1952. **4.** IBM salesman Lewis N. T. Hsu, Hong Kong, 1961. **5.** Valder Nielsen, Arne Johansen and F. Normann Jensen, Denmark, 1952. **6.** First computer dedication ceremony, Korea, 1967. **7.** T. L. Cummins (left) and Arthur Watson, Latin American management meeting, Brazil, 1957. **8.** IBM truck, Paris, 1959. **9.** Business Efficiency Exhibition, India, 1950. **10.** A. R. Dadi, Karachi, Pakistan, 1957.

11. Millionth electric typewriter, Lexington, Kentucky, 1958. **12.** System/360 shipment in Japan, ca. 1960. **13.** India kickoff meeting, 1959. **14.** Customer, Hong Kong, date unknown. **15.** Inauguration of IBM Ecuador office, 1937. **16.** Delivery to the Philippines, 1961. **17.** IBM print advertising, United States, 1935. **18.** Vienna fair, Austria, 1937. **19.** Chinese scientists visit Watson Research Center, Yorktown, New York, 1972. **20.** IBM Datamobile in downtown Copenhagen, Denmark, 1960.

For those same companies, by the nineteenth century being a global business meant shunning the closed loops of colonial empires and instead pursuing the greater economic potential of open markets. Over time they separated from their governmental parents, and the international corporation was born. In some respects, those enterprises continued the organizational architecture of their state-owned predecessors: a hub-and-spoke model, with all major operations and decisions located in the home country, and sales offices overseas. But though their organization charts might have looked similar, their purpose was different. Instead of serving the interests of one empire, these corporations sought economic opportunity for themselves wherever it presented itself.

This system worked for half a century. And then, just when many had come to believe that the international order in both politics and economics had been stabilized by a combination of market mechanisms and the balance of powers in Europe, those beliefs were blown up by World War I, the Great Depression and World War II, leading to a new fragmentation of the world economy.

IBM came on the scene just as this disruption was about to hit. The corporation's predecessor companies had established toeholds in Canada, the United Kingdom, Germany and a few other countries before Watson Sr. took charge, but it was under Watson's reign that the company aggressively expanded to Asia, Latin America and Africa. And his international ambitions took visible form in 1924, when he renamed C-T-R as International Business Machines.

If World War I was a shock to the system of world trade, the Great Depression and World War II were even stronger aftershocks. Once again, being global was redefined. In response to wartime interruptions in trade—which were then exacerbated by the increasing imposition of protectionist tariffs—companies began establishing self-sufficient businesses in each of their major markets around the world, complete with local back-office operations and manufacturing plants. By building strong national subsidiaries, corporations learned their foreign markets well. In some cases, they kept the complexion of domestic companies, enjoying nationalistic brand loyalty, plus tax and trade advantages. This is the multinational model. In 1949, it took on organizational form at IBM, when Watson created the IBM World Trade Corporation, a wholly owned subsidiary to manage these proliferating operations.

Through this period, IBM learned the same lessons other multinationals were learning. For starters, it was no longer possible to roam freely in a comparatively peaceful and open world marketplace (as in the international era). Rather, companies had to operate in a landscape pockmarked by trade barriers and increasingly nationalized economies. Businesses came to realize that they had to hire local people who understood the local business environment and culture. In addition, they had to train their global leadership teams in the requirements of managing vastly more complex organizations and relationships. And in the middle of this, they had to maintain ethical business practices, no matter how corrupt some local officials or businesspeople may have been, or how outbreaks of political chaos or war may have disrupted business.

——

MANAGING THE TENSION between the centrifugal force of local viability and the centripetal pull of global integration was one of the key skill sets developed by twentieth-century corporations. And the burden fell primarily on local, in-country management teams. Their ability to resolve these inherent conflicts had a lot to do with whether a company was able to succeed as a global business. Through decades of global expansion and experience, IBMers around the world have learned something that many others still find hard to accept: patience, adaptability and shared values are crucial to succeeding through such major historical transitions.

Take Latin America. Over the past century, countries in the region have been shaken by crisis after crisis—economic, political and military. "If we ran from a crisis, we would have been out of Latin America 50 years ago," said Bruno Di Leo, IBM's general manager of growth markets, who earlier in his career was general manager of the Latin American region. In the 1980s and early '90s, for example, Argentina, Brazil and Peru had bouts of hyper-inflation—sometimes as high as 6,000 percent per year. This could have had a devastating effect on IBM's employees, but Di Leo and his colleagues came up with inventive ways of deflecting the blows. Because bursts of inflation often occurred on traditional paydays, IBM began paying employees a day earlier than other employers. It installed bank branches in its facilities so employees could cash their checks immediately and hand the money to their spouses or other family members, who would rush to the store to buy groceries. In this way, they would gain up to 30 percent of purchasing power each payday. In addition, IBM increased salaries as often as once a month. "We had to be flexible and sensitive to the needs of the people. By being quick we gave them the opportunity to maximize their money," Di Leo said.[160]

IBM stuck it out in South America but made a different decision in India, with negative consequences. The company began selling products there in the 1930s, and the manufacturing of products began in 1951. All was well until the mid-1970s, when Indian regulators started requiring foreign-owned companies to sharply reduce their equity ownership by taking on local partners. IBM refused to go along with the new rules, and in 1978 it shut down operations in India.[161] After India began liberalizing its economy in 1991, IBM reentered in a joint venture with a subsidiary of the Tata Group conglomerate, and later it reestablished a wholly owned subsidiary. But during the time IBM was out of India, other technology companies had moved into the country and expanded via joint ventures, and IBM had to rebuild from scratch.[162] "IBM lost out. They struggled to reestablish in India. They were behind the competition," said Shyam Aggarwal, a longtime technology entrepreneur who had been a manager at IBM India during the 1970s.[163]

In the long run, IBM India has become a success, but the path there was a winding one.

A more wrenching experience of the tensions inherent in the emerging multinational model occurred in Germany in the 1930s and '40s. In 1922, C-T-R purchased a controlling interest in Deutsche Hollerith Maschinen Gesellschaft, a German company that manufactured and leased accounting and tabulating machines in Europe. In the 1930s, as international tensions rose and war in Europe loomed, Watson led a campaign to head off hostilities. He argued that disputes between Germany and its neighbors—and even the new Nazi regime's racial and social policies, such as its treatment of Jews—could be resolved through negotiation and arbitration. He adopted the slogan, "World Peace Through World Trade," urging the leaders of world powers to open up markets and avoid warfare.[164] Watson misjudged Adolf Hitler's intentions. After Watson was elected president of the International Chamber of Commerce in 1937, he and the former ICC president accepted Germany's Merit Cross at an ICC meeting in Berlin. After a one-on-one meeting with Hitler, he was convinced that the Nazi leader didn't want war.[165] In this conclusion, he was far from alone—and when Hitler's intentions became clear, Watson corrected his mistake. Immediately after Germany invaded France in 1940, he returned the medal to Germany, writing Hitler in a letter that "the present policies of your government are contrary to the causes for which I have been working."[166]

During the period when Watson was urging diplomacy, Dehomag, as IBM's German affiliate was known, gradually became estranged from its parent. The managers, all Germans, pressed headquarters in New York to transfer voting control to them so Dehomag could continue to get product orders from the German government. Headquarters refused but increased local management ownership to 16 percent in an attempt to avoid government expropriation of the business. Several Dehomag managers joined the Nazi Party, later claiming that they did so to keep the company out of the hands of the government. IBM lost all influence over Dehomag in 1941 and didn't regain full control until 1948. Shortly after the war ended, an IBM representative visited Dehomag facilities and learned that one of the company's machines had been used at the Dachau concentration camp.[167]

Watson's and IBM's principles and loyalties were not in question, but the chairman's judgment had been mistaken. More to the point, IBM was struggling with tensions endemic to the decentralized multinational model. These manifested themselves again decades later in another part of the world. In the 1970s, IBM, along with other major American companies, came under pressure from church groups and universities to stop doing business in South Africa, where the governing regime discriminated against non-whites. Uncertainty over how to respond—to withdraw or seek to promote change by engaging—was evident in remarks made by CEO Frank Cary at IBM's 1973 annual meeting: "Racial discrimination of any type is contrary to the policies of IBM.... While our presence in some ways does support the government of South Africa, we believe we should not leave, that we are a force for good there, and that we would fail our employees and our stockholders if we left."[168] Four years later, Cary hosted a historic gathering of corporate leaders that authored the so-called Sullivan Principles, a set of guidelines for American companies doing business in South Africa aimed at improving the lot of black South Africans. The document was later revised to call for an end to apartheid. When South Africa's government failed to respond, IBM was one of 70 companies that left the country. It sold IBM South Africa to a trust set up to benefit South African employees in 1987. Ultimately, partly because of such economic pressures, apartheid crumbled. After resistance leader Nelson Mandela became president of South Africa, IBM gradually bought back 100 percent of the company.

While these examples show the struggles that IBM and other multi-nationals experienced, other stories show how the company's global expansion had positive effects on some developing countries, such as helping to introduce computing and raise standards of living. For instance, even though IBM didn't have an office in Nepal in 1970, it helped the mountain kingdom conduct its first computerized census. Ravindra Marwaha, who was an IBM India sales manager at the time and later became the general manager of Indian operations, traveled via a small airplane to Kathmandu and laid the groundwork for the project, which included the first installation of a computer in the country. There were no software programmers, so he set up a system for recruiting and training them. "We got it done. IBM had a remarkable influence," Marwaha said.[169] This was such a milestone for the government of Nepal that officials arranged to ink the contract in a room in a former palace normally reserved for treaty signings.

Today, critics of globalization blame multinational businesses for many of the ills of the world, including labor abuses, environmental degradation and government corruption. There's plenty of ammunition for their claims, but, in truth, these issues are not best understood as questions of good or evil. Forms of economic organization are not inherently either. The more useful questions to ask are: How does any given type of commercial or political organization manage the tensions in its era? And which organizational forms are optimal for simultaneously creating near-term economic value, long-term organizational sustainability and broader societal progress? IBM's shift over the past two decades toward becoming what it calls a globally integrated enterprise offers an instructive indication of how those questions will be answered in the new century.

———

BY THE TIME LOU GERSTNER arrived at IBM in 1993, the company's organizational structure reflected the company's legacy as a classic multinational, with semi-independent operations in nearly 100 countries. In terms of both IBM's internal coherence and its ability to adapt, the independence of these subsidiaries had become a major hindrance. The company was so compartmentalized when Gerstner arrived that the all-powerful country managers kept vital information secret from the top managers.

Nigeria, 1965

Italy, 1933

Brazil, 1952

To put down roots, a company needs to do more than set up sales offices.

———

IBM sought to build local skills, workforces and knowledge, training employees and clients in the new technologies and processes of the Information Age.

"I declared war on the geographic fiefdoms," Gerstner wrote in his memoir, *Who Says Elephants Can't Dance?* In their place, he organized IBM around global teams focusing on a dozen major industries. Some managers were so upset that they warned he was destroying the company. That didn't happen. By shifting from being a country-centric, product-focused company to a global, client-oriented organization, IBM was able to spot business problems sooner and respond more quickly to shifting customer needs. Gerstner was reintegrating the organization. And so began IBM's transformation into something different from a multinational company.

Although this new corporate form hadn't been defined yet, it was clear that the institution of the corporation needed to undergo major changes. Indeed, Watson Jr. himself gave Gerstner his blessing to radically transform the company. Gerstner recounts in his book that one morning when he emerged from his home to be driven to work, he found the 79-year-old Watson, who lived nearby, waiting in the backseat of his car. Watson was agitated as the two men rode together. He told Gerstner that he was angry about what had happened to IBM and urged him to shake it up "from top to bottom," Gerstner wrote.[170]

Gerstner did—ironically, by deciding *not* to change IBM's basic organizational form. Swimming against the tide of conventional wisdom, he kept IBM together rather than allowing it to break up into a handful of "Baby Blues." It was the signature decision of his tenure. Within two years, after a lot of tough love, IBM had returned to financial stability.

Venezuela, 1952

Japan, 1959

Indonesia, 1950

Said Palmisano of Gerstner: "Without him, I don't think we would have survived. We needed somebody with that tough mind and analytical skill."[171]

The next stage of global transformation came just a few years later, in reaction to the communications revolution. In the mid-1990s, the emergence of the Internet and the laying of a network of data communications cables around the world had begun to intensify the reglobalization of world trade that was already under way. This sparked a major and rapid shift in the global economy, which started to show up over the following decade. Engineers in Bangalore were doing the same work as their counterparts in Silicon Valley but at about 20 percent of the cost. The same was true for other office work, including accounting, customer service and even scientific research. This revolution gave rise to a new force in the world of business. Aggressive Indian companies, including Infosys, TCS and Wipro, offered high-quality outsourcing services at lower prices than those offered by IBM and other Western tech companies. Once again, IBM faced a serious threat. What got the company's attention, specifically, was a brash prediction by Nandan Nilekani, an executive at Infosys, that the Indian tech services companies would have the same crippling effect on the American tech services giants that Japan's auto companies had on Detroit's Big Three automakers.[172]

Nilekani's prediction was further impetus for IBM to evolve into a globally integrated enterprise. IBM rapidly began hiring people in low-cost countries and now employs more than 100,000 people in emerging markets. The initial impulse was to respond to the challenge of the Indian tech services upstarts. "If we didn't shift work to lower-cost countries, we wouldn't have been able to compete," said IBM chief financial officer Mark Loughridge.[173] But there was an added bonus: IBM found that by locating its offices in important population centers around the world, it could engage tens of thousands of the best and brightest young minds on the planet.

IBM's tapping of India's talent pool has been unprecedented in scale, but not in principle. The company has long recognized the importance of hiring bright people outside the United States. In the late 1980s, for instance, the PC division began shifting design and engineering work to a laboratory in Yamato, Japan, which had been established years earlier to develop products specifically for the Japanese market. Based on their superior skills, the engineers in Yamato landed the coveted assignment of producing IBM's first ThinkPad notebook PC in the early 1990s—and nearly every version thereafter. Engineering manager Arimasa Naitoh and his team meshed well with IBM design consultant Richard Sapper, who lives in Italy, and the product marketing team in the United States. The Japanese excelled at teamwork and global collaboration. One of their engineering break-throughs, working with Sapper, was turning the ThinkPad keyboard into an easily opened door so people could conveniently upgrade the components inside.[174] At the time, the small and light notebooks were confoundedly difficult to design and engineer. "It was like the early days for airplanes," Naitoh said. "Try—and crash. Try—and crash. The ThinkPad was a surprise to all of us. It was flying and not crashing." In fact, ThinkPad went on to become one of the best-selling notebook computer franchises ever—a triumph of technology, design and global integration.[175]

Today, scientists at some of IBM's newest research locations in China and India are already contributing scientific advances. IBMers in Delhi, India, for instance, have developed voice recognition and networking tech-nologies that make it possible for people who are illiterate or who don't have access to computers to use any telephone to set up or use voice-operated websites, something IBM calls the Spoken Web. Using this simple, intuitive system, consumers can buy food or get medical advice, and farmers can check the weather and find the best prices for their crops. Now the researchers are working with IBM executives and telecom companies to turn their technologies into businesses. "Eventually, this could have a huge impact all around the world. This is what's driving us," said Arun Kumar, the IBM researcher in Delhi who came up with the Spoken Web idea.[176]

Would scientists in New York have come up with a breakthrough like that? Perhaps. But there's no question that people with a fresh perspective were at an advantage to spot a new use for technology that could help improve the lives of perhaps a billion illiterate people around the world.

IBM's adventures in India in recent years demonstrate the huge revenue growth opportunities that exist for global companies in emerging nations. Shanker Annaswamy, who arrived from GE Medical Systems in mid-2004 to run IBM's Indian subsidiary, recalls his first meeting with Palmisano, who visited Delhi that November. Annaswamy had spent hours preparing a presentation. He nervously reached for it when he and Palmisano sat down for a dinner meeting at the Taj Mahal Hotel, but Palmisano waved him off. He had already read the presentation. Instead, he laid out his grand ambitions for India. He didn't just want to tap India's vast pool of college-educated, English-speaking young people. He also wanted IBM to be the leader in India in services, software and other key product categories.[177]

This strategy proved to be highly successful. By providing tens of thousands of jobs for Indians, IBM aligned itself with the Indian government's national economic agenda. By tailoring services and products to India, it soon became the leader in technology services—beating out multi-national and local rivals. But it also made gains in other segments, including high-performance UNIX servers and external disk storage, according to market researcher IDC.[178]

The seriousness with which Palmisano regarded success in India was dramatized in June 2006, when he kicked off an IBM employee town hall meeting far from the company's New York headquarters—in a pavilion erected on the grounds of the Bangalore Palace, in the heart of India's equivalent of Silicon Valley. Palmisano told a crowd of 10,000 IBMers that the company had expanded its Indian workforce from 9,000 to 43,000 in just two years and planned on investing $6 billion in the country over the next three years.[179]

This mammoth retooling of the corporation came just a decade after the company had pulled back from the brink of ruin. But for Palmisano, it was just another day at the office. Ever since IBM's turnaround took hold, the company has been on a journey of continuous reinvention. Global integration was a big piece of that—but it was not the only piece. The company sold off commodity businesses one by one, including disk drives, printers and personal computers, while beefing up its high-value and high-profit businesses, including technology services, business consulting and software. "What Sam has done is the hardest thing to do—to take a successful platform and continually evolve it," Gerstner said. "Sam took a successful company and made it far more successful."[180]

There's nothing like a near-death experience to make you pay attention and not take success for granted. The lessons from 1993 are now part of IBM's understanding of itself. The company realizes that, at one level, it shouldn't think of itself as being in the computer server business, the software business or technology services. Rather, it is in the business of innovation, on a global scale—the business of making the world work better. That self-definition informs the company's Smarter Planet strategy, and it extends to the continual renewal of IBM itself.

Palmisano's idea of the globally integrated enterprise was captured in an article he wrote for the May/June 2006 edition of the policy journal *Foreign Affairs*: "The emerging globally integrated enterprise is a company that fashions its strategy, its management, and its operations in pursuit of a new goal: the integration of production and value delivery worldwide. State borders define less and less the boundaries of corporate thinking or practice," he wrote. The article was something of an emancipation proclamation for the borderless, networked corporation.

But it's one thing to lay out a bold new strategy and another to make it work in the trenches. At IBM, the process of turning itself into a globally integrated enterprise has been under way for half a decade, and it's not nearly done.

Palmisano launched IBM's global makeover in mid-2005, aiming to build on the company's previous success in wringing $5 billion per year in inefficiencies from its global supply chain. The goal was to use a combination of business process redesign, technology upgrades and redeployment of global labor to improve quality and responsiveness and drive annual productivity gains of 10 percent to 15 percent across the company's entire services portfolio.[181] Over the next two years, the company set the plan in motion, shifting work to low-cost countries in Asia, Latin America and Eastern Europe and setting up giant global service delivery centers that were capable of serving clients—and IBM's own business units—scattered around the world. For instance, a former IBM manufacturing plant in Hortolândia, Brazil, serves global services clients who speak Portuguese, French, Spanish and English. Service delivery managers and consulting project managers use an online database and sophisticated analytical tools to identify the best staff or open positions on projects. For IBM's Global Business Services division alone, those tools have delivered major benefits. The percent of unassigned people—called the bench—at any given time has dropped from 8 percent to 3 percent.[182]

Gradually, the notion of shared services spread to other parts of the organization. Prompted by an idea in one of the company's global jams, the sales force set up so-called Deal Hubs to help salespeople worldwide consolidate and coordinate the multiple processes required to deliver client service once a deal is signed. The technology and consulting groups combined to set up technical centers of excellence designed to address specific problems. For instance, in 2008 the company opened a Global Center of Excellence for Water Management in Amsterdam.[183] All told, the shared-services initiative cut annual costs for such tasks from $16 billion in 2005 to $11.5 billion in 2010.[184]

The Journey to Global Integration

Mid-nineteenth to early twentieth century:
The international corporation

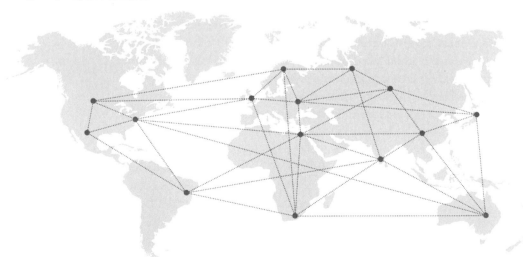

Most operations were centered in
the home country, with overseas
sales and distribution.

Mid-twentieth century:
The multinational corporation

The multinational created smaller versions
of itself in countries around the world and made
heavy local investments.

Twenty-first century:
The globally integrated enterprise

Integrated through common values and processes,
the globally integrated enterprise locates operations
and functions anywhere in the world based on
the right cost, skills and business environment.

The mantra is "radical simplification." Over the coming five years, IBM expects to save $8 billion through a combination of locating work where it can best be performed, continuous improvements through the use of analytics and focusing its integrated opportunities on high-value advisory activities.[185]

In its full-tilt drive to become a globally integrated enterprise, IBM is not alone. Many corporations—including some that have been international businesses for even longer than IBM—are now making this shift. Consider HSBC. Today, it refers to itself as the "world's local bank"—and it's being literal. The 145-year-old financial services company, which is now one of the world's largest banking institutions, was originally formed in Hong Kong as the Hong Kong and Shanghai Banking Corporation, but it now has headquarters in London and some 8,000 offices in 87 countries and territories—including a branch in the tiny Cook Islands in the South Pacific. Two of the top managers are based in Hong Kong, including chief executive Stuart Gulliver; three are in London. HSBC has lived through all of the major shifts in globalization that have affected the world's corporations over the past two centuries. It was founded to finance the growing trade between Europe, India and China. Then it went international, gradually opening operations in other major countries. And now it is becoming truly global—not just in scope but also in philosophy.[186]

———

ONCE A COMPANY HAS HIRED SMART PEOPLE around the globe, one of the key challenges is to coordinate their activities—overcoming differences in time zones, language and culture. Rogério Oliveira, general manager for IBM Latin America, recalls what it was like when the globally integrated enterprise system first came to Brazil in 2006. He was the country manager there at the time. At first, his global service delivery people were being hit from all sides by requests from IBM's product and industry groups all around the world. They didn't know what was coming, and he didn't know how many people to hire or train.

Oliveira felt intense pressure—especially around the end of each quarter. He had a sales quota to meet, but at the same time he also had to oversee this new stream of globally delivered services. "I felt like I was being torn in two directions," he said. Over time, though, new planning and management systems came into being that made the job easier. Also, he said, the company's culture helped. "You have a culture and values that are common to everybody in the company. These things make it easier to deal with the global pressures," he recalled.[187]

Since the early days of the globally integrated enterprise, IBM has devised a management system that encompasses a broad array of tactics. These include leadership training programs, the use of the latest collaboration software and setting up special teams of high-powered global executives to help local managers in emerging-market countries get major projects off the ground.

One example: IBM launched 13 Global Engagement Teams between 2008 and 2010 in countries as diverse as Brazil, China, Turkey and South Africa. These four- or five-person teams of executives mentor country managers and help them build relationships with major clients. In addition, they take on one or more major initiatives designed to develop the skills of local managers and bring IBM's global resources to bear in a country. In South Africa, for instance, Mark Hennessy, then the corporation's chief information officer, helped local leaders advise government officials on how to design an integrated financial management system to span all of the country's agencies. He tapped his network of IBM contacts to get assistance from top software architects with expertise in designing such systems. That made it easier for the government to move ahead with its project. Within months, IBM had won contracts for pieces of the system. "The team brought new insights through new connections," said Katharyn White, marketing vice president for IBM Global Business Services, who heads up the South African GET team.[188]

Most large companies provide leadership development training for a few hundred managers. IBM, because its staff is so widely scattered, realized that it needed to develop superior management skills deep in the organization. So in 2009 it set up a program called the Leadership Effectiveness and Development System, which uses software analysis tools to help identify 60,000 high-potential employees. These IBMers are given career counseling and training as global leaders, and they're put on a list that is used to select people for management positions anywhere around the world.[189]

The work that these people manage is different from the work any of their predecessors have handled. Consider how IBM put together the most recent version of Lotus Symphony, its package of PC software applications. Starting in mid-2007, software programming teams in Austin, Texas; Raleigh, North Carolina; Beijing, China; and Boeblingen, Germany, began working on the program. For the first time ever, the Beijing team was heading up a global project. To establish open communications and trust among people who had never met in person, the scattered teams used IBM's SocialBlue application, its own internal version of Facebook. The Chinese programmers were culturally conditioned to expect explicit instructions from managers, so Helen Dai, the project leader, who was born in China but educated in the United States, taught them to be more self-directed and to set priorities. "Pretty soon they were operating just like a development team anywhere else would," recalled Michael Karasick, a vice president in IBM's software group who at the time ran software development operations in China. The product was released in May 2008, on time and on budget.[190]

Being a global IBMer is not just about skills. It's also about culture. IBM has an especially strong tradition of culture on which to build—from Watson Sr.'s championing of women, minorities and the disabled to Watson Jr.'s pioneering equal opportunity policy in 1954 to an array of diversity programs launched in the 1990s. They focused on eliminating barriers in the workplace based on race and gender so that minorities and women would feel free to express their differences rather than try to fit into a traditional white male culture. The results are in: in 2010, IBM was ranked number one on DiversityInc's list of "Top 10 Companies for Global Diversity." It is the only company to be selected for *Working Mother Magazine*'s "100 Best Companies" list every year since the inception of the list in 1985.[191]

Now, in a third wave, the company's human resources managers are taking aim at cross-cultural and cross-generational issues. They call it Diversity 3.0, and it includes a Cultural Adaptability wiki where employees can contribute and find information and advice about national and regional cultural differences. They also created a web-based tool called Global Navigator that IBMers can use to select a country and learn ways to enhance their interactions with coworkers or clients who live there.[192]

――――

OVER THE COMING DECADES, IBM expects to continue expanding and integrating globally at a rapid pace—in both the clients it serves and the talent it taps. It set up a business unit in 2008 to target emerging markets, and it expects the percentage of its revenues from those countries to grow from 18 percent that year to nearly 30 percent in 2015, contributing 50 percent of the company's revenue growth over this period. For instance, in Africa and the Middle East, where the company had just 10 branch offices in 2000, by 2010 it had 23 offices and expects to expand to 40 by 2015.[193]

Some of these countries are rough places for business. The idea is to place bets that will pay off years or even decades from now. Take Iraq. IBM began doing business there at the height of the war, in 2004. Takreem El-Tohamy, an Egyptian who is IBM's general manager for the Middle East and Africa, remembers flying into Baghdad on an airplane that nosedived into the airport with its lights turned off to avoid becoming a target for rockets. He would wear a flak jacket and a helmet whenever he ventured out of his hotel to visit potential customers—and sometimes he'd even sleep in protective gear. The first big sale was of computers to the University of Baghdad, where the engineering department was limping along with out-of-date gear. "IBM being there early, establishing a presence, helping to define the IT strategy in the country—it wins the hearts and minds of the people," El-Tohamy said. "Over the long haul, this will be a very good business for IBM."[194]

In emerging countries in the Middle East and Africa, IBM plans on first establishing relationships and selling there, then making locations in some of those countries nodes in its global talent network. The company's 2010 contract to provide IT and customer-management services for Bharti Enterprises's expansion in Africa means IBM will be providing services in more than a dozen countries—including several in which it never operated before. It already has a 1,000-person global delivery center in South Africa and plans on using it as a training ground for future employees in Nigeria and other countries with large populations and promising economic futures.[195]

Western corporations face thorny political challenges as they globalize their workforces. Millions of manufacturing and engineering jobs have been created in Asia and other low-cost areas, and millions of Americans, Japanese and Western Europeans have lost their jobs. For example, more than 2 million American manufacturing jobs were lost to China between 2001 and 2007, according to the Economic Policy Institute.[196] Carlota Perez, author of *Technological Revolutions and Financial Capital: The Dynamics of Bubbles and Golden Ages*, has called for governments and businesses to band together and invest in new technologies and skills training.[197]

IBM and some of its corporate brethren are responding. In the United States, IBM has opened technology service delivery centers in Dubuque, Iowa; East Lansing, Michigan; and Columbia, Missouri. It is helping its employees retool their skills for the jobs of the future, and assisting universities that are developing new curricula for educating the next generation of knowledge workers. In addition, IBM joined with the state of New York, the State University of New York at Albany and corporate partners to foster economic development centered on nanotechnology in upstate New York, where the company operates one of its two chip fabrication plants. It's a cluster of companies, research consortia and educational institutions that, with financial support from the state, pool research facilities, equipment and ideas. The companies that participate have their roots in a number of countries in addition to the United States, including Japan, Germany, Singapore and Abu Dhabi.[198] This alliance could become a powerful model for economic renewal in the world's developed economies.

The alliance also demonstrates that the globally integrated enterprise of the future won't likely be contained within the walls of a single company— no matter how aggressively it expands around the world. Companies will not just interweave their own far-flung operations but integrate themselves into the global community of businesses of all sizes, governments and universities.

These kinds of arrangements promise not only economic growth but also a significant contribution to global security and order. Maybe Watson was ahead of his time with "World Peace Through World Trade." Or perhaps a globally networked economy is about something more than trade. One thing is clear: companies will invest in global systems of production only if they believe the countries in which they're operating are on the road to lasting stability. At the same time, they can't just stand by and hope governments can avoid wars, suppress corruption and educate large populations of poor people. The globally integrated enterprise can—indeed, must—be a force in helping to solve such problems. Palmisano said as much in his *Foreign Affairs* manifesto:

> *Government leaders will find in business willing partners to reform health care and education, secure the world's trade lanes and electronic commerce, train and enable the displaced and dispossessed, grapple with environmental problems and infectious diseases, and tackle the myriad other challenges that globalization raises....*

The shift from multinational corporations to globally integrated enterprises provides an opportunity to advance both business growth and societal progress. But it raises issues that are too big and too interconnected for business alone or government alone to solve.

Going global has meant many different things through a century packed with historic change. And yet certain underlying approaches, skills and practices have remained essential, and they promise to do so in the increasingly integrated economy of the twenty-first century. Modern corporations need country leadership that can translate global strategies into local practice—and vice versa. They need to embrace global diversity—in people, skills, thinking and resources—reflecting the reality that the rising middle classes of the world's former colonies are now its engines of economic growth and the source of new generations of innovators. They need to adopt horizontal, distributed management systems for increasingly networked supply chains, where no one organization can determine its own fate. And they need to embrace new forms of leadership development to shape a new generation of global professionals and global citizens.

• • •

How Organizations Engage with Society

After an economic crisis hit Mexico in the mid-1990s, the country's largest building materials company, CEMEX, whose business model had always been business-to-business, decided to start marketing its products directly to the millions of Mexicans who build or add onto their own homes. The thinking was that this segment might be more stable than others in times of crisis. The company sent researchers out into the field to interview homeowners and understand the market. It found that in order to sell to this group of people, many of whom were poor and lived in small, crowded shacks, it would have to come up with a new way of doing business. Out of his work, in 2000, came an initiative called Patrimonio Hoy, which means "property today."

A new global economy requires a new kind of global citizen.

One of the first teams for IBM's Corporate Service Corps pioneered a new way to unite leadership training and global citizenship. Helping spark business development in Ghana in 2008 were (from left): business process specialist Ritu Bedi, of India; technology architect Pietro Leo, of Italy; supply chain manager Julie Lockwood, of the United States; interactive community builder John Tolva, of the United States; videographer Charlie Ung, of Canada; and project manager Arindam Bhattacharyya, of India.

From 2008 to 2011, a thousand Corporate Service Corps participants were deployed in 100 teams in 24 countries to work on community-driven economic development projects: **1.** Textile worker in Ghana, 2008. **2.** CSC members Evelyn Bailey (left) of Canada and Michele Grieshaber of the United States in Ho Chi Minh City, Vietnam, 2009. **3.** Member Clara Challoner Walker of the United Kingdom in Ho Chi Minh City, 2009. **4.** Member Dan Delos (left) of the United States in Ho Chi Minh City, 2009. **5.** Artisan in Ghana, 2008.

6. Member Charlie Ung of Canada in Ghana, 2008. 7. Member Jordan Olivero (left) of the United States in Chengdu, China, 2009. 8. Arindam Bhattacharyya of India during business training, Ghana, 2008. 9. Produce store in Ho Chi Minh City, 2009. 10. Grieshaber in Ho Chi Minh City, 2009. 11. Member Guru Banavar (left) of India in Ho Chi Minh City, 2009. 12. Ho Chi Minh City, 2009.

Through the initiative, CEMEX began selling cement and other building materials directly to poor people—but that was only one piece of a complete solution that included financing, advisory and logistics services. Families typically pay $15 per week, and the program typically reduces construction time by 60 percent and cost by 35 percent. Local so-called promoters, who live in the communities, sell the package of materials and services—akin to Avon's independent beauty product representatives. The program started off as a business initiative, but the company's leaders quickly saw that it could become something much more: a way to help poor Mexicans improve their quality of life and, in the case of the promoters, to put extra money in their pockets. "We saw that this would be a huge opportunity to present a solution not just for the people but for the government—reducing social pressure and providing people with better housing," said Israel Moreno, a 20-year veteran of CEMEX who has run Patrimonio Hoy since its inception.

Since then, the program has served 300,000 Mexican families—or about 1.5 million people (CEMEX has expanded it to Colombia, Costa Rica, Nicaragua and the Dominican Republic). It's selling 100,000 tons of cement through the program in Mexico each year. But the impact is still small. Moreno intends to eventually serve 50 million Mexicans. "We have a long way to run," he said.[199]

The program is just one example among many today of companies that have begun selling products and services to the 2 billion people in the world who up until now have been part of informal local economies—scraping by at a subsistence level on little work and less money. By devising strategies that make their products affordable for this target market, yet profitable for them, companies not only create markets today but also lay the groundwork for increased prosperity for broader populations and much larger markets for their products and services. "This is the largest growth opportunity the world has ever seen," said the late C. K. Prahalad, author of *The Fortune at the Bottom of the Pyramid.*

Patrimonio Hoy also represents the leading edge of a major shift in the way corporations engage with society. Rather than seeing corporate social responsibility as an ancillary activity that companies engage in out of guilt or altruism, many leaders now see it, in its newest manifestations, as integral to their business activities and essential to their company's success. This shift, if fully realized, could change not just the nature of corporations but also of business itself. "We have the potential to create a values-based capitalism that puts a sense of purpose to make a difference in the world at the center of how businesses operate," said Harvard Business School professor Rosabeth Moss Kanter, author of *Supercorp: How Vanguard Companies Create Innovation, Profits, Growth, and Social Good.*[200]

Why has this shift happened? For the same reason the other shifts in the modern corporation have occurred—because of changes over the past century in how value is created, how people are managed and how enterprises become global. Businesses now have a different relationship with society as well—in large part because the concept of society now means something very different from what it once did.

Starting with the Renaissance and stretching into the twentieth century, the concept of a society largely referred to the relations among political institutions. Early on, monarchs, nobles and church leaders made the rules for all of the people within their spheres of influence and controlled society's economic resources. The rise of capitalism brought a major new force to bear. In the seventeenth century, economist Adam Smith's "invisible hand" of the market was a progressive force that challenged the old sources of power—the church, state-based military power and the mercantile regimes of imperialist commerce. Indeed, as capitalism grew in influence and global reach in the twentieth century, it increasingly rivaled the power of the state. Yet business leaders generally didn't see themselves as being responsible for social outcomes.

At the dawn of the twenty-first century, we're at another inflection point—one that's likely to be as consequential as the shift from feudal society

to the Renaissance and the Enlightenment. The combination of globalization, digital technologies and the empowerment of citizens through
access to more and better information is creating what IBM calls a smarter
planet. The way the world works is a function of the relationships among
many interconnected global systems—political, commercial, societal and
natural. Our planet is becoming a system of systems that cut across the
boundaries of nations, industries and existing fields and disciplines.

So "society" now means a global network of interconnected interests,
melding all types of human activities and purposes, including commercial.
And both economic growth and societal progress increasingly depend on
the ability of governments, business leaders and individuals to work together
to optimize those global systems for the health, wealth and sustainability of
the whole.

At IBM, this has led to the belief that acting in a socially responsible
way can no longer be seen as separate from the company's core business
activities. It is seen as being a similar kind of activity—and as essential to the
company's success. As Sam Palmisano put it in the introduction to IBM's
2009 Corporate Responsibility Report, "Addressing the issues facing the world
now—from clean water, better healthcare, green energy and better schools,
to sustainable and vibrant cities, and an empowered workforce and citi-
zenry—does not pose a choice between business strategy and citizenship
strategy. Rather, it represents a fusion of the two." That is, the systems of a
smarter planet—including its corporations—operate in a shared arena for
both economic growth and social progress, a global commons. The modern
corporation doesn't engage with society merely out of a desire to "do good."
Its leaders do so because of the way the world now works.

With its exhibit at the 1964/65 New York
World's Fair, IBM aimed to capture a generation's
imagination by showcasing the possibilities
of technology to make the world work better.

———

The IBM pavilion had six sections, including a giant theater called the
"Information Machine" that was designed for 16,000 visitors a day.

They also do it because of the values, culture and mindset of the next generation of thinkers, innovators and employees. "Social responsibility is deeply connected to IBM's values," said Stanley Litow, vice president for corporate citizenship. "Being socially responsible helps us attract and retain the best talent, which is how you sustain greatness. True social responsibility makes the company more effective for our clients. It minimizes risk to the company and maximizes returns for shareholders, employees and the community." [201]

In this new world, it is now clear that business and society are not separate, and that neither can be optimized without the other. An individual corporation can actually change the world, can drive progress—in ways that Jeff O'Brien describes in this book's final chapter. This does not mean that we've reached some idyllic state of economic and societal unity. Indeed, the new challenges we face may be even greater than the old ones.

The journey from individual philanthropy to social business was one of gradual exploration. Watson's conviction that business has a societal responsibility was little more than a gut instinct, without clear management models or common practices. IBM and other progressive corporations had to make it up as they went along. And they were at odds with the dominant economic theories. This conventional wisdom held that business had neither the capacity nor even the right to pursue societal progress. In this view, it was the moral responsibility of a corporation to serve the interests of its shareholders, period. Economist Milton Friedman laid out the rationale for that approach a generation ago. He wrote: "There is one and only one social responsibility of business—to use its resources and engage in activities designed to increase its profits so long as it … engages in open and free competition without deception or fraud." [202]

But there's growing evidence that this view of both economics and society no longer describes the real world. In the first decade of the twenty-first century, we witnessed a pattern of systemic crises that are inherently global, and inherently both economic and societal—in spheres ranging from climate to food, from retail to national security, from energy to finance. When the market and society and the planet are merged, there's no such thing as minding your own business.

AT THE TIME OF IBM'S FOUNDING, this systemic view was unknown. Even the idea that civic virtue should be expressed not just by individuals but also by companies was relatively new. American industrialist Andrew Carnegie, for instance, had struggled to reconcile his personal principles with his policies as the chief executive of the world's largest steel company. Personally, he supported the right of workers to organize in unions, yet when push came to shove, he ordered his lieutenant, Henry Clay Frick, to break the union organizing workers at Carnegie Steel's mill in Homestead, Pennsylvania.[203] That resulted in a bloody gun battle between strikers and a private police force hired by Frick. Carnegie argued in books and essays that the life of an industrialist should be neatly divided into two parts: his role as a business person, where he concentrates on the accumulation of wealth; and his role as a philanthropist, after he retires, where he focuses on giving his wealth to worthy causes. "Under its sway we shall have an ideal state, in which the surplus wealth of the few will become, in the best sense, the property of the many," he wrote.[204] After Carnegie sold his steel company in 1901, in addition to funding countless public libraries and schools, he established a pension fund for retirees of Carnegie Steel.

In 1886, the US Supreme Court had granted corporations the same rights as individual citizens under the terms of the country's Fourteenth Amendment to the Constitution. At the most obvious level, this was simply a recognition that corporations were no longer arms of the state—as they had been during the era of mercantile empires—but rather subjects of the state, to be governed by the same laws as its citizens. However, the analogy had deeper implications. If a corporation has some of the same legal rights as a citizen, might it also have some of the same moral or social responsibilities?

Watson Sr., for one, believed it did. He made no distinction between the responsibility of the wealthy individual and the responsibility of the company. Though Watson doesn't refer to the 1886 case in his writings, he argued often that companies should act like responsible citizens. In some respects, he was adopting the legacy of the Progressive movement, but applying it to the nascent science of business management. The Progressives believed that science, education and better government could address society's weaknesses and abuses. They helped elect a new generation of government leaders who instituted wave after wave of reform, including antitrust laws, regulations curtailing market speculation and expansion of world trade. Some business leaders marched alongside the Progressives. Henry Ford, for instance, recognized that by doubling the wages of his workers, he could attract and retain the best engineers and assembly workers in Detroit. He also understood that by paying working people good wages, industrialists would create mass markets for automobiles and other big-ticket items.

At IBM, Watson became a reformer, too. The reasons, perhaps, lie in his career up to that point—because he had run into trouble at NCR. After rising through the ranks of its sales force, he was asked by the company's management to run a subsidiary that sold used cash registers and operated without having to make a profit. That strategy drove some of NCR's competitors out of business and cleared the way for the company to dominate the market in city after city. Ultimately, Watson was one of more than 30 NCR managers who were accused of antitrust violations and put on trial. He was found guilty, but the verdict was later thrown out. After a series of disputes with NCR's innovative, strong-willed founder, John Henry Patterson, Watson left the company in 1913.[205]

Watson always denied that he broke the law, yet historians believe that he spent the rest of his life seeking redemption—indeed, more than redemption—even though he never stated it publicly. He was a man on a mission. After he was hired to run the fledgling C-T-R, he sought the high ground in one facet of business after another.

In a lecture that he delivered to audiences in the 1920s and '30s, he said: "Business leaders are not just 'doing business.' They're knitting together the whole fabric of civilization. Its harmony, pattern, design and mechanism are due to their clear thinking, ingenuity, progressiveness, imagination and character. For this reason, business leaders must be equally interested and proficient in all of the elements which go to make up a civilization which is seeking to find peace, prosperity and happiness through united effort."[206]

Watson and other like-minded CEOs pursued their beliefs in two different ways. First, they developed the notion of giving back to society through corporate philanthropy, modeled on the private philanthropy of their nineteenth-century predecessors. Second, they aimed to be socially responsible within their own four walls, adopting progressive workforce policies and practices.

Through the tenures of both Watsons, IBM was a leader in corporate philanthropy and socially conscious policy. As a result, by the late 1980s, IBM was contributing almost $200 million a year to charity worldwide. The elder Watson was the company's conscience early on, and, as IBM expanded internationally, so did Watson's own understanding of and concern for the world's poor and downtrodden. In 1950, he traveled by ship to Latin America to visit IBM facilities. One meeting was arranged in the steamy port city of Buenaventura, Colombia. There, dressed in his dark formal suit and vest, he took a stroll after lunch through the city's muddy, unpaved streets with long-time IBM executive Luis Lamassonne. Watson was shocked by the filth and

Thomas Watson Sr. believed that business organizations had a responsibility not just to their employees, but also to the communities in which they operated. When he toured the streets of Buenaventura, Colombia, with IBM executive Luis Lamassonne in 1950, the poverty he saw hit him hard, leading to a child-aid program within IBM.

poverty in which Buenaventura's children lived. Lamassonne recalled that Watson told him: "We have a responsibility here. We have to help them get education and improve their lives." In response, Lamassonne set up a child-aid program within IBM, which included sewing circles where the wives of IBM employees made clothing for children.[207]

A decade later, Thomas Watson Jr. would take up the cause of racial equality. IBM had long hired black people on an equal footing with whites, and in 1944 it became the first corporation to support the United Negro College Fund. In 1953, when IBM was negotiating with government leaders in Kentucky and North Carolina to establish factories there, Watson Jr. informed them that he planned to fully integrate the plants. This was 11 years before the Civil Rights Act outlawed racial segregation in businesses, schools and places that served the public. "I told those guys I wouldn't tolerate separate-but-equal in my company, and, if you insist, I'll take my plants elsewhere," Watson recalled in 1990, in a meeting with J. T. Childs Jr., then the head of diversity programs at IBM.[208] To put added pressure on the governors, Watson issued a letter to IBM managers formally establishing IBM's policy of hiring people without regard to race, color or creed, making it the first US corporation to issue such a mandate. Articles about the letter were published in the local newspapers. The governors backed down, and both plants were opened in 1956.[209]

The nation was deeply divided along issues of race, but IBM came down on the side of equal opportunity again and again. In 1968, at the urging of Senator Robert Kennedy, the company established a 300-person manufacturing plant in New York City's poor and predominantly black neighborhood of Bedford-Stuyvesant. It was a time when many companies were shuttering factories in the inner cities.[210] Inequality was also on Watson's mind when he penned an op-ed column for the *New York Times* in 1970. Citing the fact that nonwhites had a life expectancy six years shorter than that of whites, he called for universal health insurance. He had opposed the idea of socialized medicine when President Harry Truman proposed it in 1949, but he had since changed his mind. "We must bring the fullness of American medical care to all the American people," he wrote. "As the greatest nation in the world I believe we can do no less."[211]

When it comes to environmental protection, IBM's approach has been consistently active. Nearly 40 years ago, Watson Jr. mandated that IBM should be a leader in protecting the environment. In 1978, after the company discovered groundwater contamination at its plant in Dayton, New Jersey, it voluntarily implemented a program that required all manufacturing facilities to investigate and control contaminants in groundwater, and this was well in advance of regulations requiring such activities. Over the years, IBM has broadened its focus from pollution control to pollution prevention and to innovation for the environment. For instance, it has developed Smart Grid technology to help electrical utilities manage energy more efficiently and add alternative sources to their systems, including wind and solar. "Good environmental management is not only an imperative for the societies of which we're a part; it also makes good business sense," said Wayne Balta, vice president of corporate environmental affairs and product safety. "Businesses that do not properly handle their environmental responsibilities are neither efficient nor sustainable."[212]

———

THE SHIFT TO A GENUINELY GLOBAL ECONOMY AND SOCIETY, which accelerated dramatically with the emergence of the World Wide Web, changed the company's focus. Starting in the mid-1990s, IBM's leaders began to rethink how a company could most effectively contribute to helping the world work better—more efficiently, more creatively and more sustainably. Instead of just handing over money or setting an example with its own policies, the new strategy was to lead with IBM's technology and expertise, and to become directly involved in social betterment.

The first target for this activist approach was education. The education systems in America and elsewhere were, for all their successes, under increasing strain. In 1994 the company began working directly with school districts to improve their efficiency and effectiveness—ultimately engaging with 25 districts in the United States and 12 in other countries in a $75 million, multiyear initiative. Also, Gerstner organized the National Education Summit, held in 1996, which was attended by President Bill Clinton, numerous educators and corporate leaders and the governors of all 50 US states. It was the first large-scale education policy meeting convened by a corporation. And it got results. The participants left having arrived at a consensus: to improve public education, accountability would have to be improved. That helped inspire efforts that continue today to measure school performance, as well as initiatives such as charter schools.

This move from philanthropy to direct action has been accelerated by IBM's shift toward the Smarter Planet agenda. The company is integrating its research, business and societal strategies, on the way to devoting 50 percent of its research to Smarter Planet science and discovery.[213] It is spending billions of dollars to help develop smarter systems for government, education, healthcare, energy, food, water and other essential aspects of society's infrastructure. It is applying smarter capabilities and technologies to societal initiatives in new ways—such as the World Community Grid, which harnesses free time on individuals' personal computers to take on big number-crunching research projects, like developing clean energy, finding a cure for HIV/AIDS and formulating more nutritious varieties of rice, a staple in poor areas of the world. And it has systematized and scaled employee volunteerism in pioneering ways—via the On Demand Community, a program that gives more than 150,000 employees and retirees a rich set of software tools and information that they can use to apply their expertise to help their communities. Since 2005, the program has tracked more than 10 million hours of volunteer work. And IBM continues to be

IBM has consistently pursued the large-scale challenges of its time—which often involve issues spanning all of society.

For generations, IBM has been using data to improve healthcare. In 1969, the company helped Dr. Stanley Patten Jr. (above) of Strong Memorial Hospital in Rochester, New York, correlate instances of cervical cancer with urban poverty. Today, the health of premature babies at the Hospital for Sick Children, in Toronto, Canada, is monitored with IBM stream computing technology and advanced analytics research by the University of Ontario Institute of Technology (depicted in this image from an IBM advertisement).

among the most generous, socially responsible corporate contributors, handing out an estimated $185 million in a combination of cash, products and services in 2009.[214] It contributed more than $3 billion from 1986 to 2009.

––––

IN RECENT YEARS, more and more corporations have looked for ways to integrate their business activities and their social efforts—from Salesforce.com's commitment to contribute 1 percent of the company's equity, 1 percent of its products and 1 percent of the employees' time to good causes,[215] to Coca-Cola's help in creating more than 2,500 small businesses employing more than 12,000 people and generating $500 million in annual revenue in hard-to-reach areas of Africa.[216]

Indeed, it's becoming increasingly difficult to tell where a company's self-interest ends and its social responsibility begins. IBM set up its Corporate Service Corps in 2007 as an element of its Global Citizen's Portfolio—a collection of policy and program innovations intended to enable IBMers to be effective twenty-first-century global professionals and global citizens. The CSC in particular aims to develop the skills and experience of a new generation of leaders. It organizes small groups of high-potential IBMers with diverse talents and sends them into developing countries to help craft economic development strategies, beef up government services and improve systems such as transportation and health. In 2010, the company sent 430 potential future leaders and 36 executives on CSC assignments.[217]

In May 2010, IBM sent a team of six executives to Katowice, Poland, to help government leaders develop a plan for revitalizing not just the city but also the entire region of the country. They conducted dozens of fact-finding interviews throughout the region before producing a series of recommendations. During a press conference at the end of the team's three-week visit, Katowice mayor Piotr Uszok, a former engineer who had entered politics after Poland became a democracy, said his view of IBM had changed. Previously, he knew the company only as a well-respected technology leader. "Because of this program, we have seen the other face of IBM," he said. "This firm is not only focused on its own technology projects and making money, but it also helps people and governments function better in the modern world."

Similar things are happening elsewhere. In Vietnam, members of a CSC team mapped out a plan that could help Ho Chi Minh City become one of the most technologically advanced cities in Asia. In Ghana, another team helped local artisans market their crafts globally via a website and connected them with importers in the United States and Europe.

That experience was especially gratifying for one IBMer. Charles Ung, an IBM videographer who works in Vancouver, Canada, was a Cambodian refugee as a child. He was thrown from a boat by pirates into the South China Sea—then saved by his father, who jumped in after him. Ung knows how fortunate he was to survive and to be able to relocate to Canada with his family. "Going to Ghana was important to me. I wanted to make a difference in somebody's life, and IBM helped me do that," Ung said.[218]

The urge to make a difference in another person's life is an impulse as old as humanity itself and is the foundation for charity. But now, by harnessing both the power of capitalism and the will to do good, companies, governments and nonprofits have better opportunities to make progress on seemingly intractable problems such as poverty, disease and environmental degradation. A more prosperous, healthy and environmentally balanced world is a better place to do business, of course, but right now, in the wake of the dot-com bust and the global financial meltdown, these kinds of activities present another opportunity for businesses as well. "We can restore the role of business leaders as some of the most respected members of the community," said Harvard's Rosabeth Moss Kanter.[219]

THIS IS A TIME OF EXPERIMENTATION AND SOCIETAL INGENUITY—both for large corporations and emergent forms of community and business. For instance, global food company Danone has formed a joint venture in Bangladesh with Grameen Group. The new company, called Grameen Danone Foods, produces nutritious yogurt targeted at poor children ages 3 to 8—about 14 million people. Child-size portions sell for 5 and 7 cents. Because one of the company's objectives is to reduce poverty, it sources its ingredients from local businesses and uses local women entrepreneurs as distributors. It's a *social business*—a term coined by Grameen founder and Nobel Peace Prize winner Muhammad Yunus for businesses that plow their operating profits back into expanding their activities rather than returning them to shareholders.

For Danone, the joint venture has three objectives. It helps fulfill Danone's mission of "bringing health through nutrition to as many people as possible." It is a source of inspiration and lessons for other social business projects around the world. And it teaches lessons the company can use in its traditional businesses. For example, the joint venture set up its first factory in Bangladesh for a cost of just $700,000, compared with the more typical cost of up to $20 million for Danone to build a new factory. "Managing a social business forces us to challenge our usual ways, exploring new approaches to doing business," said Corinne Bazina, a Danone employee for 15 years who is the executive director of the Grameen Danone joint venture.[220]

In a speech at Britain's Chatham House in early 2010, Palmisano issued a call to action, urging business and government leaders to band together to take on the world's problems—to use the capabilities now at their disposal to build a smarter planet. His speech was pragmatic, emphasizing the how-to of building smarter systems. Nonetheless, he was unconsciously echoing Thomas Watson Sr.'s admonition in the 1920s that business leaders shouldn't just be doing business; they should be "knitting together the whole fabric of civilization." [221] Thanks in large part to the progress of technology and the evolution of social relations and institutions, including the modern corporation, businesses and governments now have a vast wealth of knowledge about how the world actually works—far more than in Watson's time. "With this knowledge," Palmisano said, "we can reduce cost and waste, improve efficiency and productivity, and raise the quality of everything from our products to our companies to our cities." [222]

Seen this way, the engagement of businesses with society takes on a character that's much more powerful and sustainable than mere altruism. Social engagement becomes the ultimate expression of how a company creates value—for itself, its customers and the world.

•   •   •

The financial shock that struck in late 2008 shook the foundations of the world's banking systems, commercial trade and capital markets, and its effects will doubtless be felt for years to come. But it is merely one manifestation of a deeper shift. Whether we're looking at a natural environment imperiled by climate change or the geopolitics of oil and other resources or threats to security from terror or crime, we can see that the changes that took form over the past century now must coalesce into a new pattern of human enterprise—of the *work* we do, whether in commerce, in governance or in daily life.

Henceforth, work will be global, its value will be based on the quality of thinking, its mode will be collaborative. The organizations that master the new approaches to work will be those with distinctive and enduring cultures. This will be true regardless of how local a business, community or effort may be. This new reality means that we will need to evolve new systems of governance and new institutional forms—to confront the challenges of creating economic growth and societal progress on our shared global commons. The modern corporation will be one of them, building on its innovations of the past century.

As technological advances have made the world smaller, more interconnected and more dynamic, the impact of corporations on the whole of society has grown enormously over the past 100 years. There are only a few things, among them war, revolution and climate change, that can affect the whole of humanity as profoundly as the activities of the organizations that harness the world's resources and talents and put them to work. In this way, companies, along with universities, governments and nongovernmental organizations, can be a driving force for progress—or against it.

Each organization has to find its own way, but IBM's leaders believe that the economic and social pressures of today and the business opportunities ahead will affect most companies sooner or later—and probably sooner. So IBM anticipates a broad, secular shift to come in the way companies define themselves and operate. And it's not enough just to pose the fundamental questions, peer into the murky future and guess what will be required of leaders and organizations 10 and 20 years hence. Leaders have to study the evolution of business, of capitalism and of the modern corporation to understand where they're going. "The thing that ensures that we'll have a future is an awareness of the past," said documentary filmmaker Ken Burns.[223]

The modern corporation will continue to evolve in the twenty-first century. Just as it did when it came into being 100 years ago, it will be shaped by leaders who answer the foundational questions in new ways. How will the organization create value? How will it manage and motivate employees? How will it operate? And how will it engage with society? Because of promising forces now being unleashed, the best corporations of the future have a historic opportunity to create value across all the dimensions of the human enterprise.

• • •

Making the World Work Better
Jeffrey M. O'Brien

M ore than a decade after his fateful operation, Mike May still tends to close his eyes for long stretches of conversations. It's a habit that developed in the weeks and months after he underwent an experimental stem cell procedure to restore his vision. After 43 years without sight, May was suddenly confronted by a torrent of imagery that flooded his navigational system and toppled his understanding of the world. As a blind man, May had been an independent, productive, self-assured member of society. Then he was crippled by vision.[224]

Blinded by a freak chemical accident at age 3, May spent decades making sense of the world using incomplete information. He became an accomplished technologist and inventor of a GPS navigation device for the blind, an avid traveler, a husband and father of two boys and a world-class skier capable of barreling down mountainsides at 65 miles an hour. Regaining sight in one eye (the other was damaged beyond repair) changed everything—and not always in a good way. Many everyday scenarios became too disturbing to bear. People's moving lips, contorted facial expressions, wild gesticulation—they all rendered conversation difficult. Skiing became far more dangerous when complicated by mountaintop vistas, bluebird skies, towering shadows and the appearance of other skiers. So May began closing his eyes to help him concentrate. "I am sure there will come a time when all this visual communication will mean more to me," May wrote in the *Guardian* not long after the operation, "but for now it is just distracting."[225]

As amazing as the procedure was from a medical standpoint, it was just the beginning of the incredible story, chronicled in the best-selling book *Crashing Through*, of a man traveling from self-sufficiency to functional paralysis and back.[226] We don't usually think of seeing as a learned process because it occurs so early in life. But as May's tribulations demonstrate, seeing is a journey in itself. Overload wasn't the only complication. New visual data challenged May's long-held perceptions. Crashing waves were particularly confounding. His ears told him that shorelines were thunderous and intimidating; his vision told him they were soft and peaceful.

May also had to rethink the way the world operates. He always imagined his surroundings in a vectored grid; vision revealed a far messier reality. Interstate highways don't travel north-south and east-west; they curve and undulate with the terrain. He had drawn diagrams of entire airports in his mind to negotiate mazes of boarding gates, escalators, baggage turnstiles and taxi lines. But those maps turned out to be woefully incomplete. They advised him how to get from A to B but ignored much of the complexity—the shops, restrooms, alternative pathways and organized mayhem—in between.

After 43 years of blindness, Mike May underwent a stem cell procedure to restore his vision. The risky operation worked, but the results were far different from what he imagined. Seeing confused everything, overthrew his navigational system and upended his understanding of how the world worked.

May is a man with a vigorous spirit and an impressive desire to do more in life than merely get by. But he's also a metaphor. We're all coping with a barrage of vision. Data is overwhelming our navigational systems and challenging our notions of how the world works. Billions of sensors, cameras, microphones, telescopes, microscopes and mobile phones are constantly capturing streams of information about everything happening around us— the smallest movements, the slightest changes in chemical composition, the subtlest activities at the farthest reaches of space, inside atoms and nearly everywhere in between. May is in a perpetual struggle to reinterpret the world in full awareness. And so are we.

If we can find the meaning in all of the data, the effects will be transformative. Again, May stands as evidence. Like many proud fathers, he holds his wife and two sons above his many other accomplishments. He never imagined that anything could make him love his family more. And then something suddenly did—it was the moment he saw, for the first time in his life, the color of his sons' eyes and the beauty of his wife's smile.

———

WHAT DOES IBM DO? It's a question that many of the company's more than 425,000 employees undoubtedly have encountered.[227] Brand recognition remains strong around the globe, but since selling the personal computer division, the business has become more difficult to explain to casual observers. Financial analysts and the media use categorical shorthand like "software and services," "information technology" or "consulting." And while all of those are at least partly true, they hardly paint a full picture of the company's enduring mission over a century. Chairman and CEO Sam Palmisano has an idea why the question can be so difficult to answer. "We've never defined ourselves by a hit product. From the beginning, the Watsons felt that IBM always had a bigger purpose," he told me at corporate head-quarters in Armonk, New York.[228] "IBM has always been about a culture of innovation and doing things that are profound. We have always tried to make the world work better. And that certainly remains true today."

IBMers make the world work better. It's catchier than "software and services"—but only marginally more enlightening. Perhaps it would help to cite some examples. Over the course of a century, IBM has established itself as an innovation partner for enterprises and institutions around the globe. The company has enabled space travel, and designed social welfare programs, smart electricity grids, travel reservation systems and more efficient supply chains. All of those projects—and hundreds of others—seem to qualify as making the world work better. But what separates them from, say, building a sexier smartphone, which in many people's eyes certainly contributes to a better world?

It's partly a matter of scale. IBM's greatest achievements involve designing and improving the sprawling architectures of our planet. There's a scientific catchall term for these architectures: complex systems. Complex systems are hugely complicated, but that's not what earns them their name. Here, the word *complex* is a synonym for "unpredictable"—or at least not easily predictable. Complex systems comprise thousands or even millions of cooperating parts whose interactions are not linear, but emergent. Working together, they produce surprising outcomes.

You know a complex system when you see one. In fact, they're everywhere. We interact with dozens every day. They exist both in nature and by design and make up the fabric of our lives. A cardiovascular system is the collaboration of a heart and lungs, veins, capillaries, blood and chemicals— all complex systems in themselves—that in turn cooperates with a digestive system, nervous system and so forth to produce a surprising outcome: animal life. Wheat is a combination of roots, stem, leaves, chaff and grain kernel, along with many molecular-level components, all of which interact with sunshine, soil and water to produce the largest source of vegetable protein in the world. An e-commerce website is the front end of a complex retail system that conspires with a supply chain, an energy grid and a financial system to deliver goods and services to customers at the click of a button. The engine, brakes and design of a car; the roads, bike lanes, pedestrians and traffic lights; trains, buses and airplanes—they're all components of a highly complex transportation system that takes us where we want to go.

We'd all like these systems to work better, more efficiently, more sustainably. But how do we get our arms and minds around something as vast as, say, education, much less figure out how to change it? A good start is determining what's wrong. Unfortunately, that alone involves analyzing myriad variables to assess the effect of everything from funding and teacher quality to age of textbooks, emphasis on standardized testing, length of a school day and year, and even nutrition and sleep cycles. Healthcare is worse. Improving overall health would go a long way toward reducing the inefficiency and bloat of our healthcare system (and vice versa). Even tackling one scourge, like childhood obesity, would free up resources to improve other aspects of the system. But where does obesity come from? A morass of factors, including nutrition, economic conditions, agricultural subsidies, self-esteem, pervasive advertising, the quality of public transit, school lunch policies and access to supermarkets, insurance and playgrounds.

Humans can be pretty impressive. Every day we combine observation and experience to navigate a complex world. But generally we're far more aware of symptoms than root causes. Even if we had the time to make sense of something as complex as global warming, we'd be ill-equipped on the strength of our own brain power to consider the relationships among seasonal weather patterns, energy efficiency, aerodynamics, ice cap degradation, pesticide usage, stock market performance and algal blooms. We can't untangle complex systems in our minds, and we can't intuit our way to a better-working world. Computers aren't much better on their own. It's pointless just to plug in a supercomputer in a back room and expect it to make a complex system work better. Computers are processors. They must be augmented with perception, reasoning, cognition and intuition. And that, simply put, is IBM's business. It's been true for a century and remains true today.

Making the world work better is about untangling and managing complexity. Doing so—whether to transform industries, markets, societies or nature—requires serious science. But curiosity and experimentation aren't enough. Solving systemic problems also requires a particular combination of vaulting ambition and profound humility—the level of ambition to tackle seemingly unsolvable problems and enough humility to recognize that no single entity can make the world work better and no single entity can control a complex system. What we're really talking about here is progress, which by definition is communal.

Over the course of more than a year, a small team of researchers and I interviewed dozens of IBM scientists, engineers, executives and partners. We immersed ourselves in the archives in Somers, New York, and studied the arc of the company's business. We were indifferent about how, when or whether IBM made money. Instead, we focused on when and how it has made the world work better. Considering both the company's centennial and the degree of system failure all around us, now seems like a good time to shed light on our findings.

Change is easy. It happens by itself. The universe, operating by the laws of natural selection, is inherently innovative. Progress, on the other hand— the form of innovation practiced consciously by human beings—is deliberate and difficult. But it's not random. Climate, transportation, healthcare and retail may seem to have nothing in common beyond inherent unpredictability. But as it turns out, there is a common path to follow when attempting to manipulate any complex system. Our exploration revealed some key steps on that path. We learned how our predecessors struggled to complete each step in their paths to progress, and we saw how new tools are augmenting our abilities to complete the journey more quickly, safely and inclusively.

Even to start on this path requires inspiration, which can come from many places—from a calamitous event or from a moment of clarity in the shower after 20 years of noodling the same problem. It can be spurred by a work order, a dream or the proverbial pebble in the shoe. But whatever initiates the desire to improve a system, the first step is always the same: seeing.

Seeing is not just about photons hitting a retina. It's about employing all available methods to collect data about a situation. Any complex system churns out massive amounts of information—about what's working, what's broken, about cause and effect. Every element of behavior, every phenomenon is a data point ready to be captured: the march of time, the steps from your desk to the coffee shop, the rotations of a sharp curveball, the radiant energy of a solar flare, the milliliters of oil on the garage floor, the contagion rate of the latest strain of seasonal flu. This data has always existed; what's changing is our ability to capture it.

But without context, data is just noise. To be useful, it must be organized. That's precisely what maps do. A map tells us where we are. It filters irrelevant information, reveals behavioral patterns and presents an argument for what to explore. A map of the galaxy shows Earth's proximity to the other planets and the sun. Calendars segment Earth's orbit into 365 equal parts. The Dewey decimal system categorizes the contents of all knowledge in a library. We've been organizing data in maps for many thousands of years. Now real-time data and visualization tools allow us to create dynamic maps from many points of view, inspiring us not just to explore but also to think.

A map shows when, where and even how often something happens. Understanding is the quest to answer why. Why is Earth the only planet we know of in our solar system capable of supporting life? Why does it take 365 days to orbit the sun—and why is there an orbit in the first place? In the process of understanding, we follow causal chains to determine what levers affect which outcomes. For much of history, this daunting process, which can span many lifetimes and transcend scientific disciplines, has been limited to the work of trial and error. But lately the process has been hastened by more advanced tools designed to help interpret maps, explain mysterious behaviors and virtually test hypotheses. Understanding is where entire fields of science reside, where Nobel Prizes are won and where urgency is born.

We may understand why something happens, but that doesn't tell us what to do about it. There are always many possible paths forward, and history's pioneers are the ones who make the best choices among them. Amid uncertainty, they find belief. Believing is about trusting the analysis and marshaling the will to overcome the status quo. History's greatest believers typically have been charismatic visionaries able to transmit their conviction and mobilize collaborators by force of personality—or force of arms. In more recent times, belief has begun to spread in other ways, particularly through the rigor of the scientific method. Lately, believers of all stripes have become enabled and emboldened by multivariate models, simulations and other visualization tools that allow us all to more effectively predict outcomes.

Last, progress requires putting wisdom and will to work. Even with consensus and a clear view of the future, acting on a complex system is hard. Taking action is not an isolated or solitary event. Sustainable progress requires organization, cooperation, precision and reaction—because our systems are alive and respond to our every intrusion. What's more, "better" is a moving target. As the world has become smaller, our complex systems have become more intertwined. This interdependence has increased the likelihood that breakage in one system will cause damage in others. It's also made it more difficult to fix anything in isolation. But we're not helpless. Increasingly sophisticated tools of networking, collaboration and automation are giving us greater insight into systemic behavior and allowing us to collectively intervene in a timelier, more directed fashion to make our systems faster, more efficient and more sustainable.

These steps, then, constitute a model for how to instigate progress: *seeing, mapping, understanding, believing* and *acting*. IBM has never articulated this model to explain its business, but as you'll see, the company—like many other enterprises, institutions and individuals over the past century—has followed this path in the course of making the world work better. Nearly every one of the dozens of scientists and executives to whom we described it—for short, we wound up calling the model *smuba* (after all, IBMers have a penchant for acronyms)—accepted it as a useful articulation of how systemic progress occurs. Some quibbled with the order, others with the boundaries. Some warned against applying the framework too rigidly. But such is the nature of debating an idea among an inordinately intelligent and accomplished set of actors. I'll attempt to address some of these objections and caveats in the course of this essay.

How Do We Master Complex Systems?

By following a discernible path:

Seeing

Every phenomenon is a set of data points ready to be captured...

Mapping

...and organized in the form of a meaningful map...

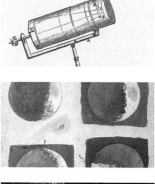

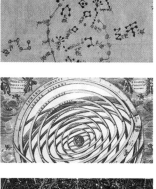

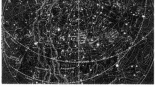

For example:

We built ever more sophisticated telescopes to accurately measure the placement and movement of celestial bodies.

By organizing those measurements, we created detailed maps of our solar system.

Understanding

... which becomes the basis for describing and anticipating complex behaviors ...

Those maps revealed behavioral patterns and spurred us to explore and articulate the laws governing astrophysics, rocket propulsion and space navigation.

Believing

... inspiring confidence that progress is possible ...

Clearer understanding emboldened us to believe it would be possible to send three astronauts to the moon — and to bring them home safely.

Acting

... and enabling forward thinkers to design, build, adapt, optimize and automate the world's systems.

A team of thousands of scientists and engineers collaborated on a historic mission: Apollo 11.

Before we dive into an exploration of large-scale changes in business, society and technology, however, consider a mundane example of progress: changing lanes on a freeway. A commuter is behind a slow-moving truck and eager to make it home in time for dinner. It's the kind of mindless problem solving that many of us engage in every day—but we actually go through the steps of smuba to make it happen.

Seeing: We gather data from the rearview and side-view mirrors. We hear the roar of a motorcycle bearing down from behind. We survey the distance to the truck ahead, notice an available space in a parallel lane and steal a quick glance at the car's blind spots. Mapping: We organize the data within our existing knowledge—our mental maps—of the rules of the road, the typical behavior of car drivers (and bikers), the horsepower underfoot, the upcoming curve of the freeway. Understanding: We combine the variables and anticipate the conditions that will allow us to safely move the car to the adjacent lane and pass the truck. Believing: We decide that, yes, we have the time, power and driving skill, and so the time to act is now. Acting: Flip the blinker, one last check of the data and make the move.

Passing one truck won't achieve the goal. To get home while the food's still hot, we must overcome a whole range of obstacles. Like the components of any complex system, cars on a freeway are in a constant state of flux and so require continual monitoring. Every time we consider another move, we complete the process again. Of course, people change lanes all the time without gathering information—or, sometimes, without any apparent knowledge of the rules of the road. But such behavior is not sustainable. And therefore it is not, in the sense of this essay, progress. A home-cooked meal (or really good takeout) is progress.

The example of changing lanes in freeway traffic illustrates another important point about our interactions with dynamic, complex systems. The path to progress is not about machines; it's about human decisions. In the changing lanes scenario, we have various tools (the car and its mirrors, and our ears and eyes), but we are the actors. Tools and technologies are here to help us, but they're not doing the driving—even if we may soon have automobiles that can do just that. When that day comes, it just means we will have mastered one more system and freed our decision-making minds to focus on bigger challenges.

• • •

Seeing

In the winter of 2010, a team of physicists at the National Institute of Standards and Technology in Boulder, Colorado, unveiled the world's most precise clock. Based on a single atom of aluminum, it ticks a trillion times in the blink of an eye and promises to slip but one second every 3.7 billion years. That's twice the accuracy of the previous record holder and many orders of magnitude better than the most advanced timepiece from 2004.[229]

Why would we ever need such a device? Officially, it's for activities that rely on extreme precision, such as space navigation, syncing telecommunications networks and, maybe one day, hands-free driving.[230] But the more honest answer might be: to be determined. What we do know is that all scientific advance starts with awareness. In the words often attributed to nineteenth-century mathematical physicist William Thomson (also known as Lord Kelvin), "If you can't measure it, you can't improve it." And the more accurate a measurement, the better it is.

Humans have always yearned to see in greater detail. We've built a wide array of tools, from the motion picture camera (left) to the Hubble telescope (above), to help us perceive the behavior of our world.

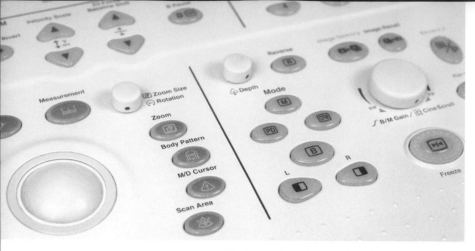

A 3-D ultrasound reveals every dimension of an unborn child.

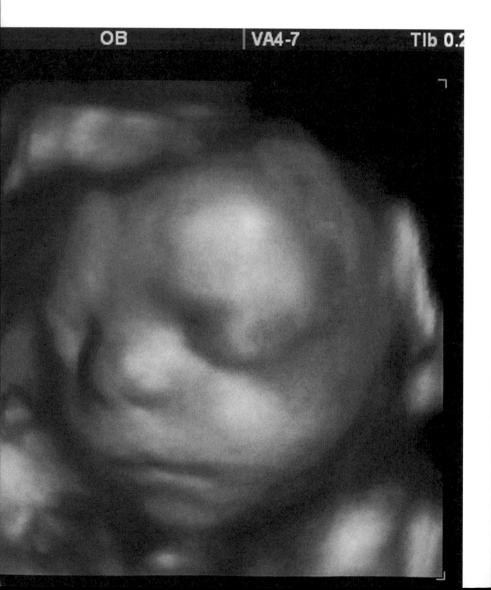

OB   VA4-7   TIb 0.2

The Compact Muon Solenoid (above), which is part of the Large Hadron Collider particle accelerator, records high-energy collisions of subatomic particles, generating data (below) that scientists hope will reveal the conditions that existed just after the big bang.

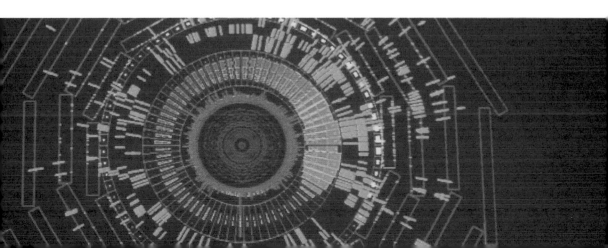

Our ability to assess the world was once limited to our five inborn senses. Then we began devising ways to augment our perception of complex systems by building tools of seeing—and we've worked steadily to increase their number, variety and sophistication ever since. The road to atomic clocks can be traced backward through millennia, from mechanical watches to quartz oscillators to spring-powered timepieces, pendulums, hourglasses and sundials. Similar paths can be drawn for tools that ascertain weight, chemical composition, movement, speed, quantity, ambience and just about any other discernible phenomenon. The earliest thermometers measured fluctuations in temperature but not degrees. In 2009, a team of researchers at the MIT-Harvard Center for Ultracold Atoms developed a thermometer that can measure trillionths of a degree above absolute zero.[231] Microscopes, stethoscopes and telescopes have allowed us to peer farther inward and outward in ever greater detail.

The trend isn't just toward greater precision. It's also about new types of tools that allow us to see behavior and phenomena that were previously invisible. The past century has brought us radar, sonar, lidar, the electron microscope and the condenser microphone. The past few decades have introduced us to GPS, RFID, digital video, chip-sized gyroscopes, fMRI and PET scans, stratospheric telescopes and even high-energy particle accelerators.

IBM has been in the seeing business since before the company even officially existed—using Herman Hollerith's punched card tabulating technology to record US census data in 1890.[232] When Thomas Watson Sr. took over C-T-R in 1914, its primary offerings, along with punched cards, were commercial scales and clocks—tools of seeing.[233] As the century marched on, IBM rolled out a family of related tools, from pencil-mark test scorers and magnetic stripes to the Universal Product Code, a now-ubiquitous barcode that gave rise to a new retail checkout and inventory tracking system, and the scanning tunneling microscope, which earned its inventors, IBM Fellows Gerd Binnig and Heinrich Rohrer, the Nobel Prize in Physics in 1986.[234]

Since then, sensors have infiltrated our natural and man-made systems. GPS chips and accelerometers track location and movement from inside our mobile phones. RFID tags do the same in our supply chains, key chains, running shoes and pets. There are chemical sniffers in airports; digital video surveillance systems in police departments; and biometric identification devices in our gyms. IBM is just one of dozens of companies working to deploy these sensors around the globe in venues as diverse as ski resorts, assembly lines, hospitals, luxury hotels, slaughterhouses and reservoirs. "Sensors are becoming both more sophisticated and less expensive to manufacture and deploy," said Harry Kolar, distinguished engineer for sensor-based solutions at IBM Research.[235] "So, they're proliferating— and they're capturing a lot of data."

Roughly 16 million inertial and magnetic sensors (e.g., accelerometers and compasses) were shipped for use in mobile phones in 2006, according to market research firm iSuppli.[236] Three years later, shipments reached 436 million—a 27-fold increase. By 2014, IC Insights projects that the semiconductor sensor market will be worth close to $6 billion.[237]

Meanwhile, as of 2010, the amount of captured data was growing 60 percent annually.[238] That was due in no small part to these sensors—but let's not forget the influence of the Internet, which encourages everyone with a phone or keyboard to contribute. In the summer of 2010, people around the world were posting to Twitter almost 64 million times daily, uploading more than 90 million Facebook photos and sending 50 *billion* instant messages.[239] According to research firm IDC, the total amount of digital information generated annually crossed the zettabyte level—a trillion gigabytes—for the first time in 2010.[240] That's the equivalent of all the information contained in a stack of DVDs reaching all the way to the moon and back. By 2020, we'll be capturing 35 zettabytes—a stack of DVDs reaching halfway to Mars.

———

WHAT'S IN ALL THAT DATA? EVERYTHING. We're seeing outward in previously unimaginable detail. Scheduled to come online in 2016, the Large Synoptic Survey Telescope will gather 140 terabytes of new data every five days.[241] The largest telescope project in existence today required a decade to gather that much astronomical data—about the same amount of time it took to detect the wobble in a star's orbit indicating the location of Gliese 581g, known as a Goldilocks planet for its Earth-like atmosphere and ostensible ability to support life.[242] "If these are rare, we shouldn't have found one so quickly and so nearby," said University of California, Santa Cruz, astronomer Steven Vogt.[243] "There could be tens of billions of these systems in our galaxy." If so, we'll soon be finding a new Goldilocks planet on the order of one a week. Meanwhile, the National Institute of Standards and Technology is building detectors to measure what happened in the first trillionth of a trillionth of a trillionth of a second after the big bang.[244] And NASA is building inexpensive 2-pound pico-satellites in hopes of opening space research to educational and not-for-profit institutions.[245]

We're seeing all forms of ambience. Our smartphones have become the planet's largest wireless sensor network, capable of monitoring traffic, the dispersion of chemical agents and the spread of everything from viral infections to invasive species. Unmanned drones fly into the hearts of hurricanes.[246] A network of solar-powered treetop video cameras designed by 10- to 12-year-old students in Tahoe City, California, sends real-time video to a central computer monitored by citizen fire watchers.[247] More than 300 sensors on the new span of the I-35 bridge in Minneapolis scrutinize concrete strength, load distribution, expansion, contraction, corrosion, temperature and even strange noises.[248] The Dutch firm Microflown

Technologies has developed microphones the size of match heads that are capable of measuring the movement of individual air particles, identifying the model of an approaching airplane and distinguishing individual voices in a crowd.[249] Shell and Hewlett-Packard have created a million-node sensor network to scout for oil underground.[250] Intel and the University of California, Berkeley, inserted pollution sensors into San Francisco street sweepers to collect block-specific measurements of carbon monoxide, ozone and nitrogen oxide.[251] New Zealand's cattle and deer are now universally tagged with RFID chips to strengthen biosecurity protection and disease tracking.[252] Many of the world's finest wineries have begun using sensor networks to monitor water usage in the vineyards, which is changing their long-held preconceptions of how a plant looks when it's thirsty. "We're training people to stop trusting only their eyes," said Thibaut Scholasch, founder of the California start-up Fruition Sciences, which has installed sensors through-out Napa Valley, "because their eyes can fool them."[253]

We're seeing into our leisure activities at a level of detail that rivals our video game play. The latest McLaren Formula One race car uses sensors to feed 300 data streams to the pit crew describing everything from the driver's heart rate to engine stress.[254] Colorado-based Vail Resorts uses RFID chips embedded in lift tickets to track the total number of vertical feet that visitors ski at six US resorts.[255] Nike+ allows runners with iPods to capture every step they take and every calorie they burn.[256] All Major League Baseball parks are now equipped with Sportvision camera systems, which identify the speed, break and rotation of every pitch at 60 points between the mound and home plate—opening a new window onto baseball for fans and professional coaches alike.[257] An extreme slow-motion video system from I-MOVIX used at the 2008 Summer Olympics in Beijing can instantly replay video at 10,000 frames per second—400 times slower than normal speed—revealing twitches and hiccups in movement that appear fluid to the naked eye. The company's tagline: "When the invisible comes to light."[258]

RFID tags have become small enough—and cheap enough—to record the movements of our world in granular detail. They track infrastructure, productivity, pharmaceutical authenticity and even the whereabouts of our meat all the way from farm to fork.

A collaboration between IBM and Ireland's Marine Institute, the SmartBay project uses sensor-laden buoys to systematically measure and collect regional data in one of the world's harshest coastal environments. That data holds the potential to reduce pollution, increase fishing stock and harness the power of the sea.

We're seeing danger. Ireland's Marine Institute and IBM have deployed sensor-laden buoys in Galway Bay to assess pollution, wind speed, air and water temperature, humidity and wave strength.[259] The FBI is developing ways to identify suspects by footprint, hand geometry and gait.[260] General Electric is working on sensors that change color when exposed to different chemicals.[261] Based on the nanostructure of a butterfly wing, these sensors may one day be attached to clothing, placed in buildings or spread over a landscape.

And we're seeing inward. A scientist at the University of California, San Diego, is printing electrochemical biosensors on soldiers' clothing to allow doctors to remotely monitor blood pressure and heart rate.[262] Researchers at Stony Brook University have designed a sensor chip using nanoparticles to detect cholesterol levels, diabetes and lung cancer by "smelling" a patient's breath.[263] University of Washington researchers have created pill cameras to scan the esophagus.[264] A German microchip allows researchers to gauge the effect of 24 potential cancer medications simultaneously on a patient's own tumor cells.[265] Beth Israel Deaconess Medical Center in Boston is using a hybrid single photon emission computed tomography/X-ray imaging system developed by Philips to pinpoint the location of infections, fractures and tumors. "For the first time, we are able to see the three-dimensional images of metabolic functions, along with the structural images provided by CT," Beth Israel physician Gerald Kolodny told *ScienceDaily*.[266] "Together they allow us to more precisely locate and determine the extent of the disease or trauma."

IBM's lab-on-a-chip, developed at IBM Research in Zurich, can test the blood of a heart attack victim in minutes—heralding a day when doctors perform such tests to quickly discern the best course of action.[267] It can even test for pandemic flu, breast and prostate cancer, and the presence of various poisons and toxins. The DNA transistor may hold even greater promise. It threads DNA molecules through a pore the size of a nanometer in a silicon chip, opening the possibility for every human to have his or her genome sequenced cheaply and quickly.[268] "There is no such thing as a human genome; there are many," said the device's co-inventor, Gustavo Stolovitzky, manager of the IBM Functional Genomics and Systems Biology Group at the Watson Research Center in Yorktown Heights, New York.[269]

"If we can make fast and cheap sequencers, something will happen that's interesting in terms of genetic medicine," said Stolovitzky. "This is an idea that will allow your grandchildren to have personalized medicine."

Together, these tools are unveiling a world that has always existed, but that we were never capable of fully seeing. In effect, they're exposing us to a new reality. Technophiles like to call it augmented reality. "The Internet has changed things because it has allowed us to think with shared memories. We're now able to have collective memory and think using that shared memory," said author and game developer Jesse Schell, in his keynote address, "Seeing," at the Augmented Reality Event 2010. "Augmented reality allows us to see with shared eyes."

• • •

Mapping

Meriwether Lewis and William Clark had their own set of seeing tools when President Thomas Jefferson sent them off on one of the most famous mapping missions in history, from the Mississippi River to what is now Astoria, Oregon. The year was 1804, and, according to the Lewis & Clark Fort Mandan Foundation, the men brought a camera obscura to trace landscape imagery, a chronometer to measure time, an octant for celestial navigation, candle lanterns, sextants, surveyor's chains, circumferentors and compasses.[270] Today, we don't think of Lewis and Clark and their Corps of Discovery as data gatherers. They were explorers on an expedition to map a commercial route to the West Coast.

It's an important distinction. The relationship between data and a map is symbiotic. Without data, there is no map. Without a map, data is largely useless. By organizing information, maps reveal context, proximity, movement, and where we've been, what we know and how

Ptolemy's world map showed our knowledge of geography taking shape.

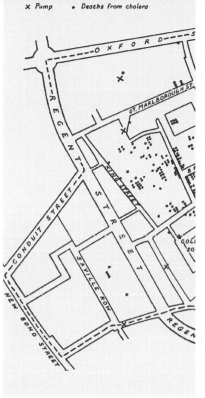

John Snow mapped a cholera outbreak in nineteenth-century London and established the basis for germ theory.

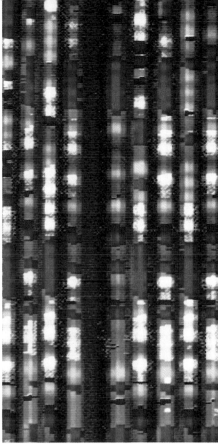

By creating a map of the human genome, we may have revealed the keys to personalized medicine.

The Dewey decimal system provided the basis for library science.

The periodic table organized the relationships of the elements and built a foundation for all of chemistry.

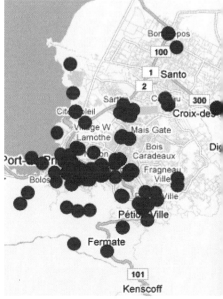

Ushahidi's Haiti map organized text messages to pinpoint trapped victims in the hours after the 2010 earthquake.

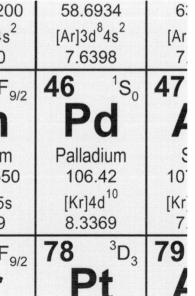

much is left to learn. They inspire further study and exploration, guide development and discovery, and spur action.

When we hear the word *map*, we think geography or maybe politics, but maps, whatever their palette or level of artistry, are, broadly speaking, a means of expressing relationships and logging resources. Recently a team of University of Zaragoza archaeologists found in a Spanish cave what could be the oldest map ever created, a clay tablet with markings for a river, a mountain, adjacent caves, deer and a herd of ibex. "We can't be sure what was intended in the making of the tablet, but it was clearly important to those who populated the cave 13,660 years ago," said researcher Pilar Utrilla in the London *Telegraph*.[271] "Maybe it was to record areas rich in mushrooms, birds' eggs or flint used for making tools." Nine thousand years later, the Sumerians used their clay tablets as early inventory systems, plotting settlements, stars, population and trade en route to establishing the world's earliest known civilization.

To be useful, any map must present data selectively. In the effort to separate signal from noise, a mapmaker decides where to focus and what to omit—which means that all maps have a point of view. Every map is an argument. The ancient Spaniards offered advice in their early map: eat here, sleep there. In the mid-nineteenth century, John Snow, now considered the father of epidemiology, presented one of the most famous arguments in the history of mapmaking after conducting door-to-door interviews and plotting a raging cholera epidemic on a London neighborhood map. More than 10,000 Londoners had died before Snow revealed a concentration of cases around a Broad Street water pump. Until he plotted his findings, no one saw the pattern. With map in hand, city officials shut down the pump and halted the epidemic.[272]

Not all maps organize dire phenomena. Some of the most important maps in history have argued for the best use of resources. The Dewey decimal system and the periodic table of elements—both maps of knowledge created around the time Snow was doing his work—are the foundations of library science and chemistry. One of the earliest modern maps of human resources was created by the Erie Railroad Company in New York in the mid-nineteenth century. An organizational chart establishing accountability from the board of directors down to the passenger, it is widely credited with turning around the fortunes of the company, bolstering the entire railroad industry and providing a staple of modern business.[273]

Then there's the census. Fittingly, IBM's first foray into mapping came in conjunction with its first foray into seeing. The data presented on punched cards for the 1890 US census would have been worthless were it not for the Hollerith Tabulator and Sorter, an early computer capable only of counting and sorting the cards.[274] The company's interest in organizing data has grown unabated ever since. In the first half of the twentieth century, the company was involved in census design and tabulation for dozens of

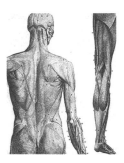

Biological maps have progressed from artistic anatomical drawings like this early musculature diagram (above) to highly detailed renderings of neurology. In 2010, researchers at IBM plotted the neural network of 383 distinct regions of a macaque brain (below).

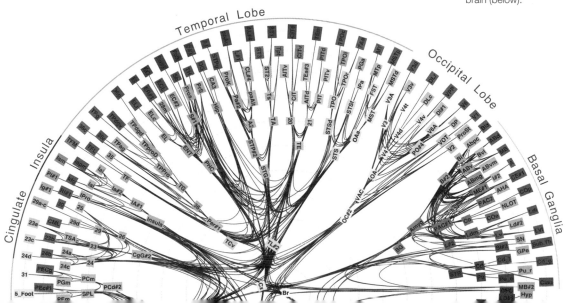

countries, from Australia to Switzerland.[275] In the 1930s, IBM worked with the Social Security Administration to organize the files of 26 million American workers.[276] In the 1960s, IBM scientists created the most precise map of the moon's orbit.[277] Donald Chamberlin and Raymond Boyce gave birth to a new mapping platform when they invented the Structured Query Language, or SQL, the software enabler for most relational databases and now one of the most pervasive and powerful forms of mapping in the world. Not long after SQL, Mitch Kapor created another mapping platform, Lotus 1-2-3, a spreadsheet, charting and database suite. And IBM's forays into mapping continue today. Last summer, IBM researchers in Delhi, India, and San Jose, California, collaborated to create what *Popular Science* called "the most complex neurological map ever seen," plotting the neural network connections among 383 distinct regions of a macaque brain.[278]

———

MAPS HAVE PLAYED AN IMPORTANT ROLE in inspiring change and shaping society. They've also been objects of great contention. The power to map is the power to define—and people fight over that sort of power. Pope Alexander VI established a line of demarcation in South America to differentiate Spanish and Portuguese territory, heavily favoring his native Spain, which is why today Brazil is the only South American country to speak Portuguese. Numerous wars have been waged about where to draw boundaries. They include the so-called Pig War of 1859 between the United States and Great Britain over the San Juan Islands in the Pacific Northwest. And, of course, the enduring conflict between Palestine and Israel is ultimately about the lines on a map.

We know our maps can never be perfect. But we also know that some frameworks, some ideas, some maps are better than others. Some are so good that they change the structure of knowledge and the course of history. Think of when Copernicus's heliocentric map of the heavens replaced the

Ptolemaic picture in which Earth had been positioned at the center of the cosmos. Or consider Sabre, a ticket reservation system that IBM created for American Airlines 50 years ago. At its core, it was a really good map—so good that it became the foundation of modern air travel.

In an era of web-based reservations and mobile phone boarding passes, it's hard to imagine that before 1960, it took a dozen employees almost three hours to book one seat on an airplane. Today, a vacant armrest feels like a gift. Back then, one of every six American Airlines seats was empty due to faulty record keeping. The airline was able to see inventories but couldn't quickly match them to passenger requests, which caused double bookings and unrecorded cancellations and ate into profits. In the company's largest commercial order up to that date, IBM designed Sabre to decrease average reservation times to less than three seconds, strip out millions of dollars of waste, boost the airline's reputation for customer service and increase profits by allowing agents to book hotels, car rentals and connecting flights.[279]

A network of 1,100 ticketing agents in 61 cities would insert paper cards corresponding to a flight into typewriter based consoles. Each agent was able to view a minute-by-minute inventory of all available seats on 1,200 daily flights and book reservations a year in advance. Thanks to the most powerful computer ever deployed for civilian use to that date, agents could also hold seats while customers were on the phone, all but eliminating the double-booking problem. The system started to shed light on customer behavior patterns, segmenting passengers by gender and travel frequency, and began to show ways to more effectively schedule flights and routes based on advanced ticket sales. The number of vacant seats plummeted from 16 percent to 7 percent—the equivalent of $13.5 million in net profits.[280] By 1964, Sabre had saved American Airlines 30 percent in labor costs.[281]

The system served as the basis for similar reservation systems that IBM developed for Pan Am, Delta, Braniff, Continental, Northeast, Eastern, Western Airlines and, later, TWA and United. In 1976, Sabre was installed

Providing the first real-time map of seat availability, Sabre increased profitability for American Airlines and reduced the passenger ticketing process from hours to minutes. Introduced in 1959, it heralded the modern era of web-based travel reservations and gave rise to Sabre's descendant, Travelocity.

in travel agent offices, allowing independent agents to make ticket purchases. In the 1980s, it became accessible to consumers via online systems such as CompuServe and GEnie. By 1996, Sabre had become an independent company and launched Travelocity.com, which brought the benefits of the system directly to the public.[282]

Today, the early Sabre system seems quaint compared with the real-time maps enabled by more powerful and ubiquitous computers, speedier networks and unlimited data. The introduction of GPS-generated maps like MapQuest and Google Maps in the mid-1990s has meant never having to ask for directions again. Now that those maps exist on mobile phones, continually updating traffic and accident information, we've been robbed of the classic excuse for being late. In early 2011, Dutch navigation company TomTom unveiled what it calls "the largest historic traffic database in the world." It spans the entire European and US road networks and includes more than 3 trillion measurements gathered from actual car movements (with 3.5 billion more added daily), making it possible to quickly analyze historical travel times and speeds on any road over any period at any time of day.[283] Shoe and clothing retailer Zappos.com presents each order, including style information and destination, on a publicly available map at the moment it's processed.[284] Breathing Earth logs birth and death rates and tracks population in real time while continually updating global carbon dioxide emissions (roughly 100,000 tons during the time it took to write that last sentence).[285]

The Internet has also greatly increased everyone's ability to access, interpret and depict raw data. With more than 10 million articles in 273 languages, Wikipedia could be seen as a simple content repository— but the online, interlinked and organized inventory of expertise is actually one of the most successful emergent, open-source maps ever created, much more than the sum of its data inputs.[286] Crisis-mapping website Ushahidi allows anyone to gather and map data via SMS, e-mail, voicemail or Twitter. In the hours and days after the disastrous 2010 Haiti earthquake, Ushahidi

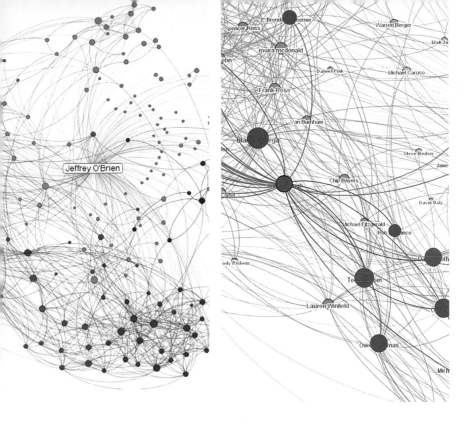

Today's maps are dynamic, collaborative and often created with a few clicks of a mouse. For example, LinkedIn Maps graphically depict relationships among a user's professional associations (left), revealing patterns that wouldn't be obvious in a mere list.

provided contextualized information about (among many other things) infrastructure damage, security threats, fires, fallen bridges, incidents of trapped victims and available services, providing a window onto the devastation for rescue workers that no army of helicopters or news crews could match.[287] "Live maps provide a new level of what the military would call situational awareness," said Patrick Meier, director of crisis mapping and new media at Ushahidi. "Now anyone can say, 'I was here, this is what I saw, this is my story,' and that presents a living representation of what's happening in the world. They say the pen is mightier than the sword. Well, a map can be mightier than the pen."[288]

With a few clicks of a mouse, social networking site LinkedIn allows any user to create a map of his or her professional associations, revealing patterns that are imperceptible in a mere list. San Francisco-based start-up Yelp taps into the opinions of millions of foodies and bar hoppers in dozens of US cities to provide an up-to-the-minute map that includes crowdsourced reviews of everything from doctors and plumbers to restaurants and hotels. Eat here, sleep there. Last year, New York City's Department of Information Technology & Telecommunications introduced the web-based NY

CityMap, which shows everything from infrastructure quality to the deployment of stimulus funding. "You can bring up the year the building was built, the square footage and any violations [or even] restaurant inspection information," Nicholas Sbordone, the DoITT's director of external affairs, told *Government Technology*.[289] "There's a whole host of things you can do just by looking at particular locations."

In 2007, IBM created its own open mapping platform. The web-based research project Many Eyes provides intuitive data visualization tools to the masses. It has attracted a diverse group of people looking to gain insight into (and make their own arguments about) proprietary and public data alike, including a community of Bible enthusiasts intent on exploring the relationships among the characters of the New Testament. They've plotted the links between every proper name, creating, in effect, a biblical social network. It's a perfect example of how the combination of readily available data and a collaborative environment encourages people to look at the things they care about in new light. "Data visualization takes on a life of its own when you allow people to explore," said Joan DiMicco, an IBM Research manager who works on Many Eyes at the Visual Communications Lab in Cambridge, Massachusetts. "They use it as a means of personal expression."[290]

A November 2010 *New York Times* article highlighted a trend among humanities researchers who are increasingly using such tools to, for example, digitally map Civil War battlefields in hopes of explaining the relationship between topography and victory, or dissect the influence of musical collaborations on jazz jam sessions. Brett Bobley, digital director of the National Endowment for the Humanities, told the *Times* that a wealth of data and user-friendly mapping tools will do for the humanities what it has already done for the hard sciences.[291] "Technology hasn't just made astronomy, biology and physics more efficient," he said. "It has let scientists do research they simply couldn't do before." Tom Scheinfeldt, managing director of the Center for History and New Media at George Mason

University, added that humanities research has moved into "a post-theoretical age" or "'methodological moment' similar to the late nineteenth and early twentieth centuries, when scholars were preoccupied with collating and cataloging the flood of information brought about by revolutions in communication, transportation and science."

No single scientific discipline has benefited more from our ability to gather and map data than genomics. When the US Department of Energy and the National Institutes of Health started the Human Genome Project in 1990, the organizations stated a number of official goals, including identifying all of the roughly 25,000 genes in human DNA, sequencing its 3 billion chemical base pairs and storing the information in databases.[292] The real goal, of course—the reason Craig Venter and Celera Genomics joined the race to sequence the genome—was both grander and more opportunistic. On one hand, decoding the genome could reveal who is predisposed to certain diseases and afflictions and enable a new age of personalized medicine. On the other, genetics-based healthcare could also open up whole new industries and bring in billions of dollars in profits.

"The first step was synthesizing the genome, and it took almost 15 years for this process. One of the things we discovered is that DNA is really the software of life," Venter said in June 2009 at the opening of the UCSF Helen Diller Family Comprehensive Cancer Center. "Another is that averages mean absolutely nothing. The model of giving the same drug to a large number of people and having it only work on a segment of the population—that has to change. The only limitation is how little we know about how to read the genome. Having one or two copies doesn't give us new knowledge. It gives us the basis for getting knowledge. Literally, tens of thousands of genomes are going to be done in the very near future. We're going to be swamped with information. The challenge is converting information to understanding."

• • •

Understanding

Data reflects behavior. Maps provide context. Seeing and mapping together paint a decent picture of what, where, when and even how. "Converting information to understanding," as Venter put it, is the process of figuring out why. It's following the chain from cause to effect. This quest can easily occupy a life's work. It's where entire bodies of science reside. It's insanely demanding. Sustainable, replicable progress is impossible without it.

There are obvious shortcuts through smuba. We can change lanes on the freeway based on a quick look over the shoulder. Even when dealing with complex systems, one piece of data can spur action. A water main break floods the streets and endangers an entire city block—the first order of systemic improvement is to fix the pipe. At other times, a bit of context will suggest a course of action. Snow's cholera diagram revealed an obvious stopgap: close the pump. But sustainable improvements require a deeper knowledge of how a system operates.

In Snow's mind, his map revealed sewage-tainted water as the source of cholera and so served as evidence of his nascent theory about how diseases spread (via microorganisms, transmitted in this case by water). City officials saw the same pattern around the well but considered it

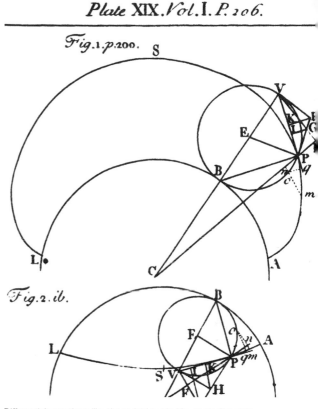

Any model is an attempt to understand complex behavior. Physical models, such as this early glider being tested by the Wright brothers, are invaluable but can be very expensive and often come with great risk.

Differential equations like those laid out in Newton's *Principia* remove risk by establishing relationships and solving for future states—but they're only as good as our mathematical knowledge.

Thanks to enormous processing power, simulations now allow researchers to repeatedly model complex behaviors and determine likely outcomes at a scale never before possible. The above protein folding simulation, performed on a supercomputer at the National Energy Research Scientific Computing Center, shows folding configurations for 156 different proteins.

proof that disease spreads via miasma (poisoned air). They took the right action for the wrong reason because they didn't understand the cause. Snow didn't give up, of course. He went on to discredit miasma as well as Aristotle's theory of spontaneous generation, and his insights became the basis for germ theory. Today, he's remembered for the cholera map, sure, but his true place in history is as the father of epidemiology. This story demonstrates how powerful a good map can be even when it doesn't explain much. Snow's map halted a disease and most likely saved thousands of lives. But the result of Snow's process of understanding—germ theory—is the cornerstone of modern medicine and has unquestionably improved and saved billions of lives.

Now let's look at how the process of understanding has transpired in a few key innovations and industries over the past hundred years—and explore how that process is being hastened by new technological tools.

American geneticist Norman Borlaug received the Nobel Peace Prize, the Presidential Medal of Freedom, the Congressional Gold Medal and the National Medal of Science, among many other honors, before dying of lymphoma in 2009 at age 95. His work developing new strains of high-yield wheat earned him the moniker "father of the Green Revolution," and by some estimates he is responsible for saving millions of lives and billions more acres of farmland.[293] Even posthumously, Borlaug remains a controversial figure for his advocacy of non-organic fertilizers. Nonetheless, his work stands as one of the great scientific achievements of all time, so it's instructive to look at how his process of following a causal chain changed agriculture as we know it.

In 1944, when Borlaug joined the Rockefeller Foundation's Cooperative Wheat Research and Production Program in Mexico, various scourges were destroying the world's wheat crops. China, India and Pakistan were on the verge of large-scale famine. Mexico suffered three stem-rust epidemics in the five years prior to his arrival. Fears were mounting that mass starvation would kill hundreds of millions and that India would never sustain itself.

In three short decades, due in large part to Borlaug's work, India and Pakistan became self-sufficient. By 2001, Indian wheat production had more than quintupled to 75 million tons. Pakistan saw similar gains, increasing output from 4.5 million to 22 million tons. Bangladesh, Turkey, Mexico and Zimbabwe all increased their yields two- to fourfold.[294]

In the simplest terms, Borlaug was a latter-day Gregor Mendel, who in the late nineteenth century spearheaded modern genetics by crossbreeding pea plants in hopes of understanding why characteristics sometimes skip generations. Rather than peas, Borlaug mixed a tall and slender wheat plant with Japanese dwarf strains to create a smaller, stiffer breed that could respond better to fertilizer, resist rust and increase yield, all without falling over from increased grain weight. It was backbreaking work. He spent days in the fields using tweezers to remove the male stamen from plants to keep them from self-pollinating. He would bag the heads to protect them from airborne pollen and then manually pollinate the plants. He'd replant the seeds and their progeny repeatedly until the characteristics of the parents began to show, usually in the fourth or fifth generation. Each time, he'd measure and log plant height and weight, stalk size, grain load, maturity at flowering, harvest date, yield, color, seed plumpness and a variety of other variables such as leaf shape, height and curvature.[295] "It was a hugely complex logistics exercise, and he did it all before the age of computers," said Noel Vietmeyer, a former National Academy of Sciences senior program officer who has written a biography of Borlaug.[296] "He would have millions of plants per season, and if any didn't match up to the combinations he was trying to achieve, he just yanked them out."

To increase the data haul, Borlaug pioneered a process he called shuttle breeding, sowing two generations of plants in separate locations over a growing season, one at an altitude of nearly 7,000 feet near Mexico City and another closer to sea level in the northwest.[297] Along with doubling output, Borlaug's method unwittingly created a variety capable of thriving in both rain-fed, low-fertility soil at high altitudes and in well-irrigated, higher-

Norman Borlaug, father of the Green Revolution, plots his observations in an effort to create a heartier wheat cultivar. He used a pair of tweezers to remove the male stamen from plants to create a new strain of dwarf wheat.

fertility soil near sea level. He exposed the varieties to different day lengths and diseases—stem and leaf rust in one location, rust and leaf blotch in another—to increase the plant's viability worldwide. The transportation issues alone were daunting. "At the beginning there were virtually no roads. He had to travel 1,000 miles, with only a month to finish harvest at one location, get the seeds packed, cleaned, treated with fungicide and dried, and then get to the next place and plant them before the season was over," Vietmeyer said. "It was just horrendous."

Borlaug also encountered challenges of his own making. Living in a pre-digital world, he logged statistics in a three-ring binder. One day at the end of the season, he and a colleague broke for lunch. "They put the notebook down on a pile of corn leaves and a dust devil flew up and lifted the notebook into the air," Vietmeyer said. "The pages went drifting off—all their year's work. After that Borlaug used big books that were clamped with metal screws."

Borlaug's quest to determine what variables affect vigor and yield obviously would have benefited greatly from a laptop and a spreadsheet. A map of the wheat genome would have allowed him to make connections at the genetic level. But those tools would arrive too late. "He didn't even know about DNA. That didn't come up until 1953. He had been running 16 cycles before he knew there was a double helix," Vietmeyer said. "He was just working from observation. Knowing what a gene was and where it was, and being able to transfer it, that was simply beyond his imagining."

Today's plant breeders don't have to imagine. We've sequenced many crop genomes in the past decade, including grape, rice, wheat, soy and canola. Last fall, confectionary manufacturer Mars Incorporated released the cacao genome to the public domain after a two-year sequencing effort that involved collaboration with IBM and several academic and government partners. Howard-Yana Shapiro, global staff officer of plant science and external research at Mars, originally approached IBM for help, hoping that a sequenced genome would aid the quest to boost the yields of the cacao tree—which produces cocoa beans, the source for chocolate—and keep it from falling prey to disease.[298]

The agricultural revolution passed by the humble cacao tree. Total production has doubled over the past 20 years or so, but only at the expense of vast stretches of tropical forests that were razed to plant more trees. Meanwhile, more than $600 million of crop value is lost every year to disease and drought. And the West African region that now accounts for 70 percent of the world's cacao production is considered highly susceptible to a fungal attack like the one that destroyed Brazil's crop in the 1980s.[299] Were that to happen, we could be facing life in a chocolate-free world.

Mars has an obvious interest in defusing this ticking time bomb. So Shapiro decided to follow Borlaug's lead. He wasn't solely interested in understanding the keys to disease resistance. He also wanted to find a way to breed trees that would produce higher-quality chocolate, adapt to climate change and increase yields for the economic benefit of the cacao farmers globally. Only problem: there's no time to untangle the relationships among cacao trees, climactic growing conditions and human taste. Borlaug didn't have the benefit of today's technology, but he did have the luxury of working with a fast-growing plant. The cacao tree grows at a snail's pace. Developing a new cultivar the traditional way takes at least a decade.

Howard-Yana Shapiro of Mars Incorporated is using a map of the cacao genome to create a higher-yielding, disease-resistant tree—and better-tasting chocolate.

Shapiro knew that by mapping the 415 million base pairs that make up the cacao genome and releasing it to the scientific community, he could hasten the process of understanding and spur development. By starting in the labs, he figured he could reduce the time it takes to breed a new cultivar to less than three years. But first he'd need help creating a map.

Shapiro visited IBM's Almaden research facility, where he met with IBM Fellow and vice president Mark Dean. "It was one of the most enlightened conversations I've ever had in my life," Shapiro recalled. "I said, 'We need your computational biology and pattern recognition software. IBM's the best in the world.' He looked at me and answered immediately: 'Yes.'"

Dean recognized that the project was important not only for its cultural and economic significance, but also because it would be a learning tool. "Cacao is a very fragile crop. It's hard to harvest and needs near-perfect conditions to grow. The goal is to determine which sequences affect yield, drought tolerance, et cetera, and find enough information to make the plant more sustainable," Dean told me shortly after the project was announced.[300] "We hope to find variants that are better at resisting certain diseases. Why is this variant resistant and this one not? There's also evidence that the flavonoids in cocoa have some health benefits. We hope to figure out why. And I'd love to find a variant that would grow beyond the equator. It would be great to grow cacao in Florida."

With IBM on board, Shapiro gathered a team of some of the world's best plant scientists, molecular biologists, geneticists and computer scientists from Mars, the US Department of Agriculture's Agriculture Research Service, Clemson University, Indiana University, Washington State University, University of California, Davis, National Center for Genomic Resources, PIPRA, HudsonAlpha Institute and Roche. The "uncommon collaboration," as Shapiro calls it, announced the project in June 2008 with a goal of sequencing the genome in five years. By September 2010, they had finished— three years early. Now comes the hard part. "It's not just the sequencing that's important, but the analysis of what genes do what," Dean said. Such analysis could have huge benefits not just for cacao. Pineapples, for example, are equally finicky, and could also benefit. So could the worlds of pharmaceuticals and finance. "There's a lot of commonality in computational methods," Dean said.

Shapiro is thinking about ramifications that extend far beyond industry or tastier candy bars. He sees a dotted line from a map of the cacao genome to an improved quality of life for cacao farmers around the world. "We identified genes responsible for disease resistance, fat content, flavor characteristics, nutrient use efficiency and tree architecture, and we're at the beginning of understanding their interactions. This is all about translating science into actions," he said. "Imagine if you could get three times as much yield from one-third as many trees. We'll use less land and diversify the crops in the region. A socially responsible, environmentally sound cacao production model could help stabilize the rural economies of West Africa and East Asia. That will be a really green revolution."

———

IF A MAP DEPICTS RELATIONSHIPS, then understanding deconstructs them. This is hardly a practice reserved for scientific researchers. For as long as there has been capitalism, companies have yearned to better understand their customers, and entire industries have recently been spawned to help, including customer relationship management, business intelligence, business process management and online analytical processing. Some of the world's biggest technology companies, including HP, Oracle, SAP and SAS, have significant interests here. Online advertising and even web searching boil down to connecting customers and data, and so Google, Microsoft and Yahoo must also be included. And, of course, IBM has a healthy presence. During the past decade, the company has repeatedly demonstrated its belief that data analysis is the wave of the future, spending more than $12 billion to acquire companies with expertise in data analytics, including Cognos, Coremetrics, ILOG, Maximo, MRO Software, Netezza, SPSS and Unica.

Each of these companies operates in a different niche, but they all have some roots, perhaps somewhat surprisingly, in the pre-Internet catalog boom of the late 1980s and early '90s and a company called Fingerhut. "That was the beginning. Fingerhut perfected database marketing. They said, 'If I take all my historical data, can I combine it to build a model that will predict who's likely to buy what next?'" said Chidanand Apte, director of analytics research at IBM's Watson Research Center.[301] Fingerhut began segmenting its database and mailing tailored versions of its catalogs to customers in

25 categories. Upon further exploration, the cataloger began seeing links from shopping habits to creditworthiness and ultimately parlayed those insights into risk-assessment tools and a credit card business. (Federated Department Stores ultimately acquired the catalog company for $1.7 billion in cash and debt, largely on the strength of its database marketing operation.[302])

Fingerhut's knack for mining its data to anticipate future behavior was hardly unprecedented. Sellers have always used anecdotal information to persuade customers to buy more stuff. But the cataloger was among the first to scale a shopkeeper's instinct across millions of customers. Now companies across all industries are modeling customer behavior to make predictions in real time. Amazon.com differentiated itself from other e-retailers early by recommending items based on past purchases. (If a shopper liked Coldplay's *Viva La Vida*, then Amazon might recommend Stieg Larsson's *The Girl with the Dragon Tattoo*.) Microsoft's search engine Bing analyzes millions of itineraries every time a customer searches for a flight and handicaps the likelihood that the fare will increase.[303] Dating site eHarmony scrutinizes the tastes and communication habits of 33 million users to find compatible love interests—and claims to be responsible for more than 500 marriages every day in the United States alone.[304] Musahino Red Cross Hospital in Tokyo analyzes 400 key characteristics of hepatitis and has identified more than 100 infection patterns. By assigning patients to the appropriate group, the hospital is better able to recommend personalized drug treatments and has boosted extermination rates from 50 percent to 77 percent. Netflix predicts how each of its more than 16 million customers will rate 100,000 movies on a five-star scale.[305] Music site Pandora examines 400 musical attributes for hundreds of thousands of songs and matches them against millions of pieces of user feedback to create customized online radio stations dynamically for 80 million users.[306] And Zillow studies 60 million real estate transactions to determine the market value of a house. The accuracy of its Zestimates varies greatly and is somewhat controversial among the brokerage and appraiser communities—which speaks both to the enormity of the task and to the idea's power to overturn the status quo. "We're trying to lift the veil off what has always been an opaque market and to understand and predict where it's headed," said Zillow cofounder and executive chairman Richard Barton.[307] "If Zillow can untangle the reasons why the market does what it does, we can provide a new value to home buyers and sellers."

Modeling isn't just for figuring out consumers' desires. Given enough processing power, it can show companies how to build better products and processes. Goodyear Tire & Rubber Company simulated and virtually tested models for the first time in 2004, a process that led to a "flurry of new tires that resulted in record profits," according to a recent report by the National Science and Technology Council. Aluminum manufacturer Alcoa virtually redesigned beverage cans and various components in the automotive, aerospace and construction industries. Golf club manufacturer Ping cut design cycles from 24 months to 8 months while producing five times as many products as a result of working with predictive models designed by the Lawrence Livermore National Laboratory.[308] In 2009, IBM began working with the island of Malta to deploy the world's first nationwide smart energy and water grid. Smart meters reduce load by providing customers near real-time consumption data on the energy and water they're using and decrease waste by helping pinpoint leakage. But the nation's energy and water utilities are also counting on the meters to provide greater insight into the links between weather patterns, tourist traffic and overall demand. It's always cheaper to plan for usage spikes than to react to them. This is especially important on an island whose energy is derived exclusively from imported fossil fuels and where half of all consumed water comes from seawater treated through the energy-intensive process of reverse osmosis.

Predictive models are also emerging as powerful tools to anticipate breakage. Manufacturers dole out tens of billions of dollars in warranty payments a year.[309] Knowing when and how a product will fail would not only save money but also improve the safety of workers and customers. This is what a Tennessee start-up called Vextec is attempting to do. Funded in part by the Defense Advanced Research Projects Agency and using a database of the world's known metals, ceramics, composites and plastics, Vextec has developed a way to predict the durability, performance and lifetime cost of machine parts by understanding the behavior of their component materials. Working for clients ranging from the US Navy to medical device manufacturers, the company simulates the workings of turbine blades, automotive axles and other machine components to reveal how various metals behave under differing levels of stress. "The problem that all industries face is that products come off the assembly line looking good, but they fail prematurely," said Loren Nasser, the company's CEO and cofounder.[310] "Product development has always been a trial-and-error process. Failure incurs bad press, warranty costs, recall costs and the loss of consumer confidence. That's what we're trying to change."

CAD software has made usage simulation possible on personal computers for years. But rather than just virtually swinging a tennis racket 250,000 times, Vextec breaks the racket down into 250 million particles and simulates stress on each particle for each of the 250,000 rackets a manufacturer will make in a given year. The company's proprietary core simulation algorithms are written in Fortran, the classic programming language invented at IBM in the 1950s, because, as Vextec vice president Frank Priscaro said, "nothing handles math quite like it—as old-time IBMers will know."[311]

Vextec's business is based on a materials library that was digitized thanks to recent advances in computational processing, such as cloud computing. Combine that information with a client's usage data, and insights begin to emerge. "As manufacturers gather more data about what they've made—from sensors, from statistical analysis, from usage profiles—our software gives them a way to make sense of it," Priscaro said. "If you know when a component is about to go, you can take steps to minimize the impact.

So things like airline maintenance will be far more efficient because they won't be guessing about how long their parts will last, or taking them out of service prematurely. They'll know."

Alcoa. Amazon. eHarmony. Goodyear. Netflix. Vextec. Zillow. These companies don't appear to have much in common. But in the back rooms, they and thousands of other enterprising companies are trying to do the same thing—to make sense of what was once written off to unpredictable behavior. By gathering, organizing and analyzing the data generated by complex systems, they're untangling the chain of cause and effect, finding rationality and reason in what was always considered chaos.

———

NO SYSTEM IS MORE MISUNDERSTOOD and more inextricably linked to our well-being than the human body. IBM works with many of the companies mentioned above and is involved in simulating everything from localized weather to nuclear stockpiles. But some of the company's most interesting modeling work is being done in an effort to make sense of what happens inside our bodies. Doing so will have obvious implications for our well-being, but it will also undoubtedly create ripple effects in many interdependent systems, from agriculture to retail to, of course, healthcare.

Treating the more than 33 million people infected with HIV/AIDS has typically involved as much guesswork as science. Controlling symptoms requires a combination of three or more anti-retroviral drugs, collectively referred to as a drug cocktail. But the proper combination of drugs varies according to the progression of the disease in the individual, as well as the patient's physiology and receptiveness to certain chemicals. Until recently, there were just two common methods to divine the most effective cocktail. Phenotypic testing involves performing in vitro tests on a blood sample to see how the virus reacts to different drugs. This approach is expensive and requires special equipment and a lot of time, which relegates it primarily to the research community.

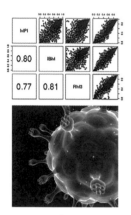

The web-based modeling tool EuResist uses the world's largest HIV database and three prediction engines to determine the probability (table above) that a drug cocktail will be effective for a patient. Personalized recommendations have proven more than 76 percent accurate— beating human experts 9 out of 10 times.

The more common clinical approach, the genotypic method, involves matching mutations from a blood sample to published scientific research and using the closest match to prescribe the cocktail. This process is scalable, cheaper and faster than phenotypic testing, but it considers only the DNA of the virus. Ignoring drug interaction and patient clinical data increases the chances that a physician will prescribe the wrong combination, which causes painful side effects and can augment the virus's already impressive knack for developing immunity. "The problem now is that the HIV virus is very smart," said Yardena Peres, a manager for healthcare and life sciences at IBM's research facility in Haifa, Israel.[312] "It replicates itself and generates variants that are not affected by the drugs anymore. Doctors have to be very careful to avoid making the virus resistant to the available drugs."

Peres is one of several IBM researchers contributing to an online modeling project called EuResist, which provides doctors with a tool to simulate various drug combinations virtually. Originally funded by the European Union, EuResist is now a nonprofit collaboration composed of the Karolinska Institute, the Max Planck Institute, the University of Siena, Informa s.r.l. and the University of Cologne, with support from the IBM Research Haifa team. The project uses IBM's DB2 software to house the largest HIV database in the world, comprising 50,000 records of AIDS patients from Belgium, Germany, Italy, Luxembourg, Spain and Sweden dating back to 1996. "Having a large database is crucial, since the analytic methods require large data sets," Peres said. "The idea is to exploit the knowledge lying in the data, and learn from past experience about what treatments were successful and what treatments failed."

The web-based EuResist tool allows doctors to input patient data and receive a recommendation for the optimal cocktail. Recommendations have proven more than 76 percent accurate—beating human experts 9 out of 10 times. "EuResist not only outperforms other prediction systems, it also outperforms doctors who are experts in HIV," Peres said.

Now is a good time to explain how a prediction engine like EuResist's works. First, a definition: any model is an abstraction from reality, a construct that helps us get our minds around what's happening in a complex system. In some cases, these models are physical, like a wind tunnel or a product prototype. Then there are nonphysical predictive models, like the one used by EuResist. These require less in the way of physical labor, materials and time, but more in the way of mathematics.

We don't need computers to build predictive models. In the days before computers, a predictive model would comprise a set of mathematical formulas, typically differential equations, which described the components of the system and the dynamic relationships among them. Scientists would analytically solve the equations to obtain predictions about behavior. Newton's second law of motion, $F = ma$, is a familiar example. By describing the relationship of force to mass and acceleration, it allows us to predict future states of a physical system. So if we know the thrust and mass of a rocket, for example, we can predict its acceleration—and, as a result, its location over time.

Mathematical models of the past were limited by the need to keep them simple enough to solve analytically. But more recently, great amounts of processing power—in the form of a supercomputer or cloud computing— have lessened the need for elegance while simultaneously increasing the ability to understand highly complex scenarios. "You can often replace human cleverness with brute force CPU power using computer simulation," said Peter Haas, one of IBM's foremost modeling and simulation researchers at Almaden.[313] Because their underlying rules aren't as precise, simulations can generate highly unlikely outcomes. But run them repeatedly and erroneous conclusions tend to fall to the far ends of the bell curve. "In the old days, you had mathematicians and statisticians coming up with sophisticated formulas, but nowadays you can keep generating new data or re-sampling existing data in relatively simple ways to make predictions in situations where analytical techniques don't suffice. And the more simulations I do, the better my answer is going to get."

As Haas noted, today's computers aren't just processing real-world data, they're actually generating it. To learn how this happens I visited William Pulleyblank, a recently retired Watson researcher who has started a new career as a mathematics professor at the United States Military Academy at West Point.[314] "Computers are having an impact on science and business in two key areas. One part is when you have the data to analyze," he said. "The second part is where you don't have much data, but you have to understand it anyway. That's where supercomputing often makes the biggest contribution."

There are times when we can't obtain data. Sometimes it's just too dangerous to do so, as with testing nuclear bombs via actual explosions. Sometimes, waiting for data to arrive is self-defeating, such as while following the spread of a highly infectious disease. And other times, we just can't get into the spaces where the behavior is occurring. By way of example, Pulleyblank offered the story of Blue Gene, the protein-folding simulation project initiated in 1998 that used the eponymous Blue Gene/L supercomputer and the principles of molecular dynamics.

Proteins are the basis of all biology. Our bodies comprise various systems—cardiovascular, respiratory and so forth—which are in turn made of organs. These organs contain cells, which rely on proteins. Before proteins conjoin as part of a cell membrane, for example, strands of amino acids must assemble into a three-dimensional form and become a protein. This process is called folding. Until recently, protein folding had been entirely mysterious—but we knew it was important because we have been able to discern patterns that link misfolding to all kinds of diseases, including Alzheimer's and many types of cancer. The reason to simulate protein folding, then, should be obvious. If we can understand the process, perhaps we can figure out why it goes wrong and increase our ability to predict and prevent such occurrences. But how do we understand a process that takes 1/1,000th of a second and happens at the molecular scale?

Blue Gene used 200,000 processors and a type of simulation called molecular dynamics, which enables algorithms to express the rules of molecular biology, physics, physiology, chemistry and other associated bodies of science, to march forward in time and anticipate how a protein goes from step A to B to C, and so on. "Suppose you wanted to know how *Avatar* ended, but I only gave you the first 60 frames of the movie and told you that everything follows logically from that. You need to reconstruct the movie frame by frame. That's what we do," Pulleyblank explained. Those 60 frames represent our basic knowledge of cellular and subcellular biology. "We start by knowing the atoms that make up the protein and knowing about the molecules that surround it. You look at each pair of atoms and determine whether they attract or repel each other. Determining where a single atom is headed depends on the forces of all the other atoms present. We need to figure out the force that each one exerts and, based on that, predict where this atom will go next. This has to be a tiny movement—if you take tiny steps, nothing gets lost—and that creates a second frame of my movie."

A typical large protein contains several thousand atoms. To simulate its behavior in the environment of the body, the protein needs to be virtually tossed in water, which requires calculating the interactions of approximately 32,000 atoms on each other—the total combined number of atoms in the protein and the surrounding water molecules. That's roughly 1 billion interactions. Computing the interaction of any pair of atoms requires 150 calculations (or floating-point operations). So moving from one frame to the next—called a time step—requires 150 billion calculations. Each time step is about one femtosecond long, and there are 200 billion femto-seconds in the roughly one millisecond it takes a protein to fold. That's a lot of calculations—3×10 to the power of 22, to be exact. "There's no name that makes sense for that number," Pulleyblank said. "It would take 1 quadrillion floating-point operations per second for a full year to do it. And, by the way, the same protein may fold differently each time. So we'd like to do this thousands of times for each protein."

Computing power has clearly advanced since Blue Gene began its work, as have some of the methodologies of molecular dynamics. Researchers have discovered ways to simulate proteins in a week or two, but Blue Gene is a great example of how simulations start. Shortcuts are much easier to find after we know the destination.

Simulations represent one of the most powerful tools of understanding we've ever had—as evidenced by the work researchers are doing around the globe. Pick up any respected peer-reviewed journal or just peruse the science coverage in a local newspaper to find ample evidence of researchers attempting to understand the mysteries of our world via computer simulations. Epidemiologists are using 2000 census data to model and track the way infectious diseases spread among 281 million Americans across the continent.[315] A team of astronomers is simulating the interactions of 75,000 dust particles from the early solar system with the outer planets, the solar wind and sunlight to better understand distant planetary systems.[316] Archaeologists are modeling the impact of thousands of years of intensive farming and animal grazing on soil erosion.[317] Meteorologists are modeling hurricanes with millions of data points, including wind speed, temperature and moisture.[318] Law enforcement agencies are filling virtual sports stadiums with 70,000 simulated fans to play out various evacuation methods in the event of an emergency or terrorist attack.[319] The Swiss Federal Institute of Technology recently announced its intention to create a Living Earth Simulator, a 1 billion euro modeling project that will attempt to foresee everything from economic cycles to pandemics to climate change.[320]

And protein folding just hints at what we can simulate in our bodies. We're trying to predict the occurrence of arteriosclerosis and the hardening of arteries by modeling blood flow through the heart based on a billion variables gathered from real patients.[321] Working with IBM Research, a team of scientists at the École Polytechnique Fédérale de Lausanne in Switzerland is developing a massive brain simulation called Blue Brain in hopes of understanding everything from cellular activity to higher order functions like memory.[322] The project began with a rat brain and the goal of simulating the human brain within the next decade. Pulleyblank sees no end to this trend. "Looking at what a single cell would do is orders of magnitude more complex than protein folding. And if I could do a cell, could I simulate a heart?" he said. "If I could do that, I could understand the effect over time of a pacemaker on an organ. If I could do that, maybe one day I could look at you and simulate over 10 years what will become of your body."

We've come a long way since Norman Borlaug arduously hand-bred individual wheat cultivars. Working in a physical realm, he made connections using a pair of tweezers, a strong back and mind, and a tireless will. He never could have foreseen the deleterious ramifications of his work—how liberally employing petrochemical-based fertilizers and pesticides would ravage intersecting systems. Now we can. We can see more broadly, map data more inclusively and understand implications more comprehensively, all to foresee such ripple effects and, ultimately, to make our inventions more sustainable.

· · ·

To put men on the moon, an entire nation first had to believe that it was even possible.

Making progress means making your case. The citizens of Stockholm at first resisted the new traffic mitigation plan—but that was before the pilot.

The path from invention to innovation is often blocked until someone shows enough conviction to see it through—as was the case with the first coronary stent.

Believing

The path to progress is rarely linear. It might help to visualize smuba as a series of gears on a five-speed bicycle. Seeing is the first gear to trigger forward movement. Its utility never goes away, but as the landscape changes, it yields to subsequent gears. And, of course, engaging any gear just once isn't sufficient. One data grab isn't enough to create a trustworthy map. Think about the 1804 map that Lewis and Clark created for Jefferson: it was as impressive as it was incomplete. Completing the map of the United States took decades of additional data-gathering missions. The same holds true during the understanding process.

Determining the cause of a traffic bottleneck could be a relatively simple matter of mapping a cluster of potholes. But if the cause lies outside the road system—say, late-afternoon sun glare—then the map needs to include ambient information, which requires more data. The process of understanding highlights the deficiencies in the map, which spurs a need for more data, and so on.

Unlike a bicycle, however, smuba is not typically powered by a single actor. Some of the examples cited so far involve capturing, mapping and analyzing proprietary data in the name of progress, but many do not. There's a wealth of public information waiting to be scoured for patterns, and there are piles of analog and digital maps ready to be interpreted and analyzed. And certainly there's plenty of opportunity for charismatic believers to make the connections after the hard work of understanding is complete.

Some of the greatest innovators in history did precisely this. Joseph Marie Jacquard wasn't the first to imagine a system to mechanize weaving. His loom was based on decades-old inventions. Henry Ford didn't invent the automobile or the assembly line; he adopted and improved upon earlier versions. It's even true of history's most accomplished technologist and inventor, Thomas Edison. Edison has more than a thousand US patents to his credit, but we remember him more for his role in the development of two ideas that weren't his own, the lightbulb and electricity. At least eight people are thought to have beaten him to the lightbulb. "It was a great technical invention, but unless you had a promoter like Edison who knew how to work the market and promote what he was doing, it wouldn't have happened. He danced on the cusp of the technical and the social, and he did it very well," said IBM chief scientist Grady Booch.[323] "In the case of electricity, he didn't wait for it to happen, he made it happen. He found opportunities for making money by selling the dynamos to produce the electricity, as well as the wires and lightbulbs—and that's how he began to electrify New York and other places."

Every inventor has a story about the moment his or her big idea hit. We devour such tales, perhaps because they give all of us hope that we, too, can be similarly struck by inspiration. But that's self-evident. Anyone can have a big idea. When talking thoughtfully about their successes, those who managed to follow an invention through to innovation tend to regard the actual idea as a commodity. Julio Palmaz, for example, was inducted into the Inventors Hall of Fame for creating the world's first coronary stent, a device that serves as scaffolding for a clogged blood vessel.[324] The idea for the stent came to him while he was listening to a speech by Andreas Gruentzig, who performed the first operation using balloon angioplasty and spoke candidly at a conference about its shortcomings. The stent didn't succeed solely because Palmaz was in the right place at the right time. There were many other people listening to Gruentzig's speech. The idea itself was emergent, the surprising product of a complex system. It would have popped up elsewhere because its time had arrived. Not that just anyone could have caught it. To imagine and flesh out the details of an entirely new device capable of shoring up arterial walls required substantial technical knowledge and creativity. But the critical factor in the success of the idea, in the creation of a multibillion-dollar industry, was a more blue-collar characteristic: dogged perseverance. "My idea was simple. Most people would say, 'I hate it. It's the obvious evolution of angioplasty, but who wants to put a piece of metal in an artery?'" said the Argentina-born cardiologist at his Napa Valley, California, winery, Palmaz Vineyards. "Innovation always meets rational negativism. Don't give me credit for coming up with the idea of the stent. Someone else would have come up with it. Give me credit for staying with it. It was my persistence that was most important."

Such persistence is the result of truly believing. There are many forms of belief, of course, including imagination, curiosity, hypotheses and intuition, and each has an important role in life. Belief is often used synonymously with faith and associated with religion, but that's not the sort of belief I'm talking about here. In the hard work of making the world work better, believing is about establishing and standing on evidence—because that's what it takes to support and pursue an idea until it's fully realized. This uniquely human capability is common among history's heroes—people who possess singular vision, drive and charisma. But it can be fostered.

The venture capital community is a mechanism designed to nurture believing. In California's Silicon Valley especially, but also around the world, venture capitalists provide a forum to breed, test and deploy big ideas. Funding is obviously a huge concern for aspiring innovators, but at their best these financiers provide more than money. They foresee pitfalls and challenge entrepreneurs while connecting them to a network of resources to inspire confidence and ambition. In short, they give those entrepreneurs a place to test and validate beliefs. Academia, of course, can also serve as a petri dish for ideas, which blossom among colleagues and eager post-doc researchers. Universities—from Harvard, MIT and Stanford to Cambridge, Oxford and McGill—have repeatedly demonstrated that the right combination of scientific acumen and market orientation can spawn systemic innovations.

Edison designed what could be viewed as the iconic modern culture of technological believing, the Menlo Park industrial research lab. He gave his multidisciplinary researchers every tool and material imaginable and tasked them with bringing new technologies to market. Many of the patents credited to Edison came from the work performed by his employees. "He built a lab structure that had lots of interesting people doing lots of cool things," Booch said. "And from the primordial soup of ideas and people experimenting, all these innovations popped out."

Corporate research and development has come a long way since. The old AT&T was known for its research labs. Xerox's iconic facility, PARC, famously gave birth to the computer mouse and graphical user interface, among many other innovations (proving again that the inventor isn't always the biggest believer). Companies as diverse as 3M, Apple, Dow Chemical, Genentech, Google, Microsoft, Monsanto and Procter & Gamble all spend billions on various forms of research and product development. IBM alone spends roughly $6 billion a year on R&D.[325] Each company has its own ideas about the mix of big-R scientific research and big-D product development, as well as strategies outlining when to foster innovation and when to acquire it. But there is a universal takeaway from these labs: invention may be a natural outcome of the scientific method, but innovation takes more than science—it takes encouragement, collaboration and integration.

Researchers at IBM's nine labs around the world generated more than 5,800 patents in 2010.[326] But patents don't make the world work better. Those researchers may believe that the application of intelligence, reason and science can improve business, society and the human condition—but progress is not possible until this belief infects hundreds of thousands of nonscientific colleagues, partners and clients. This is why IBM senior vice president and director of research John Kelly makes sure there's a steady stream of researchers going into the field and nontechnical businesspeople coming into the labs.[327] "A group of my researchers is at Mayo Clinic working on smart healthcare. I have people with boots on collecting streaming data on the shores of the Hudson River. In a sense, the lab is out there," he told me. "The business units really depend on research to be their high-beam headlights. They depend on us to be out there on the edge, trying to find the next big thing."

———

CHARISMA WILL ALWAYS BE AN IMPORTANT TOOL for convincing the troops that change is possible. But technology can play a role as well. The more precisely we calculate and visualize potential future states, the better we can

President Kennedy's moon shot speech was the spark for Apollo 11. But a lunar rocket doesn't blast into space on inspiration alone. NASA needed IBM computers and thousands of IBMers at Mission Control to calculate innumerable flight plans, anticipate every possible scenario and guard against all foreseeable complications. This work in the trenches is what made everyone believe the lunar mission was possible.

mitigate risk, and the more effective we'll be at communicating the best path forward. NASA's lunar missions offer a great example of how technology can foster the type of belief required to do something monumental—and monumentally difficult.

In 1961, President John F. Kennedy's famous moon shot address called for an effort to send an American to the moon by the end of the decade. On July 20, 1969, the 15-ton lunar module *Eagle* successfully touched down as part of the Apollo 11 mission. What made Kennedy believe such a feat was possible? Never mind the Cold War theatrics. His conviction was an outgrowth, at least in part, of the work performed decades earlier on the Astronomical Calculator donated to Columbia University by IBM in 1945. A decade later, IBM cosponsored, along with the American Astronomical Society, the Thomas J. Watson Astronomical Computing Bureau—the world's first center for scientific computation, which served as a locus for the world's astronomical community to work on the differential equations of planetary motion. This work provided a foundation for the Gemini and Mercury missions in the early 1960s, which in turn led to Apollo.

The first US suborbital manned launch, *Mercury-Redstone 3*, lasted only 15 minutes and relied on Earth-bound IBM computers to calculate proper rocket trajectories and flight paths. The first manned lunar mission, by contrast, exceeded eight days. To ensure that *Apollo 11* had the best possible navigation data, IBM researchers created a new lunar ephemeris, mapping the future positions of the moon and its orbit up to the year 2000. These calculations were 10 times more precise than anything previously available.[328]

IBM designed both the Real-Time Computer Complex in Houston, a.k.a. Mission Control, as well as the Goddard Space Flight Center in Greenbelt, Maryland. Both systems were inspired by earlier real-time tracking systems, including American Airline's Sabre, and SAGE, the Cold War-era early warning system designed to scan the skies for Soviet bombers.

Mission Control relied on five System/360 Model 75s to monitor every aspect of the rocket's condition and position and detect any deviation from the flight plan in 120 billionths of a second. Every course correction, lunar orbit, communications blackout, lunar landing, liftoff, rendezvous between the lander and capsule, and final splashdown in the Pacific was preprogrammed.[329]

In contrast to the much shorter Gemini and Mercury missions, with Apollo the computers had to make the trip, too. The 36-story, 3,500-ton Saturn V rocket was guided by a navigation computer known as the Instrument Unit. Built by 2,000 IBMers in Huntsville, Alabama, it was a feat of miniaturization and computing power unlike anything the world had seen. IBM squeezed the equivalent of a System/360 Model 50 into the size of a briefcase powered by 144 watts of electricity—less than what some lightbulbs need. The unit calculated 500 routes to the moon, each consisting of 135 equations and 6,100 instructions; continually measured the rocket's attitude, acceleration, velocity and position; and issued as many as 22 steering commands per second to ensure that astronauts maintained the most efficient path. The unit's final responsibility before being jettisoned into space was to control the burn of the third-stage rocket, heaving the command module containing Neil Armstrong, Michael Collins and Buzz Aldrin toward the moon.[330]

What does this have to do with believing? The 10 billion instructions calculated during the course of the Apollo 11 mission served as constant reinforcements—perpetual, moment-by-moment assurances—that those three men could not only make the journey to the moon, but also safely come back home.

Of course, all the technology in the world would have been worthless without the teamwork of actual humans, many of whom were IBMers. Among the biggest believers of all of them was IBMer Homer Ahr, who, in his first job out of college, manned the computers at Mission Control during the *Apollo 11* journey.[331] He remembers being particularly touched by Armstrong's famous maxim: That's one small step for man, one giant leap for mankind. "It represented all of the small steps that my colleagues and I took leading up to that small step," he said. "Because it really was a lot of small steps."

Ahr is living proof of how a team of intelligent, devoted humans can pull off just about anything. He's also evidence that there's no way to anticipate every potential complication. If we have to believe with 100 percent certainty that every action we take will be flawless, then we are doomed to stasis. But by building systems that are themselves alive, we can deal with crises as they arise. To prove the point, Ahr recalled the near disaster of *Apollo 13*, when the crew was forced to abort the landing due to a ruptured oxygen tank. "The maneuver that they did was a maneuver which, prior to that mission, could not have been computed by the ground system, could not have been targeted, could not have been told or uplinked to the crew to be done," he said, tears welling up in his eyes. "We put that capability into the computer for the first time for *Apollo 13*. And I know that because it was my office mate and I who did that."

———

SYSTEMIC CHANGE DOESN'T COME ABOUT UNILATERALLY. It takes a village. Or a nation. An entire society. Or all of humanity. Which means it takes leadership. Leadership comes in many forms. Sometimes it's a matter of convincing thousands of engineers that they can accomplish something their grandparents never could have imagined. Sometimes it's about giving away an idea to let it flourish. The personal computer is a great example. After entering the personal computer market 30 years ago, IBM opened its architecture to the world and famously decided that the software wasn't worth owning. That single act may be viewed by some as a colossal strategic blunder—after all, it effectively handed the business of operating systems to Microsoft, whose Windows division now generates close to $20 billion in annual revenue. But it was undoubtedly good for the movement (and most likely a long-term positive for IBM) because it created not just a product but also an entire industry, giving rise to Microsoft as well as clone makers and peripheral makers, from Compaq to Dell.

"If we had done it in a more proprietary fashion, it would have never become what it became. And it's funny how that happened, because we didn't do that necessarily on purpose," said IBM vice president Dean. "It's like back in the day when they would put schematics of a TV set in the back so the repairman could repair it. Well, we put the schematics in the reference manual that shipped with the PC. And thus, anybody who wanted to build a copy could easily build one. So that opened the door for a lot of people not only to build systems but to build adapters, write code—it just really provided a great platform to build on top of. That's what made it successful."

In a shrinking world standards become even more important as platforms, according to former Intel chairman and CEO Craig Barrett. "As borders become transparent, whether you are running your railroad line or your broadband connection across the border, you need to have some degree of commonality, and that's what standards ensure," he said in an interview on the company's website.[332] "The whole industry can evolve around common characteristics and innovate on top of them."

Barrett is talking about information technology and consumer electronics, but the sentiment holds true across industries, technologies and societies. By establishing limits and restrictions, standards somewhat paradoxically spur innovation by putting developers on common ground.

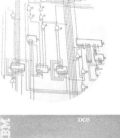

The schematic for the original IBM PC provided an instruction set for all comers to build machines of their own. This one act established a standard—and essentially gave away an enormous business—while spawning many competitors and allowing a new industry to be born.

Edison knew this when he battled Nikola Tesla over the alternating current versus direct current electricity standard. A cadre of retailers, manufacturers and installers used the UPC symbol to re-craft entire industries. The internationally recognized green-building certification known as LEED provides architects and contractors with common guidelines to spur the design and development of energy-efficient and environmentally responsible buildings. The standardization of electronic medical records is a necessary first step toward designing a more efficient, effective and transparent healthcare system—one that allows patients to access their own data, doctors to share outcomes and administrators to reduce paperwork.

Another big part of leadership comes from debate and, when necessary, putting one's reputation—or entire career—on the line for something worth believing in. One of IBM's more celebrated recent successes occurred in Stockholm, Sweden. I wrote about the city's traffic congestion pricing system in May 2009 for *Fortune*.[333] The system reduced traffic in and around Stockholm by 22 percent, curbed emissions by 14 percent and improved overall quality of life downtown. The streets became more passable for pedestrians, and buses began finishing routes ahead of schedule. But getting there wasn't easy. The biggest hurdle wasn't building a near-perfect billing system, inventing new technologies or registering cars. It was the citizens of Stockholm, who balked at the prospect of paying yet another tax.

In the face of polling data that showed a broad majority didn't want the project, the city council announced a seven-month trial, after which citizens would vote in a referendum to determine the system's fate. Gunnar Söderholm was the senior officer in city hall charged with overseeing the implementation. In effect, he and the rest of Stockholm leadership created a costly full-size model knowing that they might have to tear the whole thing down. It was a risky gambit. Overestimating the technological capabilities or benefits would have been disastrous. IBM was involved at every step, crafting a communications campaign to explain how the system would work, devising a new optical character recognition technology, aligning systems integrators and technical partners, and installing a billing system. If the Swedes hated congestion pricing, it wouldn't be because they were being erroneously charged.

In the end, the system overdelivered, and the citizens of Stockholm voted overwhelmingly to continue their less-congested, bluer sky way of life. "We started here with an empty table, designed the scheme, developed a procurement process, had the trial and referendum—all within four years," Söderholm told me in a baroque conference room at the site of the annual Nobel Prize gala in city hall. "This is one of a few examples of infrastructure investment that has immediate payback."

In a follow-up interview two years later, Söderholm noted that the citizens of Stockholm remain in favor of congestion pricing. In a November 2010 poll, two-thirds of those who had an opinion said they supported the system. And Söderholm remains proud of the scheme's accomplishment and its $450 million price tag. "Any other infrastructure to reduce traffic by 20 to 25 percent in and out of the city would have cost at least 10 times the price," he said. "The congestion tax is here to stay and is now a part of every-day life." In fact, it's spreading. Sweden's second-largest city, Gothenburg, plans to implement a similar scheme beginning January 1, 2013.

The Stockholm situation demonstrates the type of effort required to persuade the general population to accept any behavior modification without obvious payoff. This is important to remember as we address the thorny issue of climate change. MIT professor and modeling expert John Sterman gave a stirring call-to-arms at the Almaden Institute conference in the spring of 2010, imploring his peers to work harder to build public understanding that global warming is real and offering dire consequences for failure. "We are laying a table for our grandchildren that will be poor and impoverished," he said, roundly discrediting any hope that a team of scientists will save the day in a Manhattan Project-style fit of invention. "The desire for such technical solutions is understandable. By focusing enough money and genius in the deserts of New Mexico, scientists created nuclear weapons—arguably the most effective application of science and technology to affect geopolitical outcomes in our history. So you can see the appeal of a Manhattan Project to address climate change. But it can't work."

With nuclear weaponry, the public had no role (except to be afraid). With global warming, it's our own actions that are causing the ice caps to melt, the sea levels to rise, the weather to grow more extreme and fertile farmlands to turn to dust. Reducing greenhouse gas emissions requires billions of individuals to cut their carbon footprints by, for example, buying more efficient vehicles, insulating homes, using public transit and supporting legislation to promote clean, renewable energy. But many of us aren't even convinced there's a problem. Gallup's annual poll on environmental issues showed in 2010 that "48 percent of Americans now believe that the seriousness of global warming is generally exaggerated," up from 31 percent in 1997.[334] Turning this tide, Sterman argued, will require not a hermetically sealed research project, but a social crusade—something on the order of a civil rights movement that draws on distributed leadership to convince populations that our current way of life is unsustainable.

Actually, it's even harder than that. "The damage caused by segregation was apparent to anyone who looked," Sterman said. "Computer models and graphs of projected sea level rise don't provoke the same outrage as pictures of civil rights workers being beaten and attacked by police dogs because of the color of their skin." Unlike the racism that sparked the civil rights movement, the causes and effects of climate change are not obvious. With climate change, every chilly summer day or blizzard seems to dispel the notion of a warming atmosphere.

This will be the challenge of our lifetime. We have the means to gather irrefutable data, to highlight patterns emerging in real time, to understand scenarios and to simulate and demonstrate to policy makers the consequences of inaction. (IBM is even working on a model integration standard called SPLASH, which will help researchers link the dozens of models involved in simulating the effects of massively complex systems like healthcare and the climate.)[335] But is that enough to break through the public's complacency?

As a scientist, Sterman is distraught. As a human, he remains guardedly optimistic that the general population will come to recognize the enormity of the problem we're facing. "We're going to have to design our models so they have the immediacy and impact that we had in the civil rights movement. If we do that—focus not only on the technical, but also on this change process—we can address these problems."

• • •

Acting

Acting—the last step in the difficult process of making the world work better—should really be a formality. If we've gathered all the data, organized it, rooted out cause and effect and convinced the stakeholders and ourselves that there's a better way, well, then just flip the switch.

There is no switch. There's no single action to reverse climate change or strip waste out of a supply chain or eliminate obesity or get you home in time for dinner. Acting on a system is less like turning on a light and more like building a career. Picking that first job out of college is hardly sufficient. A successful career requires continual education, reassessment and reaction. If there were a progress switch—and if knowing the path and having the tools were enough—there would be no exploding gas lines, choking skies, collapsing economies, drought, forest fires or pandemics. We'd all be comfortable, well-educated, fit, well-nourished and spending a lot more time with our families in our spacious carbon-neutral homes.

But that's hardly the case. Instead, things sometimes seem to be getting worse. Our climate is warming, our viruses are getting more virulent, and our manmade systems are rapidly deteriorating. There's a school of thought that says this path will continue, that humanity is tethered to the fates of the failing quagmire of complex systems—and that nothing short of blowing them up will

Where do we begin?

Redesign or start over from scratch?

How will we find consensus?

What does it take to overcome
the status quo?

How much risk is acceptable?

Can mastering one system
shed light on the others?

do. "Even with our improved knowledge, accidents, and thus potential catastrophes, are inevitable in complex, tightly coupled systems, with lethal possibilities," sociologist and organizational theorist Charles Perrow wrote in *Normal Accidents.*[336] "We must live and die with their risks, shut them down, or radically redesign them."

That's neither helpful nor realistic. Fixing the planet is not a whole-house renovation. We can't lease a place for six months and move out while the experts build us a new one. And we humans are not particularly fond of resigning ourselves to the status quo. Our ancestors have repeatedly beaten back intractable problems and "inevitable" doom. We have scratched and clawed our way to greater wisdom, comfort and convenience. This is not meant to be a note of optimism, at least not solely. And it's not about survival instinct. Every species—humans of course included—has an innate drive to avoid perishing, to project its genes into the future, and that basic instinct serves us well. As humans, we also strive to make things better. Some of us are motivated by profits, others glory, still others altruism or greater meaning. Whatever the motivations, we have demonstrated over and over that we do not sit idly by and wait for ruin.

So how do we actually make improvements at the scale of a complex system? Acting on a system requires all the skills developed in seeing, mapping, understanding and believing. It also takes collaboration among talent, partners, and technology and, again, leadership. Good leaders are naturally great communicators. It's not just about turning a phrase. A great leader shows the masses the data and maps that have led him or her to understand and believe. It's not surprising at this point to hear that technology is helping in this regard, too. The smart meter is just one example of a technology that's giving the masses an ability to see, map, understand—and change—their habits. When communal action is required, online calendars, wikis, instant messaging, videoconferencing and personalized web portals are increasing our ability to collaborate, decreasing signal loss in our communications and enabling us to foresee consequences and contribute ideas. And we now have the technology to automate the world's systems—to notice behavioral changes as they occur, assess impact and prescribe courses of action in real time.

Another key lesson about acting: a pinpoint intervention often works better than an extreme makeover. If we can target our actions in particular areas and time those actions, we can get maximum return from minimal effort. By acting on parts of a system, we can learn lessons about how to make changes work on a broader scale. Or, even better, we can set off a beneficent chain of events that will cause the system to change itself.

Let's look at one particular scourge as an example. Poverty is both the symptom of a confluence of many deficient systems and a cause of further deterioration in those systems. It's intertwined with education, employment, social services, cost of living, crime and so forth. Eliminating poverty is an admirable but unrealistic goal. We can't blow up and rebuild all the interlocking systems that contribute to it. But we can beat it back a bit at a time.

As bad as things may have seemed in the early part of the twenty-first century, this is nothing compared with the Great Depression. Back then, things appeared truly hopeless. There was no single fix to right the economy and ensure a better future for millions of impoverished, starving and suffering citizens. Many factors eventually lifted America out of the malaise, including World War II and the jobs created by President Franklin D. Roosevelt's New Deal. But perhaps the single biggest factor in securing the sustainability of those changes was FDR's decision in 1935 to provide a social safety net to 26 million workers via the Social Security Administration.[337] It didn't decrease unemployment or increase production, but it established a floor, which limited the scope of the economy's swings (at least in their impact on individual workers). In that respect, it was a classic system intervention.

At a celebration of the 25th anniversary of Social Security's implementation, former US labor secretary Frances Perkins recounted the daunting nature of the assignment.[338] "This was a thrown-together team. We had no money," she said in an address. "It seemed as though it couldn't be done." (And many believed it *shouldn't* be done.) She borrowed people from other departments, persuaded some of the world's leading technological and

In 1935, devising a payroll tax and reimbursement scheme for 26 million workers was nearly unimaginable. And yet that's what US Secretary of Labor Frances Perkins did with "a thrown-together team and no money." IBM's role in designing and deploying America's Social Security system helped establish a belief among IBMers that any problem, no matter its size or novelty, could be addressed through the application of intelligence, science and reason.

economic minds to come to Washington—many with no salary—and stared down those American workers who were understandably less than enthusiastic about having a new tax extracted from their paychecks with no immediate benefit. She also made use of the best tools available. "I remember the day that Arthur Altmeyer, who was then first assistant secretary of labor, walked into my office and said, 'You know, I think we found it. These new IBM machines, I believe they can do it,'" she recalled, referring to the 077 Collator, a punched card machine that was invented for the project. "Out of that really inventive group, we found a way by which this could be done."

It's easy to be jaded about the sophistication of the Social Security project relative to the problems we're facing today, but it's important to maintain historical perspective. "The size was unprecedented. There had been relatively large accounting projects where tabulating machines had been used, but nothing on the scale of managing the accounts of 26 million workers," said Paul Lasewicz, IBM's corporate archivist in Somers, New York.[339] "The other thing that made it hard was the time frame. They had to go through the whole process in 16 months: solicit vendor proposals; define processes and procedures; interview, hire and train more than 2,000 employees; build the infrastructure; find the building that could hold the weight of the machines and get the machines in place; and then collect and process payroll information on millions of people."

Roosevelt called the system, which remains an important part of the fabric of American life today, the cornerstone of his administration. Pulling off a project of that magnitude put IBM on the map. "We literally changed the lives of generations and generations of people," Lasewicz said. "It was an order of magnitude jump for us in terms of visibility. They gained a great amount of credibility at a time when the government was on the verge of immense growth. The modernization of logistics as the nation prepared for the Second World War—supplying and moving armies—required accounting. Our equipment became an integral part of that effort, from logistics to personnel records to military research in the fields of ballistics and calculating nautical and astronomical tables."

The project had an even larger effect on the company's spirit, cementing a confidence and drive to take on really big challenges. It showed that intelligence, reason and science *can* improve business, society and the human condition. "IBMers like to think that the work they do is important to the world. There is this ethic of progress guiding how we think," said James Cortada, a member of the IBM Institute for Business Value and the author of dozens of books and articles on the history and management of information technologies.[340] "It's very much in the culture of the firm to create positive contributions to the world—which often turn out to be sources of good business." Enabling Social Security—"the biggest bookkeeping operation of all time"—wasn't just an intervention into America's social and economic systems. It was also a consequential intervention into the complex system known as IBM.

———

AS COMPLEX SYSTEMS OF SYSTEMS, cities are a good place to look for examples of how to make the world work better. A handful of cities around the world—including Dubuque, Iowa; Paredes, Portugal; and Incheon, South Korea—are attempting to either build an entirely new architecture from scratch or modify everything all at once. These will undoubtedly provide important lessons as the world urbanizes at breakneck speed, especially in developing countries. But for most of us, progress generally comes in increments.

In Alameda County, California, poverty remains a big problem. The social services agency, headquartered in Oakland, provides everything from food stamps to welfare, disability assistance, housing and foster care to 13 percent of the population. The agency's assistant director, Don Edwards, has no ability to change the macroeconomic factors that contribute to the county's situation. But he does have a unique insight into the social safety net—and he recently set out to change the one thing he could control.[341]

In 2005, California issued a report ranking Alameda's social services agency last among the state's counties. Only 12 percent of clients were participating in job training exercises—a supposed prerequisite for receiving benefits. The poor performance was endangering funding, but for Edwards, fixing the system had greater meaning. He grew up in a poor section of Indianapolis with his two brothers, mother and grandmother. Despite the family's limited means, Edwards's grandmother repeatedly welcomed less fortunate children for a hot meal, instilling in her grandson a sense of responsibility to help others. After stints at Wells Fargo Bank and Kaiser Permanente, Edwards left the private sector to scale his grandmother's ambitions.

In hindsight, the sources of Alameda County's social services problems seem obvious. The agency's 2,200 caseworkers were dealing with as many as 600 clients each. As recently as five years ago, case records were often filed in manila folders covered in Post-it notes. There was a wealth of analog and anecdotal data in those case files but no easy way to mine it. And none of the departments were linked, so there was no institutional grasp of program performance, system efficacy, client usage, waste or fraud. "We were data rich and information poor. We knew that many people receiving benefits weren't participating in programs, but we didn't know how bad we were," Edwards explained in his Oakland office, which overlooks a Greyhound bus station. "I wanted not just to see things at a global level, but for the workers themselves to see what's going on. If we can't empower them, we haven't empowered ourselves."

His experience in banking and insurance taught Edwards that there were technological tools to remedy such problems. He spent three years searching for the right one before settling on an IBM package called SSIRS (Social Services Integrated Reporting Service), which combines a database with various kinds of analytics and modeling software. He cashed in all the credibility he had and persuaded his bosses to allow a trial of the $1.3 million package—an almost unconscionable sum for the cash-strapped agency.

Edwards tested the system in two departments and immediately began noticing patterns. Some were simple: identical names with two or more

Social Security numbers, and payees who had been receiving benefits while living out of state. Input errors or fraud? Probably both. Then there were clients simultaneously receiving payments as clients and caregivers. SSIRS also continually monitored the system. Rather than relying on month-old reports from an outside vendor, Edwards now had reports that were "not only real-time but dead on in accuracy," providing much more reliable snapshots of the agency's performance at any given moment.

California's threat to cut social services funding to Alameda County spurred assistant director Don Edwards to overhaul the system. But his true motivation came from his grandmother, who taught him at a young age to help others.

At that point, SSIRS began speaking for itself. "We put it on the desk of executives and said, 'Here's something you can play with.' It's like what the old pet shops used to do: take this puppy home, and if you don't like it we'll take it back," Edwards told me with a laugh. "This is not rocket science. It's about touching human beings. If you can do that, you don't just get their buy-in, you get demands to do more. We went from having skeptical leaders to having champions."

According to an independent report, the system will generate nearly $25 million in direct and indirect benefits, including reduced overpayments and improved caseworker productivity.[347] And its performance continues to improve. Every time we change lanes on the freeway, we have to perform the smuba process anew. But Alameda's system is the equivalent of mapping every car on the road, anticipating where they'll all be at any given time and prescribing every necessary action to ensure that everyone gets home in time for dinner. "It's predictive and proactive," Edwards said, "like a truth serum."

Edwards was never out to save his agency money; he wanted to make the best use of his budget to better serve clients. And now he's become a systems thinker intent on bringing his methods to sister agencies, allowing city workers to track the residents of Alameda County across systems to anticipate their needs and stop them when they're headed down dangerous paths. "How can we identify kids who should be on food stamps but aren't? Foster kids who are habitually truant run the risk of crossing over into the juvenile criminal system," Edwards said. "How can we identify them and intervene? We might be able to save a kid from a criminal life."

IN HIS SEMINAL WORK, *The City in History*, historian and philosopher of science and technology Lewis Mumford posits that successful cities throughout time have provided economic opportunity, possessed a sacred core and offered a balance of culture, technology and industry.[343] Over the past century, many students of complex systems—notably Jane Jacobs, Mumford's protégé and eventual nemesis—came to see the city as humanity's distinctive intervention into the systems of our planet (in smuba terms, call it our signature action). It's no accident that both "city" and "civilization" derive from the same Latin root: *civis*. Human history is, simply put, the story of urbanization. Without cities, there would be no law, no industry, no culture and no progress.

But before we dive further into that, let's consider one essential component of this complex system of systems—and something for which every successful city provides: the safety of its citizens. Once, ensuring safety meant walling off the borders and lining them with sentries. Now, it can mean designing a system to stop crime before it happens.

In mid-2005, the Memphis Police Department under the leadership of police director Larry Godwin began a partnership with the University of Memphis called Blue Crush (Crime Reduction Utilizing Statistical History) to collate crime data and create maps of hot spots in hopes of stanching a festering wound. "Memphis has real challenges. We've got 26 percent of our population under the poverty line, 50 percent considered low income and a police department that had been fairly unstable," said W. Richard Janikowski, director of the university's Center for Community Criminology and Research.[344] "The mayor was firing police chiefs every time you blinked until he found Larry Godwin."

Blue Crush is just one of many examples of police departments turning to data to help fight crime. In the US alone, New York City, Philadelphia, Los Angeles and Baltimore all have deployed similar systems in hopes of ushering in the age of predictive policing. Doing so requires more than just turning on the data spigots. It means building a new culture. For researchers, the answers are always in the data. They tend to view police departments as treasure troves. To police officers, researchers come off as pushy, demanding, effete and self-interested. Bridging this divide in Memphis involved "going to officers and commanders, explaining what the strategy was, where we were planning to go, and trying to get feedback," Janikowski said. "Police organizations don't like change. But you have to sell the troops on the ground."

The researchers had to learn to think and communicate like police officers. "Cops carry a lot of knowledge in their heads. They can look at some of that data and say, 'Ah, yes, there's a burglary problem here, and I know there are burglars that live not too far away; we've arrested them in the past,'" Janikowski said. "It's combining that human capacity for analysis, memory and understanding with automation that produces your most effective results."

Even after the department agreed to cooperate, salesmanship remained important at every step. We all hold certain data close to our vests, and it's no different at public agencies. At first the police wanted to provide only summary information, such as the total number of aggravated assaults. The researchers wanted more, more, more. "We might argue you should be looking at an important set of variables, including socio-demographics, like poverty levels. It's making police officers into problem solvers. This takes time. It's not a magical process," Janikowski said. "Anytime you've got a collaborative, it takes a while for trust to build. It got heated sometimes, but once you build up that trust, then you can survive yelling at each other."

In 2008, Memphis deployed the real-time crime center citywide, using an SPSS analytics system, which allows cops in the field using PDAs to file reports and retrieve information immediately. The system maps incidents in real time while also incorporating non-traditional data—allowing police to understand, for example, the links between car burglaries and rainfall, or foreclosures and drug-related criminal activity.

In the four years since the program began, crime has decreased by almost 30 percent, including a 15 percent reduction in violent crime.[345] "This had never, ever been done," Godwin said.[346] "But we did some pilot programs, and the next thing we know, we're catching individuals with guns, drugs. We changed the way we did business. Man, I never dreamed it would be this promising."

Godwin announced in late February that he would be retiring in the spring. But the system that he championed will remain. Police chief Dave Martello told the Memphis newspaper the *Commercial Appeal* that Blue Crush will be Godwin's legacy. "What that did was give a lot of police officers the ability to be the police officers they always dreamed about, locking up the bad guys and making a difference in the community," Martello said.[347]

As the system matures, members of the police force are becoming increasingly comfortable guiding its evolution. "Now we're seeing commanders on their own doing their own best-practices research, coming up with new ideas, saying 'Let's try this,' or 'I read this,' or 'What is this telling me?'" Janikowski said. "That's organizational change."

———

Progress has ramifications. At San Francisco's Public Utility Commission Wastewater Enterprise, superintendent John Powell is ushering in a new era of predictive maintenance. Realizing his vision will reduce costs but also change the makeup of his workforce.

WE HAVE THE TOOLS. We know the path. So, what else should an aspiring world changer be aware of before getting started? Prepare to be surprised. Systems are ever evolving, ever growing and—no matter how well designed—perpetually suffering from wear and tear. Tinkering with them will also have ramifications on supporting infrastructures. Progress does not affect all parties equally.

The San Francisco wastewater treatment facility installed sensors along 1,000 miles of pipes and has mapped the entire system and deployed IBM's Maximo analytics software to monitor the conditions of pipelines, flow, volume, vibration, heat and performance. "Wastewater is one of the most corrosive environments in the world. If you build it, wastewater will eat it alive," said John Powell, superintendent and asset manager of the SFPUC Wastewater Enterprise, which handles about 95 million gallons of wastewater on a dry day and close to 400 million gallons of wastewater and runoff during a storm.[348]

Twenty years ago, managing the effects of corrosion meant employing a staff of mechanics to perpetually repair broken parts and pipes. That was the era of reactive maintenance. Powell's facility has since transitioned into preventive maintenance mode; parts are now systematically replaced based on their expected life spans. It's less expensive and more efficient but still not optimal, because parts are replaced based on averages. Powell's goal is to usher in an era of predictive maintenance—the industrial equivalent of personalized medicine or predictive policing. "We put together a risk model that says parts of the city are in failure mode," Powell said. "Preventive maintenance is good, but predictive is really the way to go. I want my mechanics writing work orders when they know something's going to break."

Change of this order doesn't come painlessly. The makeup of Powell's team has already morphed. Mechanics skilled at fixing broken pipes have taken a back seat to software engineers capable of monitoring, interpreting and adjusting the system. As his ultimate ambitions take hold, the forces of transparency and automation will continue to alter the makeup of Powell's workforce. He and all leaders need to anticipate skill sets to boost productivity and minimize downtime in the future. Workers, on the other hand, need to figure out how to, at the very least, keep their jobs in this new reality. There are also practical budgetary issues to consider. Businesses assume a certain amount of breakage and set aside money—and take out insurance—to cope. But whose budget does the money come from when we decide to fix something before it breaks? We may need to invent new accounting methodologies to foster an era of predictive maintenance (or personalized medicine, for that matter).

Following the smuba path has other far-reaching implications as well. Part of the challenge of the era of so-called Big Data comes from making sense of all the information available. Another part comes in determining what's off-limits. In an opaque world, we've enjoyed a natural shield of privacy and security. In a transparent world, we'll have to build the walls ourselves. This can be partly addressed with technology, but it's also a matter of cultural mores. WikiLeaks is a great example. Many people feel that distributing the contents of private conversations is a criminal act. Others feel just as passionately that sunlight, especially on government, is the great disinfectant. Whether history remembers the whistle-blower site as good or evil, it will have helped establish precedent. Data security is perhaps an even greater concern. It's often said that technology is benign. So, too, is progress. Throughout this essay I've written about people who are intent on

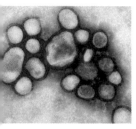

By learning how to halt the spread of H1N1, we gain insight into more than just pandemic behavior. Discouraging disease transmission may reveal the keys to encouraging the spread of ideas, tolerance or even happiness.

capturing, organizing and analyzing data in the name of positive change. Each example stands for dozens or even hundreds of others around the globe—researchers, entrepreneurs and government officials working in this manner to make the world work better. But there will always be nefarious forces using the process for ill. As tools of seeing become cheaper and more widely available, the bad guys will become more adept at gathering data that's supposed to be off-limits or generating convincing false data. Maps have always conferred power on the owner, regardless of motivations, and now they're easier than ever for anyone to make. As simulations gain recognition as tools for fostering belief, we will undoubtedly experience ever more clever and deceptive models designed to sell bad ideas—in much the way some on Wall Street sold society on subprime loans.

On a more positive note, implementing progress can be hugely profitable. In late 1936, IBM estimated that the Social Security Act's requirements had created an additional 20,000 business prospects. By the end of 1937, revenues were up 48 percent from 1935, and by 1939 they were 81 percent higher.[349] That one act of solving an extremely difficult problem established IBM as the company to go to when faced with big problems or pursuing big dreams—a reputation that continues to this day. Any entity proving similarly able to solve seemingly intractable challenges (including data security and privacy issues) will surely generate its own halo.

And open new doors. As any research scientist will point out, untangling one complex system can shed light on ways to transform the others. Sometimes the correlations are clear. By learning to anticipate the transmission of virulent flu strains like H1N1, we gain insight into the spread of various other pandemics and epidemics. But understanding a disease can also improve our understanding of systemic phenomena that aren't so obviously related. To halt the spread of H1N1, we quarantine the infected and instruct the symptomatic to cover their mouths and stay at home. With education, we perform similar actions toward an opposite end. We want to encourage the spread of knowledge. Some of our greatest institutions are designed—or at least have evolved—to cloister the susceptible and restrict interaction to minds deemed capable of "catching" big ideas. To infect future generations, we put those big ideas online and in libraries. So what? So maybe nothing. Or maybe halting disease is the opposite of fostering ideas. After all, disease and knowledge have the same vector: us. So maybe stopping H1N1 can reveal ways to build a better school system or a business environment that fosters creativity. Maybe learning how to halt negative symptoms like obesity will show us how to encourage positive actions such as exercise. Learn how to encourage exercise, and we can use those tactics to encourage, who knows, tolerance? Generosity? Maybe reducing the friction in commerce can teach us not just how to stop fraud but also to increase safety and well-being. Scientists thrive on this sort of discovery. But any curious mind can uncover systemic patterns given the right combination of tools, opportunity and experience. And success only increases ambition. Don Edwards is a great example. Learning how to bridge his agency's disconnected departments may yet show him the way to connect police, fire, transportation, education, water and energy systems into the great hyper-aware, hyperconnected city of tomorrow. At the very least, his experience has greatly increased his desire to try.

It's important to re-emphasize that the complex systems we're acting upon aren't static. They react to our interventions. This brings me back to the topic of cities. On one hand, the city is what enabled humans to become the planet's dominant large species and what made us a serious contender to fight it out with the planet's dominant small species, bacteria. But as writer Steven Johnson shows in *The Ghost Map*, his book about John Snow and the 1854 cholera epidemic, it was the city itself that dramatically enhanced bacterial reproduction by concentrating the food supply: the residents.

So we adjusted the way we managed this creature of ours, the city. We had to intervene into our own intervention. That's what Snow's map, germ theory and the then new science of epidemiology were. The good news for humans, in Johnson's view, is how powerful the city remains as an engine of progress—a smuba machine, if you will. Yes, it helped the bacteria at first—but it has helped us more.

The broader point is that progress is an iterative, dynamic process. You see, you map, you understand, you believe and you act—and then the systems of nature and society react to your actions. So you have to see, map, understand, believe and act again. And so on.

Many of the people I've talked to through the course of researching this essay know all this innately. They're systems thinkers with a penchant for recognizing similarities among seemingly unique dilemmas and following the smuba path repeatedly. Once they've mastered a complex problem, they move on to the next great challenge, ever curious, ever confident, ever willing. This ability and ambition are pervasive at IBM, allowing the company to thrive across numerous industries and to tackle a broad set of problems. Many companies build and operate thriving businesses on a single smuba principle—by helping customers gather or organize all available data, for example. But IBM plays at every step along the path. This may not have been the product of prescient design, or maybe it was. Either way, the company's business reflects the steps of progress. This is almost certainly why it continues to attract some of the world's finest minds eager to ponder ways to create electric airplanes and super-efficient photovoltaic cells, to re-imagine education, to challenge *Jeopardy!* masters as a way to understand the vagaries of human language, to fight pollution, to craft more reliable and cost-effective healthcare systems, and to solve the many modern problems that have emerged as by-products of age, increased population, jerry-rigging and best intentions.

Why stop there? It may be impossible to build a new world from the ground up. But we can build better tools to improve the one we have. Imagine if the first native app of the age of complexity were built expressly to make the world work better. That's where we're headed, according to Dario Gil, an IBM Research program director.[350] "We need a new set of tools that allows us to address the emergent problems that we never could have imagined. We need to develop computers that are not valued for MIPS [millions of instructions per second] or memory, but rather for whether they help us achieve our intended outcomes. Do we get to do what we want to do?" Gil told me. Envision computer systems that are as emergent as the problems they seek to solve. "We call them learning systems."

Learning systems will increase our abilities to gather, organize and analyze data of all sorts while simultaneously decreasing the friction between the steps on the path to making the world work better. The result will be more dynamic and effective predictions about the best course of action to eliminate fraud, curb poverty, improve education, eradicate disease, reduce waste, encourage sustainable behaviors, prolong lives or get home in time for that family dinner we so crave.

As Gil sees it, such learning systems will change society in another way, as well. By giving us all the tools to participate in a revolution, much of what has been viewed as a scientific process will be liberated and democratized. "How many people could do calculations when it required mastery of an abacus? Very few. Now, how many people can do calculations? It's almost universal," Gil said. "Today, how many people can gather data in a statistically meaningful way, order it, establish hypotheses and formulate an action that will lead to a good outcome? A very small number. But if this process becomes embodied in something repeatable, we can all use the tools of the scientific method to make progress—and that's when the hope for progress will make a huge leap."

Making the world work better has never been easy. And better is a moving target. But it's inspiring to know that there's a path to follow and tools to help speed the journey. Because, ultimately, managing complexity is far more than IBM's business model. It's humanity's collective quest to improve our quality of life. We're all in this together.

· · ·

"There's something so big about vision, almost biblical, that one thinks it should be a mechanism that doesn't need any other accompanying assets." Mike May sat across the table from me at an outdoor café near the Ferry Building in San Francisco, reflecting on his decade-long journey since a stem cell surgery restored his sight. "In the beginning, I hadn't really thought this stuff all through. I had this complex overload of information on my plate, and thought, 'What do I do?'"

May's surgery was an elective procedure that was both new and only possible under specific circumstances. He fit the necessary profile, but going under the knife wasn't the obvious choice that most sighted people would assume. He had a full and fruitful life as a blind man. Blindness was part of his identity. And while the experimental procedure offered intriguing possibilities, it also came with only a 50-50 chance of success. And even then, success would require taking a powerful immunosuppressant medication that would help prevent rejection of the new eye but also severely undermine his immune system and greatly increase his likelihood of contracting various diseases, including cancer. Was vision really worth risking his life?

Ultimately, May chose to see, and while his process of understanding the world anew has been anything but linear, he's now off the drugs and for the most part enjoying life with vision. Getting to this point required an epiphany. "I had all this visual input, and I was trying to process it and not doing a very good job. I thought I just needed more practice, but more practice didn't necessarily help," May told me.

Three years after the surgery, the scientific journal *Nature Neuroscience* published a paper stating that May's vision would not get better.[351] It concluded that his brain had lost its plasticity; he'd be stuck with visual chaos forever. It caused him to rally in ways that science didn't consider possible. "That was a big deal. At that point, I kind of thought I'd like to prove them wrong. I gotta believe. There's always a way," he said. "Believing is the absolute critical bridge you need to cross. I decided I had to be more analytical. I had to think of vision as a tool and to use it in conjunction with my other tools."

Now May, like the rest of us, has more tools at his disposal than ever. This morning he walked from his home to the Amtrak station in Davis, California, about 60 miles away from San Francisco, and then transferred to a BART commuter train in Richmond. Upon arriving in West Oakland, officials emptied the train due to an incident at San Francisco's Embarcadero station. He considered taking a taxi across the Bay Bridge to our meeting, but that would have been giving up.

He checked iBART Live on his iPhone to see a real-time map of train positions and decided to just grab the next train, which the app predicted would arrive shortly. It did. He hopped aboard. The train skipped the Embarcadero and dropped him off several blocks away from our meeting point. When he emerged aboveground, May set Embarcadero as his destination on a GPS navigation device he invented to assist blind people, and it directed him toward our table.

"It was a nice combination," he said, "of technology and human ingenuity."

• • •

Acknowledgments

The authors would like to thank Paul Lasewicz for his wealth of knowledge and guidance in researching IBM history; Mike Wing for providing a steady and thoughtful editorial hand; Teresa Yoo and Elizabeth Schaefer for their judgment and care in shepherding this project from start to finish; Jon Iwata and Keith Yamashita for guidance in shaping the themes; Pennie Rossini and Janet Byrne for scrupulous care in copyediting and fact-checking; and dozens of current and former IBMers for their contributions. Finally, we are grateful to Curt Schreiber and the VSA team for giving visual expression to our essays' ideas.

Kevin Maney thanks Steve Wildstrom, Russ Mitchell and Emerson Pugh for their help researching and pulling together the history of computing; and Dag Spicer, curator of the Computer History Museum, for his advice all along the way.

Steve Hamm thanks retired IBM executive Nicholas Donofrio for guidance and academics; Erik Brynjolfsson for insights into value creation; and Rosabeth Moss Kanter and the late C. K. Prahalad for their views on corporate engagement with society.

Jeff O'Brien thanks Stuart Luman for his undying effort and enthusiasm; Sabrina Clark, Carl DeTorres, Heui Jin Jo, Nicolas Maitret, Susana Rodriguez and dozens of researchers and engineers at the Santa Fe Institute, MIT and IBM—notably Don Eigler, Laura and Peter Haas, and Bill Pulleyblank—for their help shaping smuba; and Heather, Hugo and Henry for everything.

Notes

1 Margaret Martonosi (professor, Princeton University), interview by Russ Mitchell for Kevin Maney, June 2010.

2 Marine Institute, "SmartBay Environmental Monitoring System Installed in Galway Bay," news release, July 2010, http://www.marine.ie/home/aboutus/newsroom/news/smartbaymonitoring-systeminstalledingalwaybay.htm; IBM, "IBM and Marine Institute Ireland Netting Results in Galway's 'SmartBay' Project," news release, March 16, 2009, http://www-03.ibm.com/press/us/en/pressrelease/26922.wss.

3 Geoffrey B. Austrian, *Herman Hollerith: Forgotten Giant of Information Processing* (New York: Columbia University Press, 1982), 50–70; Paul Ceruzzi, *A History of Modern Computing* (Cambridge, MA: MIT Press, 1998), 26.

4 "Robert William Bemer," The History of Computing Project, last modified March 17, 2010, http://www.thocp.net/biographies/bemer_bob.htm.

5 M. J. Underwood, "Shoebox—A Voice Responsive Machine," *Datamation* 8 (1962): 47; "IBM Shoebox," IBM, accessed May 2010, http://www-03.ibm.com/ibm/history/exhibits/specialprod1/specialprod1_7.html.

6 "Human Language Technologies," IBM Research, accessed December 2010, http://www.research.ibm.com/hlt/html/history.html.

7 David Nahamoo (IBM Fellow), interview by Kevin Maney, June 22, 2010.

8 George Laurer (former IBM engineer), interview by Russ Mitchell for Kevin Maney, June 2010.

9 *The Trumpeter*, "ASCO's Dual-system RAMAC," October 1960, IBM Archives, Somers, NY.

10 James W. Cortada, *Before the Computer: IBM, NCR, Burroughs, and Remington Rand and the Industry They Created, 1865–1956* (Princeton, NJ: Princeton University Press, 2000), 142.

11 "A few facts about IBM storage," IBM, accessed February 2010, http://www-03.ibm.com/ibm/history/exhibits/storage/storage_facts.html.

12 J. M. Fenster, "How Bing Crosby Brought You Audiotape," *Invention & Technology* 10 (Fall 1994): 58.

13 R. Bradshaw and C. Schroeder, "Fifty years of IBM innovation with information storage on magnetic tape," *IBM Journal of Research and Development* 47, no. 4 (2003): 373.

14 Ibid.

15 Magnetic Tape file, IBM Archives.

16 M. E. Wolf, "The R&D bootleggers inventing against the odds," *IEEE Spectrum* 12 (July 1975): 38.

17 RAMAC file, IBM Archives.

18 Robert Dennard (IBM Fellow), interview by Kevin Maney, May 2010.

19 Sally Adee, "Thanks for the Memories," *IEEE Spectrum* 46 (May 2009): 48; IBM, "IBM Moves Closer to New Class of Memory," news release, April 10, 2008, http://www-03.ibm.com/press/us/en/pressrelease/23859.wss; Kevin Maney, "Every move you make could be stored on a PLR," *USA Today*, September 2004; Stuart Parkin (IBM Fellow), interview by Kevin Maney, May 2010.

20 Kevin Maney, *The Maverick and His Machine* (Hoboken, NJ: John Wiley & Sons, 2003), 359.

21 Ibid., 415.

22 Memorandum by G. M. Amdahl, "Logical Equations for ANS Decoder," December 13, 1955, Computer History Museum, http://archive.computerhistory.org/resources/text/IBM/Stretch/pdfs/06-06/102632244.pdf (accessed April 2010); Frank da Cruz, "A Chronology of Computing at Columbia University," Columbia University, Watson Laboratory, last modified September 28, 2010, http://www.columbia.edu/acis/history; transcripts, John Backus (ref. no.: X3715.2007), Charles Branscomb (ref. no: X5548.2010), Richard Case (ref. no: X3777.2006), Paul Castrucci (ref. no: X4943.2009) and Grace Hopper (ref. no.: X5142.2009), Oral Histories Online, Computer History Museum, accessed December 2010, http://www.computerhistory.org/collections/oralhistories/

23 "IBM 704 Electronic Data Processing Machine Manual of Operation," 1955, IBM Archives.

24 "The Chip That Jack Built," Texas Instruments, accessed May 2010, http://www.ti.com/corp/docs/kilbyctr/jackbuilt.shtml.

25 Peter Capek and Bruce Shriver, "Just Curious: An Interview with John Cocke," *Computer* 32 (November 1999): 34.

26 "Tribute to Seymour Cray," IEEE Computer Society, accessed June 2010, http://www.computer.org/portal/web/awards/seymourbio.

27 "The Supercomputer at Los Alamos," IBM, accessed May 2010, http://www-03.ibm.com/systems/deepcomputing/rr/.

28 "Blue Gene," IBM Research, accessed May 2010, http://domino.research.ibm.com/comm/research_projects.nsf/pages/bluegene.index.html.

29 Juan B. Cuvillo et al., "Toward a Software Infrastructure for the Cyclops-64 Cellular Architecture," CAPSL Technical Memo 55, University of Delaware, Newark, DE, 2004.

30 "The History of Superconductors," Superconductors.org, last modified October 2010, http://www.superconductors.org/History.htm; Lisa Hernandez, "The Exascale Supercomputer: 10 Million Cores in 2020," *ConceivablyTech*, September 23, 2010, http://www.conceivablytech.com/2997/products/the-exascale-supercomputer-10-million-cores-in-2020/.

31 John W. Backus and Harlan Herrick, "IBM 701 Speedcoding and Other Automatic-Programming Systems," 106 (paper presented at the Symposium on Automatic Programming for Digital Computers, the Office of Naval Research, Washington, DC, May 1954); Backus and Hopper, Oral Histories Online; Steve Lohr, "John W. Backus, 82, Fortran Developer, Dies," *New York Times*, March 19, 2007.

32 Backus, Oral Histories Online.

33 E. F. Codd, *The Relational Model for Database Management: Version 2* (Reading, MA: Addison-Wesley, 1990), 12.

34 Edward Hurley, "Q&A: An insider's view of CICS' development," *SearchDataCenter.com*, September 16, 2004, http://searchdatacenter.techtarget.com/news/1156274/QA-An-insiders-view-of-CICS-development.

35 Bruce Weber, "Swift and Slashing, Computer Topples Kasparov," *New York Times*, May 12, 1997; Feng-hsiung Hsu, *Behind Deep Blue: Building the Computer That Defeated the World Chess Champion* (Princeton, NJ: Princeton University Press, 2002), 68.

36 Clive Thompson, "What Is IBM's Watson?," *New York Times Magazine*, June 20, 2010.

37 David Ferrucci (staff member, IBM Research), interview by Kevin Maney, May 2010.

38 John Markoff, "Computer Wins on 'Jeopardy!' Trivial, It's Not," *New York Times*, February 16, 2011.

39 Ray Kurzweil, "The Significance of Watson," *Kurzweil, Accelerating Intelligence* (blog), February 13, 2011, http://www.kurzweilai.net/the-significance-of-watson.

40 Maney, *The Maverick and His Machine*, 331–332; "Calling signals for the Army," *Popular Mechanics* 82 (August 1944): 56.

41 Richard Canning, oral history interview by Jeffrey Yost, August 2002, Charles Babbage Institute Center for the History of Information Processing, University of Minnesota, MN.

42 Bob Braden (computer scientist), interview by Russ Mitchell for Kevin Maney, May 2010.

43 Larry Smarr (founding director, California Institute for Telecommunications and Information Technology), interview by Russ Mitchell for Kevin Maney, May 2010.

44 Vint Cerf to Interesting-People elist, September 30, 2000, http://www.interesting-people.org/archives/interesting-people/200009/msg00052.html.

45 Dennis Jennings, interview by Andreu Veà Baró, November 28, 2007, Who is Who in the Internet World, Palo Alto, CA.

46 Al Weis (former IBM employee), interview by Russ Mitchell for Kevin Maney, June 2010.

47 "Data, data everywhere," *Economist*, February 25, 2010, http://www.economist.com/node/1555743.

48 Maney, *The Maverick and His Machine*, 150; "Columbia University Professor Ben Wood," Columbia University, last modified April 29, 2009, http://www.columbia.edu/acis/history/benwood.html.

49 Cruz, "A Chronology of Computing at Columbia University," http://www.columbia.edu/acis/history/.

50 "IBM 1401 System 50th Anniversary," YouTube video, 125, Computer History Museum celebrates the anniversary of the 1401 on November 10, 2009, posted November 19, 2009, by ComputerHistory, http://www.youtube.com/watch?v=FVsX7aHNENo.

51 Branscomb, Oral Histories Online.

52 Emerson Pugh, L. R. Johnson and J. H. Palmer, *IBM's 360 and Early 370 Systems* (Cambridge, MA: MIT Press, 1991), 113–174.

53 "Timesharing: A Solution to Computer Bottlenecks," YouTube video, 28, MIT science reporter John Fitch at the MIT Computation Center in an interview with MIT professor of computer science Fernando J. Corbató on May 9, 1963, posted January 7, 2010, http://www.youtube.com/watch?v=Q07PhW5sCEk; John McCarthy, "Reminiscences on the History of Time Sharing," Stanford University, 1983, http://www-formal.stanford.edu/jmc/history/timesharing/timesharing.html; Martin Campbell-Kelly and Daniel Garcia-Swartz, "Economic Perspectives on the History of the Computer Time-Sharing Industry, 1965–1968," *Annals of the History of Computing*, IEEE 30 (January–March 2008): 16.

54 Bill Lowe (former vice president, IBM), interview by Bob Cringely, *Triumph of the Nerds*, PBS, June 1996; David Sanger, "Philip Estridge Dies in Plane Crash; Guided IBM Personal Computer," *New York Times*, August 5, 1985.

55 Charles Seife, *Decoding the Universe* (New York: Viking Penguin, 2006), 56–87.

56 Brenda Dietrich (IBM Fellow), interview by Kevin Maney, May 2010.

57 Kevin Maney, "Amazon's new direction: Point, click, make a product to sell to the world," *USA Today*, November 21, 2006.

58 Eric Horvitz (scientist, Microsoft Research), interview by Liane Hansen, "Meet Laura, Your Virtual Personal Assistant," NPR, March 21, 2009.

59 Sam Palmisano (CEO, IBM), interview by Kevin Maney, May 2010.

60 *1910 US Census, Populations of Cities*, US Bureau of the Census (Washington, DC), 188, http://www2.census.gov/prod2/decennial/documents/36894832v3ch2.pdf.

61 *Census 1920*, US Bureau of the Census (Washington, DC), 4, http://www2.census.gov/prod2/decennial/documents/41084484v4ch02.pdf.

62 *Computing-Tabulating-Recording-Company Report*, March 31, 1912, IBM Archives.

63 Richard Tedlow (professor, Harvard University), interview by Steve Hamm, 2004.

64 Sam Palmisano (CEO, IBM), interview by Steve Hamm, May 6, 2010.

65 Masaaki Sato, *The Honda Myth: the Genius and His Wake* (New York: Vertical, 2006), 69–81.

66 Jeffrey Smith (executive, Honda America), interview and e-mail with Steve Hamm, October 2010.

67 Honda, "Summary of 2010 CEO Speech," news release, July 20, 2010, http://world.honda.com/news/2010/c100720Mid-Year-CEO-Speech/index.html.

68 John P. Kotter and James L. Heskett, *Corporate Culture and Performance* (New York: Free Press, 1992), 11.

69 Thomas J. Watson Jr., *A Business and Its Beliefs* (New York: McGraw-Hill, 1963), 5.

70 Maney, *The Maverick and His Machine*, 145.

71 "The Man Proposition," January 25, 1915, IBM Archives.

72 Peter Drucker (management consultant), interview by Kevin Maney, 2002.

73 *Business Machines*, October 6, 1932, 1, IBM Archives.

74 IBM Archives.

75 Ibid.

76 Lisa Gable, IBM human resources, e-mail message to Steve Hamm, November 2, 2010.

77 Patrick Toole (former IBM executive), reading from a notebook given to him by C. L. Reeser, January 11, 2010.

78 Patrick Toole, interview by Steve Hamm, January 11, 2010.

79 John R. Opel (former IBM CEO), interview by Steve Hamm, January 7, 2010.

80 James Birkenstock (former IBM executive), interview by Kevin Maney, December 11, 2000.

81 Typed notes of Thomas J. Watson Sr.'s talk to IBM executives, November 18, 1929, IBM Archives.

82 Maney, *The Maverick and His Machine*, 138.

83 Ibid., 155.

84 Audiotape of IBM executive school, November, 8, 1955, IBM Archives, tape 1.

85 Ibid., tape 2.

86 Dick Wright, "1991 biography of Thomas Watson Jr.," IBM Archives.

87 *Business Machines*, October 25, 1957, 7, IBM Archives.

88 Beth Kowitt and Kim Thai, "World's Best Companies for Leaders," *Fortune*, last modified November 19, 2009, http://money.cnn.com/galleries/2009/fortune/0911/gallery.leadership_top_ten.fortune/index.html.

89 *Business Machines*, January 29, 1963, IBM Archives.

90 Michael Cronin (executive, IBM), interview by Steve Hamm, October 20, 2010.

91 Chuck Boyer, *The 360 Revolution* (Armonk, NY: IBM, 2004), 32, ftp.//flp.software.ibm.com/s390/misc/bookoffer/download/360revolution_040704.pdf.

92 Frederick Brooks (former IBM executive), interview by Steve Hamm, April 2004.

93 Watson Jr., *A Business and Its Beliefs*, 34.

94 Rachel Konrad, "IBM and Microsoft: Antitrust Then and Now," *CNET News*, June 2, 2000, http://news.cnet.com/2100-1001-241565.html.

95 Nicholas Donofrio (former IBM executive), interview by Steve Hamm, July, 23, 2010.

96 Louis V. Gerstner (former IBM CEO), interview by Steve Hamm, January 5, 2011.

97 Bernard Meyerson (IBM Fellow), interview by Steve Hamm, January 18, 2010.

98 Palmisano, interview by Steve Hamm.

99 Paul Hemp and Thomas A. Stewart, "Leading Change When Business Is Good," *Harvard Business Review* (December 2004): http://hbr.org/2004/12/leading-change-when-business-is-good/ar/1.

100 Jon Iwata (executive, IBM), interview by Steve Hamm, January 2010.

101 Diane Brady, "The Immelt Revolution," *BusinessWeek*, March 28, 2005.

102 John F. Akers (former IBM CEO), interview by Steve Hamm, December 16, 2010.

103 Palmisano, interview by Steve Hamm.

104 J. Randall MacDonald (executive, IBM), interview by Steve Hamm, January 18, 2010.

105 Newspaper clipping from unidentified newspaper, IBM Archives.

106 *Current Employment Statistics, 1950 to 2007*, US Bureau of Labor Statistics (Washington, DC, March 2008); "USA Statistics in Brief–Employment," US Bureau of the Census, accessed October 1, 2010, http://www.census.gov/compendia/statab/2010/files/employ.html.

107 Michael S. Christian, "Human Capital Accounting in the United States: 1994–2006," *Survey of Current Business* (June 2010): 31.

108 Will Hamlin and Max Eulenstein, "A Retrospective Look at U.S. Productivity Growth Resurgence" (presentation, Economics 161, Pomona College, February 3, 2009).

109 Erik Brynjolfsson (professor, MIT), interview by Steve Hamm, October 6, 2010.

110 Barry Jaruzelski and Kevin Dehoff, "The Global Innovation: How the Top Innovators Keep Winning," *Strategy + Business*, November 3, 2010, http://www.strategy-business.com/article/10408?gko=08375.

111 Michael H. Zack, "Rethinking the Knowledge-Based Organization," *Sloan Management Review* 44, no. 4 (Summer 2003): 67.

112 Computer Science and Telecommunications Board, *Funding a Revolution: Government Support for Computing Research* (Washington, DC: National Academies Press, 1999), 1, 139.

113 "Thomas A. Edison & the Menlo Park Laboratory," Henry Ford Museum, accessed January 13, 2011, http://www.hfmgv.org/exhibits/edison.

114 Audiotape of IBM executive school, November, 8, 1955, IBM Archives, tape 1.

115 Ibid.

116 "IBM's Intellectual Property History," intellectual property and licensing division, IBM.

117 *Business Machines*, January 4, 1935, IBM Archives.

118 Jean Ford Brennan, *The IBM Watson Laboratory at Columbia University* (Armonk, NY: IBM, 1971), http://www.columbia.edu/acis/history/brennan/index.html.

119 Herb Grosch (former IBM scientist), interview by Steve Hamm, January 2010.

120 Gardiner Tucker (former IBM executive), interview by Steve Hamm, August 20, 2010.

121 Gerd Binnig (former IBM researcher), interview by Steve Hamm, November 17, 2010.

122 Robert Buderi (author), e-mail interview by Steve Hamm, November 11, 2010.

123 "NSF and the Birth of the Internet," National Science Foundation, last modified July 10, 2008, http://www.nsf.gov/news/special_reports/nsf-net/textonly/index.jsp.

124 Computer Science and Telecommunications Board, *Funding a Revolution*, 1, 139.

125 National Science Foundation, *Japan Hopes to Double Its Government Spending on R&D,* NSF 97-310, (Arlington, VA: NSF, June 13, 1997), http://www.nsf.gov/statistics/issuebrf/sib97310.htm.

126 IBM, "IBM Seeks to Build the Computer of the Future Based on Insights from the Brain," news release, November 20, 2008, http://www-03.ibm.com/press/us/en/pressrelease/26123.wss.

127 Leonard Kleinrock's home page, "Leonard Kleinrock's Personal History/Biography: the birth of the Internet," last modified March 9, 2005, http://www.lk.cs.ucla.edu/personal_history.html.

128 Gartner, "Gartner EXP Worldwide Survey of Nearly 1,600 CIOs Shows IT Budgets in 2010 to be at 2005 Levels," news release, January 19, 2010, http://www.gartner.com/it/page.jsp?id=1283413.

129 Gartner, "Gartner Reveals Five Social Software Predictions for 2010 and Beyond," news release, February 2, 2010, http://www.gartner.com/it/page.jsp?id=1293114.

130 Andrew McAfee, *Enterprise 2.0: New Collaborative Tools for Your Organization's Toughest Challenges* (Cambridge, MA: Harvard Business Press, 2009), 211.

131 Francisco D'Souza (CEO, Cognizant), interview by Steve Hamm, 2009.

132 Anita Williams Woolley and Christopher F. Chabris, "Evidence for a Collective Intelligence Factor in the Performance of Human Groups," *Science* 330, no. 6044 (October 29, 2010): 686–688.

133 MIT News, "Study Finds Small Groups Demonstrate Distinctive 'Collective Intelligence' When Facing Difficult Tasks," news release, September 30, 2010, http://web.mit.edu/press/2010/collective-intel.html.

134 Linda Sanford (executive, IBM), interview by Steve Hamm, February, 2, 2010.

135 IBM InnovationJam events page, accessed January 13, 2011, https://www.collaborationjam.com.

136 Palmisano, interview by Steve Hamm.

137 Thomas W. Malone, *The Future of Work: How the New Order of Business Will Shape Your Organization, Your Management Style and Your Life* (Cambridge, MA: Harvard Business Press, 2002), 4.

138 Ibid., 93.

139 C. K. Prahalad and Venkat Ramaswamy, *The Future of Competition: Co-Creating Unique Value with Customers* (Cambridge, MA: Harvard Business Press, 2002), 49–52.

140 IBM, "IBM and Danish Hospital Pioneer Smarter Patient Records to Improve Patient Care," news release, March 10, 2009, http://www-03.ibm.com/press/us/en/pressrelease/26870.wss.

141 Palmisano, interview by Steve Hamm.

142 IBM, "IBM Analytics Streamlines Processes for Russian Prosecutor General's Office," news release, April 8, 2010, http://www-03.ibm.com/press/us/en/pressrelease/29843.wss.

143 John Kelly (executive, IBM), interview by Steve Hamm, July 15, 2009.

144 Henry Chang (researcher, IBM), interview by Steve Hamm, August 2009.

145 Spencer Ante, *Creative Capital: George Doriot and the Birth of Venture Capital* (Boston, MA: Harvard Business School Press, 2008), xiii, xviii.

146 WilmerHale, *2009 Venture Capital Report,* 2, 4.

147 Pierre Haren (executive, IBM), interview by Steve Hamm, November 2010.

148 A. G. Lafley, "P&G's Innovation Culture," *Strategy + Business* (Autumn 2008), http://www.strategy-business.com/media/file/sb52_08304.pdf.

149 Rishab Aiyer Ghosh, *Study on the: Economic impact of open source software on innovation and competitiveness of the Information and Communications Technologies sector in the EU,* (Maastricht, the Netherlands: UNU-Merit, November, 20, 2006), 50.

150 Henry W. Chesbrough, "The Era of Open Innovation," *MIT Sloan Management Review* (Spring 2003), http://sloanreview.mit.edu/the-magazine/articles/2003/spring/4435/the-era-of-open-innovation/?type=x&reprint=4435.

151 Raymond M. Wolfe, *U.S. Businesses Report 2008 Worldwide R&D Expense of $330 Billion,* NSF 10-322 (Arlington, VA: National Science Foundation, May 2010), http://www.nsf.gov/statistics/infbrief/nsf10322/nsf10322.pdf.

152 Linus Torvalds and David Diamond, *Just for Fun: The Story of an Accidental Revolutionary* (New York: Harper Collins, 2001), 158.

153 Robert Le Blanc (executive, IBM), interview by Steve Hamm, November 19, 2010.

154 Robert Sutor (executive, IBM), interview by Steve Hamm, October 2010.

155 US Bureau of Labor Statistics, "Preliminary Multifactor Productivity Trends, 2009," news release, October 6, 2010, http://www.bls.gov/news.release/prod3.nr0.htm.

156 IBM University Relations, briefing provided by Timothy Willeford, October 21, 2010.

157 IBM, "Roche and IBM Collaborate to Develop Nanopore-Based DNA Sequencing Technology," news release, July 1, 2010, http://www-03.ibm.com/press/us/en/pressrelease/32037.wss.

158 Chad Peck (researcher, IBM), interview by Steve Hamm, May 6, 2010.

159 John Micklethwait and Adrian Wooldridge, *The Company: A Short History of a Revolutionary Idea* (New York: Random House, 2003), 17–28.

160 Bruno Di Leo (executive. IBM), interview by Steve Hamm, October 5, 2010.

161 N. R. Kleinfield, "IBM to Leave India and Avoid Loss of Control," *New York Times,* November 16, 1977.

162 Shyam Aggarwal and Ravi Marwaha (former IBM executives), interview by Steve Hamm, November 2010.

163 Aggarwal, interview.

164 *New York Times,* "Arbitration Asked for World Issues," January 18, 1939.

165 *New York Times,* "'No War,' Says Hitler to American Caller," June 30, 1937; *New York Times,* "Thomas J. Watson Is Decorated by Hitler," July 2, 1937.

166 *New York Times,* "1937 Hitler Decoration Is Returned by Watson," June 7, 1940.

167 Memorandum titled "Germany," November 16, 1945, 3, Fales Library, New York University, IBM European Business Archive.

168 IBM Archives.

169 Marwaha, interview.

170 Louis V. Gerstner, *Who Says Elephants Can't Dance? Leading a Great Enterprise Through Dramatic Change* (New York: Harper Collins, 2002), 37.

171 Palmisano, interview by Steve Hamm.

172 Mark Loughridge (executive, IBM), interview by Steve Hamm, December 21, 2010.

173 Loughridge, interview by Steve Hamm.

174 Steve Hamm, *The Race for Perfect: Inside the Quest to Design the Ultimate Portable Computer* (New York: McGraw-Hill: 2008), 75–78.

175 Arimasa Naitoh (executive, Lenovo), interview by Kenji Hall, May 2, 2007.

176 Arun Kumar (researcher, IBM), interview by Steve Hamm, January 29, 2010.

177 Shanker Annaswamy (executive, IBM), interview by Steve Hamm, May 28, 2010.

178 "IBM Market Share in India," (presentation, IBM India, June 2010).

179 Manjeet Kripalani, "IBM's India Pep Rally," *BusinessWeek,* June 6, 2006.

180 Gerstner, interview.

181 Robert Moffat, "Services Competitiveness," (presentation at IBM Investor Day, May 7, 2007), http://www.ibm.com/investor/events/analyst0507/presentation/part6/part6.pdf.

182 IBM Global Technology Services, *The Road to a Smarter Enterprise* (Armonk, NY: IBM, October 2010), ftp://public.dhe.ibm.com/common/ssi/ecm/en/ciw03076usen/CIW03076USEN.PDF.

183 IBM, "IBM Establishes Global Center of Excellence for Water Management in the Netherlands," news release, February 1, 2008.

184 Bill Creighton (executive, IBM), interview by Steve Hamm, October 29, 2010.

185 Mark Loughridge, "Financial Model" (presentation by Mark Loughridge at IBM Investor Day, May 12, 2010), http://www.ibm.com/investor/events/analyst0507/presentation/part10/part10.pdf.

186 "About HSBC," HSBC, accessed January 13, 2011, http://www.hsbc.com; Brendan McNamara, e-mail to Steve Hamm, December 9, 2010.

187 Rogerio Oliveira (executive, IBM), interview by Steve Hamm, 2007.

188 Katharyn White (executive, IBM), interview by Steve Hamm, March 10, 2010.

189 Ted Hoff (executive, IBM), interview by Steve Hamm, February 24, 2010.

190 Michael Karasick (executive, IBM), interview by Steve Hamm, March 2010.

191 Gable, e-mail.

192 Ron Glover (executive, IBM), interview by Steve Hamm, January 14, 2010.

193 Loughridge, presentation.

194 Takreem El-Tohamy (executive, IBM), interview by Steve Hamm, October 6, 2010.

195 Bruno Di Leo (executive, IBM), interview by Steve Hamm, October 5, 2010.

196 Robert E. Scott, Costly Trade With China, 188 (Washington, DC: Economic Policy Institute, May 2007), http://www.epi.org/publications/entry/bp188/.

197 Carlota Perez (author), interview by Steve Hamm, 2007.

198 Steve Hamm, "Radical Collaboration," BusinessWeek, August 30, 2007.

199 Israel Moreno (executive, CEMEX), interview by Steve Hamm, September 2010; CEMEX public relations, e-mail to Steve Hamm, September 29, 2010.

200 Rosabeth Moss Kanter, "Enduring Principles of Changing Times" (speech), Long Now Foundation, San Francisco, November 9, 2007, transcript and Adobe Flash audio, http://fora.tv/2007/11/09/Rosabeth_Moss_Kanter.

201 Stanley Litow (executive, IBM), interview by Steve Hamm, January 11, 2010.

202 Milton Friedman, "The Social Responsibility of Business Is to Increase Its Profits," New York Times Magazine, September 13, 1970.

203 John Steele Gordon, "The Sunny Steel Baron and His Bootstraps Fortune," New York Times, October 30, 2006, http://www.nytimes.com/2006/10/30/books/30gord.html?ref=andrew_carnegie&pagewanted=print.

204 Andrew Carnegie, "Wealth," North American Review 148, no. 391, (June 1889): 653.

205 Maney, The Maverick and His Machine, 24–25.

206 Thomas J. Watson Sr., Think: The First Principle of Business Ethics (Waynesboro, VA: University of Science and Philosophy, 2003), 80.

207 Luis Lamassonne (former IBM executive), interview by Steve Hamm, January 8, 2010.

208 Ted Childs (former IBM executive), interview by Steve Hamm, January 2010.

209 "Policy letter #4," September 21, 1953, IBM Archives.

210 Richard E. Mooney, "IBM Plans 300-Worker Plant in Slums of Bedford-Stuyvesant," New York Times, April, 18, 1968.

211 Thomas J. Watson Jr., "The Right to Life," New York Times, December 19, 1970.

212 Wayne Balta (executive, IBM), interview by Steve Hamm, May 21, 2010.

213 Mark Dean (executive, IBM), interview by Steve Hamm, October 2010.

214 Robin Willner (executive, IBM), interview by Steve Hamm, October 2010; Willner, e-mail to Steve Hamm, October 25, 2010.

215 "Integrated philanthropy. The 1/1/1 model," Salesforce.com, accessed January 13, 2011, http://www.salesforce.com/company/foundation.

216 Jane Nelson et al., Developing Inclusive Business Models (Cambridge, MA: Harvard Kennedy School, 2009), http://www.hks.harvard.edu/m-rcbg/CSRI/publications/other_10_MDC_report.pdf.

217 Willner, interview.

218 Charles Ung (videographer, IBM), interview by Steve Hamm, January 20, 2010.

219 Rosabeth Moss Kanter (professor, Harvard University), interview by Steve Hamm, October 18, 2010.

220 Corinne Bazina (executive, Danone Grameen), interview by Steve Hamm, October 2010.

221 Watson Sr., Think, 80.

222 Sam Palmisano, "Welcome to the Decade of the Smart" (speech), Chatham House, London, January 12, 2010, http://www.ibm.com/ibm/sjp/speeches.html.

223 "Ken Burns: Citizen of the West," PBS, accessed January 13, 2011, http://www.pbs.org/weta/thewest/program/producers/burns.htm.

224 Mike May (president and CEO, Sendero Group), interview by Jeffrey O'Brien, June 2010.

225 Mike May, "Mike May regains his sight after 43 years of blindness," Guardian, August 26, 2003.

226 Robert Kurson, Crashing Through: A True Story of Risk, Adventure, and the Man Who Dared to See (New York: Random House, 2007).

227 IBM, *2010 Annual Report*, accessed December 2010, http://www.ibm.com/annualreport/2010/.

228 Palmisano, interview by Jeffrey O'Brien, May 2010.

229 National Institute of Standards and Technology, "NIST's Second 'Quantum Logic Clock' Based on Aluminum Ion Is Now World's Most Precise Clock," news release, February 4, 2010, http://www.nist.gov/pml/div688/logicclock_020410.cfm.

230 Quinn Norton, "How Super-Precise Atomic Clocks Will Change the World in a Decade," *Wired*, December 12, 2007, http://www.wired.com/science/discoveries/news/2007/12/time_nist.

231 "Super Cool Atom Thermometer: New, Reliable Ways of Measuring Extreme Low Temperatures," *ScienceDaily*, December 8, 2009, http://www.sciencedaily.com/releases/2009/12/091207173626.htm.

232 "Hollerith Tabulator and Sorter Box," IBM, accessed December 2010, http://www-03.ibm.com/ibm/history/exhibits/attic/attic_071.html.

233 "1900s," IBM, accessed December 2010, http://www-03.ibm.com/ibm/history/history/decade_1900.html.

234 "1986," IBM, accessed December 2010, http://www-03.ibm.com/ibm/history/history/year_1986.html; "The Nobel Prize in Physics 1986," Nobelprize.org, accessed December 2010, http://nobelprize.org/nobel_prizes/physics/laureates/1986/.

235 H. R. Kolar (chief architect, IBM Systems and Technology Group), interview by Jeffrey O'Brien, August 2010.

236 iSuppli, "Shipments of Cell Phone Motion Sensors to Rise Fivefold by 2014," news release, May 4, 2010, http://www.isuppli.com/MEMS-and-Sensors/News/Pages/Shipments-of-Cell-Phone-Motion-Sensors-to-Rise-Fivefold-by-2014.aspx; Jérémie Bouchaud (principal analyst, iSuppli), e-mail message to Stuart Luman, May 27, 2010.

237 Rob Lineback (senior market research analyst, IC Insights), e-mail message to Stuart Luman, May 26, 2010.

238 John Gantz and David Reinsel, *The Digital Universe Decade—Are You Ready?*, International Data Corp., May 2010, http://idcdocserv.com/925.

239 "Twitter, now 2 billion tweets per month," *Royal Pingdom* (blog), June 8, 2010, http://royal.pingdom.com/2010/06/08/twitter-now-2-billion-tweets-per-month/; "Amazing facts and figures about Instant Messaging (infographic)," *Royal Pingdom* (blog), April 23, 2010, http://royal.pingdom.com/2010/04/23/amazing-facts-and-figures-about-instant-messaging-infographic/; "Facebook: Facts & Figures for 2010," *Digital Buzz Blog*, March 22, 2010, http://www.digitalbuzzblog.com/facebook-statistics-facts-figures-for-2010.

240 John Gantz and David Reinsel, *The Digital Universe Decade—Are You Ready?*, 2.

241 "Data, data everywhere," *Economist*, February 25, 2010, http://www.economist.com/node/15557443.

242 NASA, "NASA and NSF-Funded Research Finds First Potentially Habitable Exoplanet," news release, September 29, 2010, http://www.nasa.gov/topics/universe/features/gliese_581_feature.html.

243 University of California, Santa Cruz, "Newly discovered planet may be first truly habitable exoplanet," news release, September 29, 2010, http://news.ucsc.edu/2010/09/planet.html.

244 NIST, "NIST Super-Sensors to Measure 'Signature' of Inflationary Universe," news release, May 5, 2009, http://www.nist.gov/pml/quantum/cmb_050509.cfm.

245 "NASA announces new satellite initiative," *Space Daily*, March 1, 2009, http://www.spacedaily.com/reports/NASA_announces_new_satellite_initiative_999.html.

246 "NASA Lightning Research Happens in a Flash," *Terra Daily*, August 10, 2010, http://www.torradaily.com/reports/NASA_Lightning_Research_Happens_In_A_Flash_999.html.

247 Jaymi Heimbuch, "Forest Guard Sets Up Solar Powered Warning System for Forest Fires," *Planetgreen.com*, February 29, 2010, http://planetgreen.discovery.com/tech-transport/forest-guard-solar-warning.html.

248 "Minneapolis Bridge Reopens Following Last Year's Deadly Collapse," *NewsHour*, PBS, September 17, 2008, http://www.pbs.org/newshour/bb/science/july-dec08/bridgereopens_09-17.html#_jmp0.

249 Jim Nash, "Super listening device hears and identifies any sound," *DVICE* (blog), March 9, 2010, http://dvice.com/archives/2010/03/super-listening.php; "Acoustic Vector Sensors," Microflown Technologies, accessed December 2010, http://www.microflown-avisa.com/acoustic-vector-sensors/.

250 Greg Lindsay, "HP Invents a 'Central Nervous System for Earth' and Joins the Smarter Planet Sweepstakes," *Fast Company*, February 15, 2010, http://www.fastcompany.com/1548674/hp-joins-the-smarter-planet-sweepstakes#_jmp0.

251 Agam Shah, "Intel Measures Air Quality With Sweepers," *IDG News*, July 10, 2008, http://www.pcworld.com/businesscenter/article/148205/intel_measures_air_quality_with_sweepers.html; "Deployments," Common Sense, accessed December 2010, http://www.communitysensing.org/deployments.php.

252 "RFID for All of New Zealand's Cattle and Deer by 2011," *RFID Update*, June 5, 2008, http://www.rfidjournal.com/article/articleview/6991/1/565/.

253 Thibaut Scholasch (founder, Fruition Sciences), interview by Jeffrey O'Brien, July, 2010.

254 Owen Slot, "Technology from Formula One to be used in Surrey healthcare trial," *Times of London*, April 1, 2010, http://www.timesonline.co.uk/tol/sport/formula_1/article7083337.ece.

255 "Epic Mix," Vail Resorts Management Company, accessed December 2010, http://www.snow.com/epicmix/home.aspx?intcmp=SN00009.

256 "Nike+ Dashboard," Nike, accessed December 2010, http://nikerunning.nike.com/nikeos/p/nikeplus/en_US/plus/#//dashboard/.

257 "Sportvision: Baseball," Sportvision, accessed December 2010, http://www.sportvision.com/base-pitchfx.html.

258 "SprintCam Live V2.1," I-Movix, accessed December 2010, http://i-movix.com/en/products/sprintcam-live-21.

259 IBM, "IBM and Marine Institute Ireland Netting Results in Galway's 'SmartBay' Project," news release, March 16, 2009, http://www-03.ibm.com/press/us/en/pressrelease/26922.wss; "A mirror in the sea," Economist, November 5, 2010, http://www.economist.com/blogs/babbage/2010/11/sensors_multiply_ocean_too.

260 "Emerging Biometrics," FBI Biometric Center of Excellence, accessed December 2010, http://www.biometriccoe.gov/Mcdalities/Emerging_Biometrics.htm.

261 "Wearable RFID sensors to detect airborne toxins," Printed Electronics World, February 19, 2010, http://www.printedelectronicsworld.com/articles/wearable_rfid_sensors_to_detect_airborne_toxins_00002050.asp.

262 Jacob Bush, "Biosensors in Brief," Highlights in Chemical Technology, March 25, 2010, http://www.rsc.org/Publishing/ChemTech/Volume/2010/05/biosensors_in_briefs.asp.

263 Stony Brook University, "New Sensor Nanotechnology Developed by Stony Brook University Researchers Simplifies Disease Detection," news release, September 29, 2010, http://commcgi.cc.stonybrook.edu/am2/publish/General_University_News_2/New_Sensor_Nanotechnology_Developed_by_Stony_Brook_University_Researchers_Simplifies_Disease_Detection.shtml.

264 "Camera in a Pill Offers Cheaper, Easier Window on Your Insides," ScienceDaily, January 25, 2008, http://www.sciencedaily.com/releases/2008/01/080124161613.htm.

265 "Sensor Biochips Could Aid in Cancer Diagnosis and Treatment," Physorg.com, October 22, 2009, http://www.physorg.com/news175412440.html.

266 "New Hybrid Imaging System Allows Pinpoint Locating of Problems," ScienceDaily, January 9, 2007, accessed December 2010, http://www.sciencedaily.com/releases/2007/01/070108153030.htm.

267 "IBM Scientists Reinvent Medical Diagnostic Testing," IBM, accessed December 2010, http://www.zurich.ibm.com/news/09/lab_on_a_chip.html.

268 "DNA Transistor," IBM, accessed December 2010, https://researcher.ibm.com/researcher/view_project.php?id=1120.

269 Gustavo Stolovitzky (manager, functional genomics and systems biology, IBM Research), interview by Jeffrey O'Brien, February 2009.

270 "Washington City to Fort Mandan," The Lewis and Clark Fort Mandan Foundation, accessed December 2010, http://lewis-clark.org/content/content-article.asp?ArticleID=3018.

271 Fiona Govan, "World's oldest map: Spanish cave has landscape from 14,000 years ago," Telegraph, August 6, 2009, http://www.telegraph.co.uk/news/worldnews/europe/spain/5978900/Worlds-oldest-map-Spanish-cave-has-landscape-from-14000-years-ago.html.

272 Stephen Johnson, The Ghost Map (New York: Riverhead Trade, 2007).

273 Alfred D. Chandler, Strategy and Structure: Chapters in the History of the American Industrial Enterprise (Boston: MIT Press, 1969), 22.

274 "Hollerith tabulator and sorter," IBM, accessed December 2010, http://www-03.ibm.com/ibm/history/exhibits/vintage/vintage_4506VV2139.html.

275 Ken W. Sayers, "A Summary History of IBM's International Operations 1911–2006," 2nd ed.," October 26, 2006, IBM Archives.

276 "1930s," IBM, accessed December 2010, http://www-03.ibm.com/ibm/history/history/decade_1930.html.

277 "Federal Systems Division, Lunar Landing Special," IBM News, July 24, 1969, IBM Archives.

278 Amara D. Angelica, "IBM scientists create most comprehensive map of the brain's network," Kurzweil, Accelerating Intelligence (blog), July 28, 2010, http://www.kurzweilai.net/ibm-scientists-create-most-comprehensive-map-of-the-brains-network.

279 Duncan G. Copeland, Richard O. Mason, and James L. McKenney, "Sabre: The Development of Information-Based Competence and Execution of Information-Based Competition," IEEE Annals of the History of Computing 17, no. 3 (1995): 30–55; Robert V. Head, "Getting Sabre Off the Ground," IEEE Annals of the History of Computing 24, no. 4 (2002): 32–38.

280 Walt Rauscher (vice president, passenger sales and service, American Airlines), address to Public Relations Society of America, New York Hilton Hotel, November 10, 1966, 9:30 a.m., Sabre box, IBM Archives, 27.

281 "Sabre history," Sabre Holdings, accessed December 2010, http://www.sabre-holdings.com/aboutUs/history.html.

282 Copeland, Mason, and McKenney, "Sabre: The development of information-based competence and execution of information-based competition."

283 TomTom International, "TomTom Makes the Largest Historic Traffic Database in the World Available for Governments and Enterprises via its Online Web Portal," news release, January 24, 2011, http://licensing.tomtom.com/WhyTeleAtlas/Pressroom/PressReleases/TA_CT047806.

284 "Mappos—The Zappos Real-Time Order Map," Zappos.com, accessed December 2010, http://www.zappos.com/map/#.

285 David Bleja, "Breathingearth—CO_2, birth & death rates by country, simulated real-time," Breathingearth, accessed December 2010, http://www.breathingearth.net.

286 "Our Projects," Wikimedia Foundation, accessed December 2010, http://wikimediafoundation.org/wiki/Our_projects#Wikipedia.

287 "About us," Ushahidi, accessed December 2010, http://www.ushahidi.com/about.

288 Patrick Meier (director of crisis mapping and new media, Ushahidi), interview by Jeffrey O'Brien, February 2011.

289 Hilton Collins, "New York City's Digital Map Puts In-Depth GIS Data a Few Clicks Away," Government Technology, November 18, 2010, http://www.govtech.com/e-government/New-York-City-Digital-Map.html.

290 Joan DiMicco (research manager, IBM), interview by Jeffrey O'Brien, March 2011.

291 Patricia Cohen, "Digital Keys for Unlocking the Humanities' Riches," New York Times, November 16, 2010.

292 "Human Genome Project Information," Department of Energy Office of Science, accessed December 2010, http://www.ornl.gov/sci/techresources/Human_Genome/project/about.shtml

293 Gregg Easterbrook, "Forgotten Benefactor of Humanity," Atlantic Monthly 279, no. 1 (1997): 75–82; Norman Borlaug, anniversary Nobel address at Nobel Institute, Oslo, Norway, "The Green Revolution Revisited and the Road Ahead," September 26, 2002.

294 Leon Hesser, The Man Who Fed the World (Dallas: Durban House Publishing, 2008), 28; Norman Borlaug, "Preface," in S. Rajaram and G. P. Hettel, eds., Wheat Breeding at CIMMYT: Commemorating 50 Years of Research in Mexico for Global Wheat Improvement, Wheat Special Report No. 29 (Mexico D.F.: CIMMYT, 1995), iv–vi.

295 Hesser, The Man Who Fed the World, 44–45; Noel Vietmeyer, Borlaug, vol. 2 (Lortan, VA: Bracing Books, 2009), 101.

296 Noel Vietmeyer (author), interview by Stuart Luman for Jeffrey O'Brien, October 2010.

297 Hesser, The Man Who Fed the World; Vietmeyer, Borlaug, 67–86.

298 Howard Yana-Shapiro (global staff officer, Mars Inc.), interview by Jeffrey O'Brien, November 2010.

299 Mars, "MARS, USDA-ARS, and IBM Unveil Preliminary Cacao Genome Sequence Three Years Ahead of Schedule," news release, September 15, 2010, http://www.mars.com/global/news-and-media/press-releases/news-releases.aspx?SiteId=94&Id=2460.

300 Mark Dean (Fellow and vice president, IBM), interview by Jeffrey O'Brien, February 2009.

301 Chidanand Apte (senior manager, data analytics, IBM), interview by Jeffrey O'Brien, May 2010.

302 Leslie Kaufman, "Federated Department Stores to Buy Fingerhut," New York Times, February 12, 1999.

303 "Our Technology and Data," Bing Travel, accessed December 2010, http://www.bing.com/travel/about/ourTechnology.do.

304 "About eHarmony," eHarmony, accessed December 2010, http://www.eharmony.com/about/eharmony.

305 "Press kit," Netflix, accessed December 2010, http://www.netflix.com/MediaCenter?id=5379; Netflix, "Netflix Passes 10 Million Subscribers, With 600,000 Net Additions Since the First of the Year," news release, February 12, 2010, http://netflix.mediaroom.com/index.php?s=43&item=307.

306 "About the Music Genome Project," Pandora, accessed December 2010, http://www.pandora.com/corporate/mgp; M. G. Siegler, "You Are On Pandora: Service Hits 60 Million Listeners, Adding Users Faster Than Ever," TechCrunch, July 21, 2010, http://techcrunch.com/2010/07/21/pandora-stats.

307 Richard Barton (cofounder, Zillow), interview by Jeffrey O'Brien, September 2010.

308 "Goodyear Puts the Rubber to the Road with High Performance Computing," Council on Competitiveness, accessed December 2010, http://www.compete.org/publications/detail/685/goodyear-puts-the-rubber-to-the-road-with-high-performance-computing/; "High Performance Computing Drives a 'Can-Do' Attitude at Alcoa," http://www.compete.org/publications/detail/495/high-performance-computing-drives-a-can-do-attitude-at-alcoa; "PING Scores a Hole in One with High Performance Computing," http://www.compete.org/publications/detail/684/ping-scores-a-hole-in-one-with-high-performance-computing.

309 "Warranty Claims & Accruals in Financial Statements," Warranty Week, accessed December 2010, http://www.warrantyweek.com.

310 Loren Nasser (CEO and cofounder, Vextec), interview by Jeffrey O'Brien, June 2009.

311 Frank Priscaro (vice president, Vextec), interview by Jeffrey O'Brien, August 2010.

312 Yardena Peres (manager, healthcare and life sciences, IBM), interview by Mat Honan for Jeffrey O'Brien, August 2010.

313 Peter Haas (staff member, IBM Research), interview by Jeffrey O'Brien, September 2010.

314 William Pulleyblank (professor, operations research, United States Military Academy), interview by Jeffrey O'Brien, July 2010.

315 "Census Data Aid Disease Simulation Studies," ScienceDaily, April 1, 2010, http://www.sciencedaily.com/releases/2010/03/100331141015.htm.

316 "Dust Models Paint Alien's View of the Solar System," ScienceDaily, September 26, 2010, http://www.sciencedaily.com/releases/2010/09/100923111528.htm.

317 "Advanced Geographical Models Bring New Perspective to Study of Archaeology," *ScienceDaily*, May 17, 2010, http://www.sciencedaily.com/releases/2010/05/100514094838.htm.

318 "Supercomputer Reproduces a Cyclone's Birth, May Boost Forecasting," *ScienceDaily*, July 23, 2010, http://www.sciencedaily.com/releases/2010/07/100721121701.htm.

319 "Evacuating 70,000 Sports Fans in Less Than an Hour? Rehearse It With 70,000 Avatars," *ScienceDaily*, April 12, 2010, http://www.sciencedaily.com/releases/2010/04/100410160121.htm.

320 "Europe's Plan to Simulate the Entire Planet," *The Physics arXiv Blog*, April 30, 2010, http://www.technologyreview.com/blog/arxiv/25126/?a=f.

321 "3-D Model of Blood Flow by Supercomputer Predicts Heart Attacks," *ScienceDaily*, May 24, 2010, http://www.sciencedaily.com/releases/2010/05/100520102913.htm.

322 "About the Blue Brain Project," École Polytechnique Fédérale de Lausanne, accessed December 2010, http://bluebrain.epfl.ch.

323 Grady Booch (chief scientist, IBM), interview by Stuart Luman for Jeffrey O'Brien, August 2010.

324 Julio Palmaz (cardiologist), interview by Jeffrey O'Brien, June 2010.

325 IBM, *2010 Annual Report*.

326 IBM, "IBM Earns Most U.S. Patents for 17th Consecutive Year; Will Offer Licenses to Patent Portfolio Management Know-How," news release, January 12, 2010, accessed December 2010, http://www-03.ibm.com/press/us/en/pressrelease/29168.wss.

327 John Kelly (senior vice president and director, IBM Research), interview by Jeffrey O'Brien, March 2009.

328 "Federal Systems Division, Lunar Landing Special," *IBM News*.

329 Ibid.

330 Ibid.

331 Homer Ahr (retired programmer, IBM), interview by Errol Morris, October 2010.

332 "Craig Barrett on the Importance of Global Standards," Intel, accessed December 2010, http://www.intel.com/standards/execqa/qa0904.htm.

333 Jeffrey M. O'Brien, "IBM's Grand Plan to Save the Planet," *Fortune*, May 4, 2009.

334 Gallup, "Americans' Global Warming Concerns Continue to Drop," news release, March 11, 2010, http://www.gallup.com/poll/126560/americans-global-warming-concerns-continue-drop.aspx.

335 Paul Maglio (manager, Smarter Planet Service Systems, IBM Research) and Peter Haas (staff member, IBM Research), interview by Jeffrey O'Brien, August 2010; "SPLASH: Smarter Planet platform for Analysis and Simulation of Health," IBM, accessed December 2010, http://www.almaden.ibm.com/asr/projects/splash.

336 Charles Perrow, *Normal Accidents* (Princeton, NJ: Princeton University Press, 1999), 354.

337 "Legislative History: 1935 Social Security Act," Social Security Administration, accessed December 2010, http://www.ssa.gov/history/35actinx.html.

338 "Social Security Anniversaries: 25th Anniversary Article from OASIS," Social Security Administration, accessed December 2010, http://www.ssa.gov/history/25annoasis.html.

339 Paul Lasewicz (corporate archivist, IBM), interview by Jeffrey O'Brien, August 2010.

340 James Cortada (member, IBM Institute for Corporate Value, and author), interview by Jeffrey O'Brien, June 2010.

341 Don Edwards (assistant director, agency administration and finance, Alameda Social Services Agency), interview by Jeffrey O'Brien, May 2010.

342 "ROI Case Study: IBM SSIRS, Alameda County Social Services Agency," Nucleus Research, August 2010, http://nucleusresearch.com/research/roi-case-studies/roi-case-study-ibm-alameda-county-social-services-agency.

343 Lewis Mumford, *The City in History: Its Origins, Its Transformations, and Its Prospects* (New York: Harcourt Brace Jovanovich, 1961).

344 W. Richard Janikowski (director, Center for Community Criminology and Research, University of Memphis), interview by Stuart Luman for Jeffrey O'Brien, August 2010.

345 IBM, "Memphis Police Department Reduces Crime Rates with IBM Predictive Analytics Software," news release, July 21, 2010, http://www-03.ibm.com/press/us/en/pressrelease/32169.wss.

346 Larry Godwin (director, Memphis Police Department), interview by Stuart Luman for Jeffrey O'Brien, August 2010.

347 Amos Maki, "Memphis Police Director Larry Godwin Says He'll Retire in April," *Commercial Appeal,* February 25, 2011.

348 John Powell (superintendent, SFPUC Wastewater Enterprise), interview by Jeffrey O'Brien, July 2010.

349 Lasewicz, interview.

350 Dario Gil (program director, IBM Research), interview by Jeffrey O'Brien, January 2011.

351 Ione Fine et al., "Long-term deprivation affects visual perception and cortex," *Nature Neuroscience* 6, no. 9 (2003): 915–16.

Photography Credits

Index

About the Authors

Steve Hamm has been a journalist for 30 years. Before joining IBM's corporate communications department as a writer and videographer, he was a senior writer at *BusinessWeek* and spent two decades covering the computer industry, first in Silicon Valley and then in New York. He is the author of *Bangalore Tiger* and *The Race for Perfect*. He lives in Pelham, New York, with his wife and son.

———

Kevin Maney is the author of *Trade-Off: Why Some Things Catch On, and Others Don't, The Maverick and His Machine: Thomas Watson Sr. and the Making of IBM* and *Megamedia Shakeout*. He was a reporter, editor and columnist at *USA Today* for 22 years and a contributing editor at *Condé Nast Portfolio*. He has been a contributor to *Fortune* and *Wired* magazines, the *Atlantic*, NPR and *ABC News*. He lives in Centreville, Virginia.

———

Jeffrey M. O'Brien has been a senior editor at *Fortune* and *Wired* magazines. His work has appeared in *The Best of Technology Writing*, *The Best American Science and Nature Writing* and *The Best American Science Writing*. He lives with his wife and two sons in Mill Valley, California.